From Factories to Palaces

FROM FACTORIES TO PALACES

Architect Charles B. J. Snyder and the New York City Public Schools

Jean Arrington

With Cynthia Skeffington LaValle
Foreword by Peg Breen

EMPIRE STATE EDITIONS

AN IMPRINT OF FORDHAM UNIVERSITY PRESS
NEW YORK   2022

Funding for this book was provided by:
Furthermore: a program of the J. M. Kaplan Fund.

Frontispiece: C. B. J. Snyder at his desk in 1898, drawing by Hector Janoska from a photo published in the 1898 *Architectural Record*

Copyright © 2022 Fordham University Press

All rights reserved. No part of this publication may be reproduced, stored in a retrieval system, or transmitted in any form or by any means—electronic, mechanical, photocopy, recording, or any other—except for brief quotations in printed reviews, without the prior permission of the publisher.

Fordham University Press has no responsibility for the persistence or accuracy of URLs for external or third-party Internet websites referred to in this publication and does not guarantee that any content on such websites is, or will remain, accurate or appropriate.

Fordham University Press also publishes its books in a variety of electronic formats. Some content that appears in print may not be available in electronic books.

Visit us online at www.fordhampress.com/empire-state-editions.

Library of Congress Cataloging-in-Publication Data

Names: Arrington, Jean, author.
Title: From factories to palaces : architect Charles B. J. Snyder and the New York City public schools / Jean Arrington, with Cynthia Skeffington LaValle ; foreword by Peg Breen.
Description: Empire State Editions. | New York : Fordham University Press, 2022. | Includes bibliographical references and index.
Identifiers: LCCN 2021062258 | ISBN 9780823299164 (Hardback) | ISBN 9780823299171 (ePub)
Subjects: LCSH: Snyder, C. B. J., 1860–1945. | Public schools—New York (State)—New York—History. | School buildings—New York (State)—New York—History. | Architecture—New York (State)—New York—History. | Education—New York (State)—New York—History.
Classification: LCC LD7501.N517 A77 2022 | DDC 371.0109747—dc23/eng/20220223
LC record available at https://lccn.loc.gov/2021062258

Printed in the United States of America

24 23 22   5 4 3 2 1

First edition

to Kate, Louise, and Anne,
Sylvie and Marion

CONTENTS

Foreword by Peg Breen   ix

In Memoriam   xiii

List of Figures   xv

Introduction: Hidden in Plain Sight   1

1 The Making of an Architect 1860–1945   15

2 Auspicious Times for Snyder's Public-School Mandate   28

3 The Creative Decade 1891–1900:
   Making Revolutionary Change   49

4 The Prolific Decade 1901–1910:
   Building a World-Class Public-School System   99

5 The Standardizing Decade 1911–1922:
   A Dimming of the Glory   166

   Epilogue: Retirement and Successors   197

Lists of Snyder Public Schools   205

Glossary: Architectural Terminology 237

Acknowledgments 243

Notes 247

References 263

Index 273

FOREWORD

Peg Breen, President,
The New York Landmarks Conservancy

NEW YORK CITY boasts an impressive array of buildings by noted architects through the years—from Richard Upjohn to McKim, Mead, and White, Bertram Goodhue, Cass Gilbert, Mies van der Rohe, and Lord Norman Foster. But no architect has created more distinguished buildings and promoted more social good than C. B. J. Snyder.

Architect Robert A. M. Stern praised Snyder in his book *New York 1900: Metropolitan Architecture and Urbanism 1890–1915*. The 408 schools and additions Snyder designed during his long tenure as the city's superintendent of school buildings from 1891 to 1922 are beloved by generations of students and community residents. But Snyder has never enjoyed the widespread recognition he deserves. This book should correct that.

This welcome assessment of the man and his buildings presents the full picture of his genius. He played a major role in a progressive era that treasured education. Social reformer Jacob Riis was a fan. Before Snyder's tenure, schools resembled tenements—dark and overcrowded. Students spent their days on backless benches. Snyder's schools welcomed waves of immigrant children and offered them light, air, beauty, and modern technologies. The years in which Snyder had free rein, backed by mayors and the superintendent of schools, read like a lost, golden era. Sadly, and not surprisingly, a tangle of politics and bureaucracy finally caused him to resign.

I was introduced to Snyder and his work in the late 1990s. My office at the New York Landmarks Conservancy was besieged with calls asking us to stop the city from tearing down Snyder's P.S. 109, a Collegiate Gothic beauty on East Ninety-Ninth Street in Manhattan. The city closed the school for repairs in 1995, then permanently shut it two years later. Parents and community residents were outraged.

We succeeded in getting the State Historic Preservation Office (SHPO) to stop the demolition. The city failed to notify SHPO and was using public money to demolish a building clearly eligible for listing on the State and National Registers of Historic Preservation.

The city ignored community pleas to reopen P.S. 109 and left it vacant. Finally, a nonprofit developer transformed the building into affordable live/work apartments for artists and their families, as well as community space.

We got similar pleas for help at that time from teachers and parents at P.S. 31, Bronx, another Snyder beauty. An individual city landmark, it was known as the "Castle on the Hill." The building had a mosaic entrance floor, eighteen-foot ceilings, and a wood-paneled auditorium highlighted by stained glass.

"As soon as you walked in, you had respect for the building, and for education itself," a P.S. 31 teacher said at the time. "This was like a church."

We discovered that the city had hired inexperienced contractors to perform repairs. They emptied the school unnecessarily and created more damage. We worked with the school principal, parents, and community residents to pressure the city to repair and reopen the building.

Plans eventually were drawn to repair the school and build a rear addition to house a modern cafeteria and gym. Then the city administration changed, and the funding was withdrawn. The building was demolished in 2015 over the fierce objections of the city's own Landmarks Preservation Commission, preservation groups, and the community.

These experiences prompted us to persuade the city council to hold a hearing on the city's treatment of Snyder schools. Robert A. M. Stern agreed to make the case for their preservation in an op-ed piece in the *New York Times*.

We became such cheerleaders for Snyder schools that a Department of Buildings engineer gave us a gargoyle that had to be removed during repairs at P.S. 33 in the Bronx. We named it "Snyder," and it sits in a place of honor in our office. We talk about it with interns we host from Bronx International, a Snyder high school.

Through the years, we've given our annual Lucy G. Moses Preservation Awards to the city for restoration of some Snyder schools and for the reuse of others as housing and community centers. One of our "Tourist in Your Own Town" videos highlights several of his buildings.

We plunged into advocacy again in 2020 when fire damaged Snyder's first school building. Built in 1893, the former P.S. 23 was known as "the heart of Chinatown." Once again, residents with treasured memories pleaded for saving what remains of the exterior. The city has yet to announce the building's fate.

Buildings engender fierce devotion because they hold stories. Snyder's buildings contain the collective memories of generations. More than 200 of his designs still serve as schools. Others still serve their communities in various ways. Sadly, the city has discarded or ignored several others.

The debate over New York City's public education continues. Perhaps this book's reminder of what C. B. J. Snyder and the city accomplished—this picture of New York at its best—will inspire us again. In any event, we are fortunate that Snyder's buildings still anchor neighborhoods throughout the city. I look forward to this book introducing this remarkable man to many more New Yorkers and generating the acclaim he deserves.

IN MEMORIAM

OUR MOTHER, JEAN ARRINGTON, arrived in New York City in the summer of 2005 after a full career of teaching in the United States and abroad. She had taught in New York as a young woman, before family and work and life took her to Raleigh, North Carolina, for almost thirty years, and she had dreamed of returning one day. When Annie, our youngest sister, left home for college, it finally felt like that time. Her primary work goal, she imagined, was to land one final, part-time position that would allow her to continue teaching and give her time to explore the place in the world that excited her the most. She did end up teaching at Borough of Manhattan Community College and at Long Island University, both as a professor and as a mentor to New York Teaching Fellows. But it was in walking the city in search of employment that summer, visiting schools and meeting principals, that she developed a wonder of and then a passion for the magnificent turn-of-the-century buildings that still serve the majority of New York's public school students. This wonder quickly led to an obsession with the neglected historical figure behind this architecture—C.B.J. Snyder.

Our mother had no business writing this book. Although her experience in education was extensive, she had no expertise in architecture or New York history. So she simply turned herself into the person capable of writing it. She became an avid student, taking history and architecture classes at New York's universities, going on frequent tours with the New-York Historical Society and Pratt University (tours she was very quickly leading), forging relationships with and support from New York's most accomplished architectural historians and seeking out the living relatives of C.B.J. Snyder. She visited every one of the more than 278 still-standing schools that Snyder designed, befriending teachers, principals, and custodians. For many years, every Christmas included homemade gifts with Snyder's face. When we would delicately ask after a date she may have had, she would reply, "Oh, it was lovely, but I don't have time for another primary relationship. I'm married to Snyder now."

In 2016, after a series of inexplicable falls, our mother was diagnosed with Parkinson's. A year later, the diagnosis was amended to Multiple Systems Atrophy, an even more quickly debilitating disease. The physical toll was devastating, and by the time the manuscript was rejected with an extensive list of necessary changes, our mother was no longer capable of typing on a computer. Although it was Covid-19 that ultimately caused her death in January 2022, three months prior to the publication of this book, it was also Covid that gave her the opportunity to complete this work. Through the marvel of Zoom and the opportunity of quarantine, Cindy LaValle, Snyder's great-granddaughter, would become our mother's hands as well as her devoted and tireless partner. It is due to the dedication of these two remarkable women that we are elated to have and hold this book and to tell the story of C.B.J. Snyder, a genuine champion of New York's children.

Anne, Louise, and Kate Arrington Bauso

FIGURES

1	Morris High School Ornamental Close-ups: Grand and Imposing	4
2	Number of Structures Completed per Year	5
3	Number of Schools per Borough per Decade	5
4	GS 1M, 1899: Creative First Decade Renaissance-Revival and Collegiate Gothic Style	7
5	PS 36X, 1902: Prolific Second Decade, Italian Palazzo-Style	8
6	PS 189M, 1923: Standardized Third Decade, Simplified Collegiate Gothic Style	9
7	The Snyder Family Home in New Rochelle, New York	23
8	Snyder Ad in the *New Rochelle Pioneer* from 1890	24
9	The Snyder-Designed House Pictured in the 1895 Building Edition of *Scientific American*	25
10	The Snyder Bakery on Fifty-Eighth Street, Manhattan, Demolished	25
11	Army of 610,000 Children Went to School	31

12	Charles B. J. Snyder, from "How New York City Has Solved Some Trying School Building Problems," by Snyder, in *School Journal*, 1902	34
13	Appropriations for Running the Schools	38
14	Appropriations for New Buildings	38
15	Chicago's 1893 Columbian Exposition	41
16	Miscellaneous Ornamentation	44
17	Snyder at Desk as Portrayed in the 1898 *Architectural Record*	45
18	Bushwick High School, 1913: Door Handle	51
19	PS 2M: Pre-Snyder School with Tenement on Henry Street	52
20	PS 67M, 1894: Signed Snyder Drawing	53
21	PS 67M, 1894: then High School of Performing Arts, now Jacqueline Onassis School of International Studies: Landmarked	54
22	PS 25M, 1894, now PS 751: Dutch Renaissance Revival	55
23	PS 158M, 1899: Italian Palazzo-Style	58
24	PS 160M, 1899: Italian Palazzo-Style	60
25	PS 20M, 1899: Queen Anne and Gothic Cathedral Elements	60
26	PS 27X, 1898: Italian Palazzo-Style	61
27	PS 25X, 1898: Gothic/Flemish Renaissance Revival	61
28	PS 31X, 1900: Landmarked and Demolished	62
29	PS 166M, 1900: Collegiate Gothic: Landmarked	62
30	PS 165M, 1900: First Extant H-Plan Design, First Floor Plan	64
31	PS 165M, 1900: Second Floor Plan	64
32	PS 165M, 1900: 108th Street Façade	65
33	PS 165M, 1900: 109th Street Façade	65
34	Board of Education and the City of New York Seals	67

35	PS 7M, 1893: Italian Palazzo-Style	69
36	"Superintendent C. B. J. Snyder, who builds our Beautiful Schools"	70
37	PS 24K: Scissor Stairways Drawings	74
38	Stairway Pictured in Riis's *The Battle with the Slum*	75
39	PS 90M, 1907	76
40	PS 186M, 1903: H-Plan	76
41	PS 186M: Minerva Statue	77
42	PS 11R: Clerestory Windows	80
43	PS 11R: Plenum Ventilation	81
44	Bushwick High School: Details of Blower Apparatus	82
45	PS 23M: Drawing with Four Floors and an Attic	88
46	PS 23M: Renovated to Five Full Floors	88
47	PS 38M, 1906 (Later Became West Side Vocational High School)	89
48	West Side Vocational High School	89
49	PS 166M, 1900: Fifth-Floor Gymnasium	91
50	PS 8X, 1898: Assembly Rooms with Partitions	93
51	Girls in Cooking Class	94
52	Boys in Design Class	94
53	Letter from President Hubbell	98
54	Four-Part Snyder Article, Part I	101
55	PS 132K, 1902: Institutional Italian Palazzo-Style	105
56	PS 132K 1902: Close-up Views of Front and Side	105
57	PS 130K, 1903: Institutional Italian Palazzo-Style, Marion's School	106
58	PS 130K: Entrance	107

xviii · FIGURES

59	PS 130K: Interior Entrance Foyer	107
60	PS 108K, 1894: James Naughton School	109
61	PS 102K, 1901: Three-Story Naughton Tribute School	109
62	PS 136K, 1902: Four-Story Naughton Tribute School with Ventilators on Roof	110
63	PS 126K, 1902: Four-Story Naughton Tribute School	111
64	PS 85M, 1906: Institutional Italian Palazzo-Style, East Harlem	112
65	PS 62M, 1905: For 7th & 8th Graders, Institutional Italian Palazzo-Style	113
66	Former PS 80Q, 1903: City View Inn	114
67	PS 32R, 1902: Two Entrances	115
68	PS 35X, 1902: Institutional Italian Palazzo-Style	117
69	PS 6X, 1904: Institutional Italian Palazzo-Style	117
70	*Real Estate Record and Guide*, June 1912	118
71	PS 126K, 1904: Girls' Playground on the Roof	124
72	PS 102K, 1901: Bathing	128
73	Great Hall at Cooper Union	129
74	Stuyvesant High School, 1908: Auditorium with Skylights	132
75	Former DeWitt Clinton High School, 1906: Auditorium and Stage	133
76	PS 135M, 1895: Open-Air Classroom with Balcony	135
77	PS 102M Annex, Jefferson Park: Open-Air Class in Warmth-Providing Bags	135
78	PS 170M, 1901, Drawing: Chateau-Type H-Plan above NE Corner of Central Park	141
79	PS 179M, 1901: Chateau-Type H-Plan	141
80	Wadleigh High School, 1902	142
81	PS 63M, 1906: Baroque	144

82	Former DeWitt Clinton High School, 1906	145
83	PS 90M, 1907: Drawing by Brandon Phillips, Unfinished	147
84	Bushwick High School, Brooklyn, 1913	148
85	Flushing High School, Queens, 1915	150
86	Curtis High School, Staten Island 1904, with Leap of Faith Ornamentation	154
87	Erasmus Hall High School, Brooklyn, 1906, West Side	155
88	Snyder's Masterpiece: Morris High School, Bronx, 1904. Landmarked Outside and Inside	156
89	Commercial High School, Brooklyn, 1906	162
90	Erasmus Hall High School, Brooklyn, 1906	165
91	Sidney Lanier High School, Montgomery, Alabama	165
92	Accolades from Employees, the NYC Board of Education, and the American Institute of Architects	167
93	PS 29K, 1921: Sylvie's Elementary School	173
94	PS 97Q, 1917: Simplified Collegiate Gothic Entranceway	174
95	PS 93Q, 1917: Simplified Collegiate Gothic, 7 Bays, Quadruplet Tudor-Arched Windows	175
96	Normal College, 1913, Now Part of Hunter College	177
97	Washington Irving High School, 1913, 8 Stories	179
98	Manhattan Trade School for Girls, 1917, 10 Stories	179
99	George Washington High School, Completed by Gompert, 1925: Eagle Ornamentation Surrounds Cupola	180
100	Bushwick High School, Brooklyn, 1913: Fourth-Floor Specialty Areas	184
101	Washington Irving High School, 1913: Auditorium	189
102	Washington Irving High School Auditorium after 2014 Renovation	189
103	Flushing High School, Queens, 1915: Music Room	192

104	PS 47M, 1925: School for the Deaf	193
105	Snyder in His Later Years	198
106	Harriet and Charles	199
107	Granddaughters Elizabeth Orr and Shirley Skeffington	201
108	The *Babylon Leader*, November 12, 1945	202
109	Snyder's Grave at Woodlawn Cemetery	202
110	Snyder Family Members and Author at Gravesite	203

From Factories to Palaces

INTRODUCTION

Hidden in Plain Sight

Every schoolhouse should be a temple, consecrated in prayer to the physical, intellectual, and moral culture of every child in the community and be associated in every heart with the earliest and strongest impression of truth, justice, patriotism and religion.

—Henry Barnard

Snyder schools are among the great glories of our city.

—Robert A. M. Stern

EVERY SCHOOL DAY thousands of New York City students and teachers walk into 235 public-school buildings that were revolutionary in conception, design, and execution at the turn of the twentieth century. Through these buildings one man, Charles B. J. (C. B. J.) Snyder, as superintendent of school buildings from 1891 to 1922, elevated the standards of school architecture in New York and across the nation. He translated Progressive-Era school-reform and City-Beautiful tenets into brick and stone, in the process improving the educational experience of students and leaving New York City a rich visual legacy: "The pervasive, powerful presence of our existing school buildings,"[1] as a president of the Architectural League of New York noted. Snyder schools still make people stop and look. They still mold the waking hours of 20 percent of public-school students. Yale University architectural historian Robert A. M. Stern calls them "people's palaces, . . . everyday masterpieces of a talented, historically overlooked architect."[2]

Of course, Snyder didn't perform this magic alone. He worked side by side amid a group of like-minded, hardworking individuals. Together, this New York City squad of city and school board officials, administrators, teachers, Building Bureau draftsmen, builders, custodians, and various other school system employees managed this feat. In this book his name is often used as shorthand for himself and others working at the core of this finely oiled machine.

They were working in a country that, from its inception, has had a love affair with education. The founders of the fledgling United States felt that education, as John Adams wrote in 1786, "must become the national care."[3] He argued, "The whole people must take upon themselves the education of the whole people and be willing to bear the expense of it."[4] Henry Barnard, widely viewed as the father of education in this country, described schoolhouses and their moral importance in religious terms.[5] By 1850 a greater percentage of Americans under the age of fifteen attended school than in any other country, and by 1860, 800 colleges had already been founded. The United States, alone among twentieth-century empires, established public-school systems even in its colonies.[6] No wonder the little red schoolhouse, like the stars and stripes, is familiar as a national icon. Twentieth-century scholar Paul Turner sees "boundless enthusiasm for education" as "a particularly American trait,"[7] and educator Herbert Kohl goes so far as to assert that the United States invented public education.[8] Snyder was part of a mainstream, deeply valued undertaking.

And nowhere is public education more prominent than in New York City, which now and always has had the largest public-school system in the country, perhaps in the world. Moreover, despite all the problems and shortcomings that inevitably accompany a huge system, the city's public schools have an impressive history, having, for example, many graduates who went on to win the Nobel Prize. But what about the buildings in which this phenomenon occurred? What role has the architecture of the city's public schools played in that achievement? Since World War II, the New York City Department of Education has brought in to design public schools some of the nation's leading architects, such as Harrison & Abramovitz and Edward Durrell Stone. But this emphasis on the best isn't new. More than a century ago, the city faced a public-school crisis that was mitigated by Charles Snyder's progressive school buildings.

In the second half of the nineteenth century, the city's public schools lagged behind those of the rest of the country. It was partly because of the lack of interest on the part of the ruling political bloc, Tammany, the machine controlling much of New York City and state politics, but mainly because of the overwhelming population influx. Walt Whitman in "Manahatta" had written in the 1850s about "immigrants arriving, fifteen and twenty thousand in a week," pouring into lower Manhattan.[9] By 1890 that number had more than doubled.[10] The most the city could do was struggle, unsuccessfully, to provide enough "sittings" in factory-like elementary schools. Providing attractive buildings and new educational practices like those being offered in other cities was more than New York could even imagine. Also contributing to the educational morass was the decentralized system that had evolved under Tammany, wherein, for each of twenty-two wards, five politically appointed trustees made all the hiring and curriculum decisions for the schools in their ward. It was this dynamic, corrupt, diverse, inefficient system that Snyder joined and sought to improve.

Snyder's is a success story of the progressive socially responsible vision. A Progressive himself, working for a supportive Board of Education for the span of the Progressive Era, he addressed the school situation on three fronts: appearance, construction, and function. Instead of blending in with the surrounding buildings as earlier schools had, Snyder's were grand and imposing: "He does that which no other architect before his time ever did or tried: He builds them beautiful,"[11] wrote the consummate reformer of the age, Jacob Riis (fig. 1). Also, Snyder and the Building Bureau improved the construction of the buildings. For example, in response to an investigation that found "three-quarters of the public school buildings in New York . . . defective or unsanitary to a greater or lesser degree," they worked to fireproof them, to redesign them for greater light and air, and to improve their sanitary facilities.[12] They focused on quality-of-life issues such as water fountains and heated cloakrooms, attention not previously accorded schools. Finally, they started making available in New York design features that Progressive educators had been introducing in the rest of the country, such as high schools, kindergartens, and, to support a more relevant, practical curriculum, gymnasiums and manual-training rooms. In all, Snyder and the board strove to change the prevailing metaphors for schools from prisons, factories, and barracks to "people's palaces" and "cathedrals of culture."

In addition to unprecedented quality, Snyder also brought to New York schools unprecedented quantity. Arguably, he designed more public schools than has any other single architect in a single city. He built an average of thirteen schools per year, with a high of twenty-nine in 1906 (see the chart "Number of Structures Completed per Year," in fig. 2). In total, he left New York City 408 schools and additions—about 130 each in Manhattan and Brooklyn, sixty in the Bronx and Queens, twenty-three on Staten Island (see the chart "Number of Schools per Borough per Decade," in fig. 3).

Figure 1. Morris High School Ornamental Close-ups: Grand and Imposing. Arrington photo.

Brooklyn has been the best steward of its Snyder schools, with 81 percent still standing, while Manhattan has been the least concerned about preservation. Of the 267 extant buildings, the vast majority—235—still function as public schools. The others are now private schools, arts complexes, health facilities, shelters, senior-citizen housing, apartments, and condos, with one now a church and one a motel in Queens. Twenty of Snyder's schools have been landmarked, and six are on the National Register of Historic Places.

Despite the extent of Snyder's accomplishment, little attention has been paid him. Participants on walking tours to look at Snyder schools often make comments to the effect that "I've walked by this school a hundred times but never really noticed it." In addition, architectural and educational historians have not explored the far-reaching effects of Snyder's contributions to school

INTRODUCTION · 5

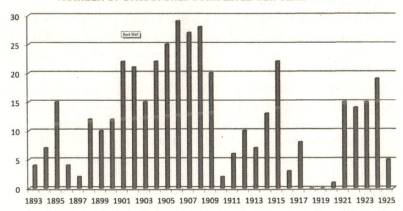

Figure 2. Number of Structures Completed per Year. Arrington table.

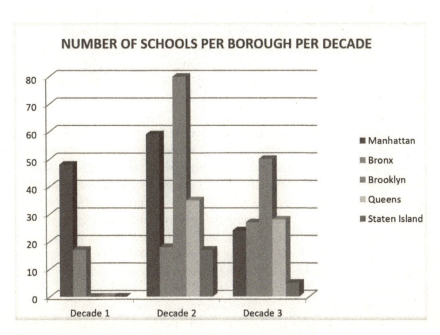

Figure 3. Number of Schools per Borough per Decade. Arrington table.

design. His schools remain hidden in plain sight in more ways than one, an oversight this book strives to rectify.

Chapter 1 looks at the ways in which Snyder's life prepared him for the career at which he would excel. Growing up in the affluent vacation community of Saratoga Springs, New York, but in strained circumstances himself, he came to build grand public schools in numerous historical styles for a largely immigrant population. Also, his firsthand experience of the ravages of fire, which during his youth leveled six of the huge wooden hotels along Saratoga Springs' main street, led to his designing the first fireproofed schools in the nation.[13] His experience as a student at Cooper Union molded him to see idealism and practicality as symbiotic, not polarized. By his mid-twenties he had established himself as a commercial and residential architect, and in 1891, when he was thirty-one, despite having had no experience with schools, he was elected by the Board of Education to the position of superintendent of school buildings.

Chapter 2 shows the many ways that Snyder was encouraged and sustained in this position by the historical moment. Late nineteenth-century Progressives viewed education as the panacea for the ills of industrialization that were afflicting large cities in the United States—New York, in particular. As much from fear of anarchy as from philanthropy, Progressives undertook many reform efforts in the 1890s to ameliorate the difficult life of the disadvantaged—settlement houses, public health initiatives, public baths, public parks, public libraries, and—what seemed the lynchpin in improving society and transforming immigrants into model American citizens—improved public schools. Snyder worked on fertile ground, and Jacob Riis's influential *The Battle with the Slum* (1902) championed his new schools.

In addition, the historical moment was right for a public-school architect such as Snyder in that the 1893 Chicago's World's Fair and consequent City Beautiful movement catapulted the arts into prominence. Nicholas Murray Butler, founder of Columbia's Teachers' College, fought and won, in 1896, a war to centralize and professionalize the New York City school system, supplanting the inefficient and inequitable ward-trustee arrangement. And just two years later the city consolidated with Brooklyn and the towns in Queens and Staten Island to become Greater New York.[14] Now the second-largest city in the world, New York became committed to having world-class schools, in deed as well as word: the city increased the funding for the schools dramatically. In fact, each of these Progressive improvements has characterized the operation of the New York City public-school system for over 100 years.

Given Snyder's background and this range of philosophical, practical, and financial support, he moved New York City from public-school laggard to national leader. The following chapters detail the three phases of his thirty-one-year career: creative (1891–1900), prolific (1901–10), and standardizing (1911–22).

Chapter 3 details the startling creativity of his first decade. Perhaps it was the open-mindedness of his Dutch heritage, abetted by his lifelong membership in the Masons, that led to schools that showed a whole new way of thinking—on the outside, in the way they were built, and on the inside, in the way they functioned. In other words, his buildings transformed the look of New York City schools, exhibited the most current construction techniques, and provided specialized spaces for the most current educational practices (fig. 4). While the look of the schools he inherited had little to distinguish them from tenements, Snyder designed Renaissance-Revival and Collegiate Gothic buildings that drew attention to themselves and to the importance of education and of students. While the earlier schools had been load-bearing masonry buildings, Snyder dared to employ the newly introduced steel-skeleton technology, which allowed for fireproofing and

Figure 4. GS 1M, 1899: Creative First Decade Renaissance-Revival and Collegiate Gothic style. *New York City Board of Education, Bureau of Finance, Annual Financial and Statistical Report, 1906–8* (hereafter *NYC BOE AFSR 1906–8*).

huge windows. While earlier schools had typically consisted of classrooms alone for a strictly academic curriculum, he added specialized spaces such as gymnasiums, rooftop playgrounds, and manual-training rooms to accommodate progressive pedagogies that incorporated play, the arts, and learning by doing. In all, he was innovative on every front—designing flamboyant but dignified buildings, using new construction techniques that promoted health and safety, and broadening the schools' functionality. Also, he designed and put out for bids his own versions of many items such as student desks and ventilation machines because commercial versions were prohibitively expensive.

If creativity is the key to Snyder's first decade, abundance describes his second. Most striking is how prolific he was: he more than tripled the number of schools he had erected during his first decade. Chapter 4 shows how he again transformed the look of the New York City public schools, moving to an Italian palazzo-style (fig. 5). He honed and expanded innovations that were now standard, and he continued to design innovative features, adding, for instance, other specialized spaces such as auditoriums, science laboratories, art studios, and music rooms. It also focuses on his unique, celebrated H-Plan schools, the majority of which he built during this decade. This

Figure 5. PS 36X, 1902: Prolific Second Decade, Italian Palazzo-Style. *NYC BOE AFSR 1906–8.*

–chapter further details his collaboration with Irish-born Superintendent of Schools William Maxwell (1852–1920) to provide New York's first high schools. By the end of the decade, he and his bureau had built twelve, half of his career total. Even though under tremendous time constraints, he made each building visually distinctive, relying on his experience designing Collegiate Gothic and H-Plan elementary schools.

Snyder's third decade (1911–22), discussed in Chapter 5, represented a falling off not only in the number of schools constructed, but also in the public perception of his career and its accomplishments. Although he continued to be innovative, especially with high schools, and received accolades associated with his twenty-fifth year as superintendent and later his retirement, he also faced criticism and discouragements. The overall number of schools built dropped by a third. Another new look, the Simplified Collegiate Gothic style, dominated elementary schools, representing large-scale standardization (fig. 6). The decade involved difficulties for the country as a whole—the 1910 recession and the Great War—and for Snyder himself, both personal and professional, ending with political pressures forcing him to resign.

Certain qualities and beliefs account for Snyder's far-reaching accomplishments. He was a thoroughgoing Progressive, Democrat, and champion of immigrants and the working class. He saw himself as an artist, innovator,

Figure 6. PS 189M, 1923: Standardized Third Decade, Simplified Collegiate Gothic style. Arrington photo.

and problem-solver, not just a builder or bureaucrat. His historicist, eclectic buildings grew out of his love and respect for children: he wanted the school to be an oasis, a space distinctly different from the city streets they inhabited. Finally, he was an expert at balancing the demands of both the students, faculty, and staff who occupied the schools on the one hand and, on the other, the Board of Education and City of New York. These constituencies often had conflicting values, the immediate consumers wanting quality, the city wanting to keep costs down. To satisfy the first group, Snyder surveyed the opinions and desires of teachers and principals and openly proclaimed his faith in students—that they wouldn't, for example, destroy the landscaping. At the same time, while building schools with the future in mind, not just the present, he documented his frugality to satisfy the educational bureaucracy, assuring the city that he was providing "goods that give us the greatest service."[15]

Snyder brought New York's schools into the twentieth century literally and figuratively. During his thirty-year career, more changes occurred in school design in New York City and across the country than have in the subsequent century as the simple nineteenth-century schoolhouse morphed into the complex twentieth-century school building. His schools were modern in that they constituted what we now think of as a school—a building with amenities such as auditoriums, gymnasiums, cafeterias, art studios, science laboratories, and indoor bathrooms. In the decades that he participated in a nationwide movement toward modern schools, his "skill and genius," said the president of the Board of Education at the time of the 1898 Consolidation, placed him "at the head of the department of scholastic architecture in the country."[16]

Snyder and public-school architecture are both ripe for study. Except for Gary Hermalyn's *Morris High School and the Creation of the New York City Public High School System*,[17] a chapter in Michele Cohen's *Public Art for Public Schools*,[18] and several of Christopher Gray's "Streetscape" columns in the *New York Times*,[19] the phenomenon of Charles B. J. Snyder has not been addressed, nor had public-school architecture in general. Although schools are among the most numerous and easily identifiable public buildings in the United States, their architecture is the least studied. Dolores Hayden, in *The Power of Place*, shows how urban schools are particularly ignored.[20] Although schooling has become, according to City College architectural historian Marta Gutman, "the central experience of modern children and schools the central site where modern childhood is lived," she observes that the comprehensive critical history of school buildings in the United States remains to be written.[21]

Public-school architectural gems are hidden in plain sight. Walking-tour participants say that for the first time they are really looking at the building, taking in its beauty and complexity. The public tend to dismiss and overlook schools, the general assumption being that they are "cookie cutter." The neglect of the subject on the part of scholars may be due in part to a prejudice against education as a relatively recent field of study at universities. Certainly, the hierarchy is rigid as far as teachers go: college professors garner the prestige, while secondary and then primary teachers are distinctly second- and third-class citizens within the educational realm. The same hierarchy carries over to architecture: while designing a college academic complex or campus might be attractive to architects, few grow up dreaming of becoming a public-school architect. As for architectural historians, Nicholas Pevsner's canonical handbook illustrating seventeen building types doesn't so much as mention schools.[22]

However, this state of affairs seems to be changing. American Studies major Anjali Balaikrishna at Yale University has written both her junior and senior theses on Snyder under Delores Hayden. Marta Gutman has chosen schools and other child-related architecture as the focus of her research, which has led to her anthology *Designing Modern Childhoods: History, Space, and the Material Culture of Children*.[23] Other recent significant works to examine the history of school design in the United States are *Small Wonder: The Little Red Schoolhouse in History and Memory*, by Jonathan Zimmerman of New York University, and Dale Allen Gyure's *The Chicago Schoolhouse: High School Architecture and Educational Reform, 1856–2006*.[24] Most recently appeared the self-published *C.B.J. Snyder, New York City Public School Architecture, 1891–1922*, by Jennifer Nadler Wright, with photographs of schools by her husband, Roy Wright.[25] *From Factories to Palaces* contributes to this new conversation by adding in-depth analysis of the origins of and patterns in the architecture of this brilliant man who—suffused with the optimism of the Progressive Era and his own can-do attitude, supported by a series of school boards and mayoral administrations—designed remarkable public schools that influenced subsequent school design in New York City and in the country as a whole.

Explanation of the Naming of the Schools

A note on nomenclature: At the founding of the New York City Board of Education in 1843, a distinction was made between a primary school (PS) for grades one through five and a grammar school (GS) for grades six through eight. Some school buildings, such as PS 1 in Chinatown, housed four departments with four principals: primary boys, primary girls, grammar boys, and grammar girls. Then in 1897, on the eve of the Consolidation of the Boroughs, to simplify the system, every school became a PS, meaning "Public School." Now we've come full circle in that many Snyder buildings in the twenty-first century house several small schools instead of one large one.

As for the numbering, each borough has a separate sequence, so there can be as many as five PSs with the same number. Therefore, to distinguish among boroughs, the letters M, X, K, Q, or R, standing for Manhattan, Bronx, Kings County (or Brooklyn), Queens, and Richmond (the former name of Staten Island), can be added to the school's number—for example, PS 160M or PS 160K. When the Bronx became a separate borough instead of an annexed district of New York, its schools were renumbered in 1902, #60 becoming #1 and, at the other end, #182 becoming #36. Originally the numbers indicated the order of the schools' construction; however, as buildings were demolished or decommissioned and their numbers reused, the order lost its chronological accuracy. At one point, an alternate philosophy led to some schools being numbered according to the crosstown street of their location: PS 189M, for example, is on 189th Street. In 1916, the attempt was made to replace with meaningful names what was viewed as the sterile numbering system. A *New York Times* editorial resorted to sarcasm about this effort:

> The Board of Education is now contributing to enlightenment by slapping new names on the public schools. It forgets, in its zeal for innovation, the love which thousands of men and women in this city, thousands scattered over the country, feel for "Old Public School, Number" So and So.[26]

All primary schools therefore now have both a name and a number. High schools originally were named rather than numbered; at some point in the 1960s they were also assigned numbers. PSs are still referred to primarily by number, high schools as well as junior high schools by name. This study refers to each school primarily by its original number or name, which in some cases has now been changed. Although Snyder did reconstitute some of his elementary schools to become junior high schools, he never designed one per se, the first custom-built junior high school being the 1932 Herman Ridder in the Bronx.

Finally, a note about class sizes: Snyder sought to reduce them and succeeded to a degree. PS 25M tells the story: his 1894 addition had 15 classrooms for 975 "sittings," which computes to 65 students per classroom, while his 1908 addition had 16 classrooms for 800 sittings, or 50 students per classroom. In other words, Snyder changed the formula for the number of "sittings" per classroom from the 65 he had inherited to hover around 60 in the latter 1890s; then in the wake of Consolidation fervor in 1900, he brought it down to 45; it later rose back to 50. Elementary classes remained at 50 for the rest of his career; high school classes were somewhat smaller. Today the same buildings typically support only half the number of students for which they were built.

Chapter 1

The Making of an Architect
1860–1945

HOW DID A poor boy from Saratoga Springs, New York, come to make a lasting change on the face of New York City? How did an architect working in the particularly conservative field of education become an innovator in a city whose architectural scene was not hospitable to innovation? Although no personal papers or library, no sketchbooks or journals seem to have survived, we can still start to answer these questions by looking at the life and work of Charles B. J. Snyder. His first thirty years made him sensitive to the difficulties of poverty and the ravages of fire, leading him to place equal value on practicality and idealism and imbuing him with the optimism of the Progressive Era and the excitement of turn-of-the-twentieth-century New York City.

The Early Years

His parents, who traced their British and Dutch lineage back to this country's early settlers, were living in humble circumstances in the mid-nineteenth century. After marrying in 1857, Charity Curtis Shonts and George Snyder, like George's older brother Earl Stimpson Snyder and his wife, settled in Stillwater, New York, a booming mill town on the banks of the Hudson. Charity and her one brother, a railroad conductor, came from a family of Saratoga County farmers. George, the second-oldest in a family of eight whose own father had died in 1850 when George was seventeen, worked as a harness maker. But in 1862, when their firstborn, Ella, was five years old, Charles two years old, and Charity pregnant with Kitty, George enlisted as a foot soldier with the 77th Regiment to fight in the Civil War. Charity moved back with her two children to her parents' home on Van Dam Street, just a few blocks from the center of Saratoga Springs.

One crucial aspect of Charles's life—a key to his later creation of palatial schools in immigrant neighborhoods—was that, born November 4, 1860, he grew up poor in one of the wealthiest, most opulent vacation communities in the country. In 1853 a second railroad line had been built into the center of Saratoga Springs so that in a mere three hours, Manhattanites could come to gamble, bet at the racetrack, and drink the waters, with no fewer than fifteen spas offering healing draughts and sociability. Mammoth hotels with three-storied porticoes, grand venues for people to see and be seen, lined Broadway. Charles must have felt like an outsider in his own hometown. He and his friends could saunter the streets, looking at the flurry of trunks being delivered and at the lavish dress and behavior of out-of-towners.

This attractive life of the well-to-do was foreign to Charles. His father, home in 1864 one year before the end of the Civil War, apparently could never recover from his war experiences and tried unsuccessfully to reestablish himself as a harness maker. The Snyders were able, probably with the help of Charity's parents, to buy a nearby house on Van Dorn Street according to the 1865 census. Small, wooden, modest, the house was valued at $800 in a neighborhood of $5,000 to $6,000 houses, including that of Charity's parents. Two blocks away was the children's warm, sturdy, two-story brick public school. On Sundays they walked ten blocks to attend the imposing downtown Methodist-Episcopal church on Washington Street. Charity took in boarders, and George found work as a laborer and as a clerk. But a year later he moved out and boarded in downtown Saratoga Springs, after which, when his son Charles was thirteen, he disappeared, perhaps joining another brother, Orris Snyder, in Bergen County, New Jersey, perhaps moving to New York City. Again, Charity and the children moved back with her parents.

A year after George's disappearance, seventeen-year-old Ella found work in a milliner's shop to help support the family, but the following year she stayed home, possibly because of poor health. The year after that, having returned to work, she died when Charles was sixteen. Four years later the children's grandfather Jeremiah died. Charles's youngest sister, Kitty, was kept home until she was a mature, healthy twenty-four before starting work as a salesclerk. Against the background of this affluent Gilded Age mecca for the well-to-do, the Snyders's experience of struggle and heartache was a connection to the immigrant public-school children in New York that may account for Snyder's passion for providing them beautiful schools.

Another seminal aspect of Charles's youth in small-town Saratoga Springs was calamity caused by fires: From the time he was four until he left at eighteen, twenty-seven major fires occurred in this small town, including seven that destroyed behemoth wooden hotels. Such regular devastation must have been frightening and disruptive for a boy, but particularly affecting was the loss in 1865, when Charles was five, of the Marvin House Hotel in the heart of town on the corner of Broadway and Division, owned and run by cousins Philip, Adam, and Daniel Snyder. Perhaps it was no coincidence that when Charles was thirty-five, he would build the first fireproofed public schools in the United States, employing techniques beyond those simply required by law.

Saratoga Springs offered a budding architect other valuable experiences. Its residential streets constituted a virtual architectural primer of styles—Greek Revival, Romanesque Revival, Italianate, French Renaissance, Queen Anne. Jobs were plentiful not only to provide goods and services for vacationers but also to rebuild the highly profitable hotels destroyed by fires, including the Marvin House. As an adolescent Charles would have had the opportunity of working in construction but may have tended toward bookkeeping instead, perhaps at his cousins' hotel. This experience likely led to his being hired as a notary public in a publishing firm when he moved to New York after high school. He attended Saratoga Springs High School, and, although the records are lost for the class of 1878, the fact that he was accepted by Cooper Union suggests that he did graduate. The school's 1853 building he attended was replaced in 1886 by a new school that, according to historian Evelyn Barrett in the *Chronicles of Saratoga*, had

> well equipped physical and chemical laboratories, separate gymnasiums for both sexes, a commodious auditorium, seating 420 persons ... a union free school library with 2,000 volumes, and a valuable reference library ... accessible to students at all times.[1]

This new state-of-the-art school, which he would have seen on visits home, became the model of the type he would provide for New York City schoolchildren.

First Years in New York City

Of course, a young man with talent and aspiration would have wanted to be in the city at the center of the universe. And his mother also would have wanted her promising son to go to the place of opportunity for higher education and high-quality apprenticeships rather than stay home supporting her and his younger sister. At eighteen, in 1878, he headed for New York, a move that was made possible through family connections.

Charles's mother's first cousin, Ellen Louise Curtis, had lived almost literally a movie star's life. In 1850 her father had set her up in her own milliner's shop in Saratoga Springs. Bright and successful, she had progressed from there to Troy, to Philadelphia, and finally to New York City, the fashion capital of the country. She moved her shop up from Grand Street to Twelfth Street, then to 17 East Fourteenth Street, just a few doors down from the fashionable Delmonico's Restaurant, on Fourteenth Street at the corner of Fifth Avenue at that time. Along the way in 1858, she had married the publishing magnate William Jennings Demorest. She and her husband created a little empire through stapling paper dress patterns, her major contribution to fashion history, into the center of his popular magazines with titles such as *Demorest's Illustrated Monthly Magazine* and *Mme. Demorest's Mirror of Fashions*—"Madame" alluding to Empress Eugenie, the French fashion magnate of the time. Ellen did not patent the tissue-paper dress pattern she had invented (William, by contrast, who also saw himself as an inventor, filed two individual patents, for a sewing machine and for a velocipede bicycle). In keeping with the free-thinking traditions of Ellen's Dutch heritage and of the Masons to which her husband belonged, she hired African American women and treated them as equals, telling customers who objected, no matter how wealthy, to go elsewhere. She cofounded Sorosis, a New York City women's club of liberal bent, and she and her husband were avid temperance advocates.

The Demorests were supportive of eighteen-year-old Charles in the practical logistics of living in a new expensive city, but perhaps even more importantly as role models of independent thought. He moved into a rooming house three blocks away from his cousins' office and emporium at 17 East Fourteenth Street, and we can assume Demorest provided him a day job while he attended Cooper Union at night. But not until 1885 is he listed in the New York City Directory as a notary at Demorest's office. Demorest may well also have arranged an apprenticeship for him with a carpenter/architect who rented an office in the Demorest Studio Building at 6 West

Fourteenth Street, diagonally from Demorest's own office. Charles would come to display the social conscience, principled independent thought, and inventiveness the Demorests exemplified, with Charles providing his own designs for public-school ventilating machines, desks, heated cloakrooms, water fountains, and more, although he, like Ellen, never filed for patents.

He was living near Union Square in what was then the political, cultural, and retail center of the city. He lived with seven others in a Greek Revival home turned boarding house at 155 West Thirteenth Street, a few doors west of the imposing Greek Revival Village Presbyterian church. A block further to the west was the 1877 PS 16, for which in 1899 he would design an addition. Around him was the heart of New York. On East Fourteenth stood the original Tammany Hall, the political hub. Next door was the Academy of Music, the center of New York's social scene for the last third of the nineteenth century, featured in the opening scene of Edith Wharton's *The Age of Innocence*. Union Square was also the classical music district; Carnegie Hall was still more than a decade in the future. In addition to the Academy, people went to George Post's Chickering Hall at Fifth and Eighteenth or to the original Steinway Hall on East Fourteenth Street, the venue of Charles Dickens's and Oscar Wilde's tremendously popular lectures. To the north on Twenty-Third Street were Bryant's and Pike's Opera Houses and to the south the Astor Place Opera House, scene of the notorious 1849 riot. For drama, one went to the Booth Theater on Twenty-Third Street, the Union Square Theater, or Alexander Saeltzer's Theatre Française on West Fourteenth Street. Across from it stood the Renwick mansion in which the Metropolitan Museum of Art was located until 1880. This was also the heyday of New York's first major shopping area, the Ladies' Mile. The opening of the Sixth Avenue Elevated, the year Charles arrived in town, brought crowds to the mercantile granddames, whose former buildings still dominate the area—Arnold Constable and Lord & Taylor on Broadway and, on Sixth Avenue, the emporia of Macy's, Seigel-Cooper, Ehrich Brothers, and Adams Drygoods.

Walking the streets, young Snyder, without even leaving his immediate neighborhood, would have learned from the great architects of the time: McKim, Mead, & White, Richard Morris Hunt, Ernest Flagg, Henry Hardenbergh, R. H. Robertson, Edward Kendall, C. C. Haight, William Schickel. They all designed buildings in the Union Square area during the fourteen years Snyder was working for Demorest.

During Snyder's first year in New York, when walking just the two blocks of Fourteenth Street between his rooming house and workplace, he would have witnessed the erection of three W. Wheeler Smith commercial buildings and, in his second year, the completion of David & John Jardine's Baumann's Dry Goods.*

As a young man, Snyder would have seen firsthand several dramatic moments in the city's history: in 1879 the first electric streetlights on Broadway from Fourteenth to Twenty-Sixth Streets, in 1883 the opening of the Brooklyn Bridge, in 1886 the unveiling of the Statue of Liberty. He would have lived through New York's transformation from a city of one- to six-story buildings to a city of skyscrapers. He would have followed the startling emergence of Madison Square Garden (1887–90) and of three college campuses—Columbia, New York University in the Bronx, and City College. He would also have watched the demolition of grand buildings, e.g., Andrew Jackson Davis's English-Collegiate-Gothic first home of New York University on Washington Square in 1890. A more exhilarating time and place for a young newcomer would be hard to imagine.

Right on schedule, in 1881 Charles earned a three-year Certificate in Practical Geometry from Cooper Union. Three years later, the same year the college started a four-year program in architecture, he earned a second three-year certificate, this time in Elementary Architectural Drawing. Instead of the plain "Charles Snyder" on his earlier degree, the second certificate read, "Chas. B. J. Snyder." What the initials "B. J." stand for remained a mystery for years. Charles added them perhaps to give himself an air of distinction (like the architect C. P. H. Gilbert, for example), perhaps to distinguish himself from two Charles Snyder cousins in Saratoga Springs

---

*Simply to mention some buildings that went up during that period and still stand: Edward Kendall's Methodist Book Concern (1888–90) on Fifth Avenue and Twentieth, southwest corner; his Gorham Building (1884–86) next to Lord and Taylor; C. C. Haight's Brooks Brothers (1883–84) across Broadway from Lord and Taylor; Ernest Flagg's downtown Scribner's store (1893–94) at 153 Fifth Avenue; McKim, Mead, and White's Judge Building (1888) at Fifth and Sixteenth; Stanford White's Goelet Building (1886) on the southeast corner of Broadway and Twentieth; catty-cornered from it, his Warren Building (1890); Napoleon Lebrun's East Eighteenth Street firehouse; a wealth of R. H. Robertson buildings—the Rand School (1885–87) on West Fifteenth, the Lincoln (1889–90) at the corner of Fourteenth and Union Square West, the YWCA (1890) on West Sixteenth, the Mohawk (1891) on West Twenty-First, and the McIntyre (1890–92) on East Eleventh; Henry Hardenbergh's Western Union Building (1882–83) on Madison Square; Charles Rentz's Webster Hall on East Eleventh (1886); William Schickel's Century Building (1880–81) on Union Square North; Richard Morris Hunt's 1888 Jackson Free Library, a crow-gabled Dutch guildhall on West Twelfth near Greenwich Avenue (Hunt's 1857 Studio Building stood at 15 West Tenth Street). George Post's 1877 Hospital stood on the block between Fifteenth and Sixteenth Streets and Fifth and Sixth Avenues.

or from a rash of Charles Snyders of dubious repute in New York City newspaper stories. Whatever the reason for his adding those two initials with their aristocratic ring, they were probably a nod to his paternal grandfather, Benjamin, and to his maternal grandfather, Jeremiah.* Professionally, Snyder was known as C.B.J., judging from references in newspaper articles and the way he signed blueprints, drawings, articles, and letters. To his mother, he was Charlie.

A description of his blueprints as engineering plans of architectural structures suggests that the six years at Cooper Union prepared him as both engineer and architect; but in addition to the training he gained from his courses, the whole spirit of Cooper Union became an important underpinning for his career. For one thing, the school's atmosphere of practical idealism—grappling with problems "by promoting the power and the means of their solution, rather than dogmatizing upon theoretical methods"[2]— instilled a solution-seeking, can-do attitude. For another, Peter Cooper's egalitarian vision—"to instruct, elevate, and improve the working classes in the city of New York [through] branches of knowledge which are practically applied in their daily occupations"[3]—confirmed his unflagging drive to provide public schools for primarily working-class families and to promote the newly introduced manual-training curriculum. Finally, even as the 1884 Cooper Union Trustees "doubt whether at any time, or anywhere in the world, results of equal value to the community have ever been achieved with so small an expenditure of money,"[4] similarly throughout his career, Snyder would build schools at sometimes half the cost per child of schools in other American cities. The founding and operating principles of Cooper Union resonated deeply with C. B. J. Snyder.

In addition to working for Demorest and studying at Cooper Union, young Snyder apprenticed himself to master carpenter William Bishop (1826–88). Perhaps Bishop felt a particular affinity for Charles because Bishop's first wife and child had died; the son would have been almost exactly Charles's age. Bishop, a volunteer fireman who lived and worked mainly in the West Village, was a Mason, as was Demorest. Charles's association with this minor New York City carpenter/architect/volunteer fireman reinforced his concern about fire and gave him practical experience on a higher order than the day-labor jobs rebuilding Saratoga Springs hotels would have.

---

*Benjamin had died in 1850, ten years before Charles was born; Jeremiah Shonts was the main stable male figure in Charles's early life. He lived down the block at the corner of Van Darn and what was then Pearl Street; the Snyders lived at the corner of Van Darn and Van Dorn.

Even before Snyder had completed his second three-year certificate from Cooper Union, Demorest must have realized that his wife's talented cousin could be far more useful to him as an architect than as an accountant. From 1882 until 1891, when he officially became superintendent of school buildings, Snyder filed thirty-five alteration jobs with the Manhattan Department of Buildings. Almost all were in the Fourteenth Street/Ladies' Mile area, the majority for Demorest or one of his sons, thirty for less than $2,000, four averaging $11,000 each, and one for $75,000 but with no completion date. Snyder was willing to do the often-thankless work of commercial alterations—experience that served him well: high schools he later designed would be commended for their similarity to new Broadway office buildings. The 1888–89 New York City Directory was the first to list his profession as architect.

Snyder may even have contributed to the practice of architecture in locations as distant as Central America. The book *History and Commerce of New York City*, 1891, includes the following:

> [Mr. Snyder] has developed a large business in Central America. He is the designer of the earthquake-proof buildings which have been erected in such large numbers in Costa Rica and other points in that section. . . . Mr. Snyder was the first to discover the true principle on which such buildings should be erected, and his success in solving this difficult problem is alone sufficient to establish his skill and ability as an architect.[5]

Such a claim would seem hard to make up, but then this is the only reference to such work, and the entry as a whole is rather grandiloquent, not a measured, formal biographical statement.

By age twenty-six, Snyder was sufficiently established to set up his mother, sister, and grandmother in a fancier lifestyle than they had been eking out in Saratoga Springs—or, at least, one closer to him. The sale of the family farm may also have made the move possible. In 1886 Snyder bought a lot in the popular commuter suburb immortalized by George M. Cohan's "Forty-five Minutes from Broadway," the newly subdivided, garden-type community of Iselin Park near downtown New Rochelle. Its Saratoga Springs–like resort aspects must have made the Snyder women feel at home there. The *New York Times* reported in 1896 that J. P. Morgan and other prominent families had opened their handsome cottages at Premium Point: "The village is rapidly assuming its lively Summer aspect."[6] For his family Snyder designed the house, with its big front porch, that still stands at 157 Elm Street (fig. 7).

Figure 7. The Snyder Family Home in New Rochelle, New York. Arrington photo.

He gave up his room on Thirteenth Street to live there with his family for six years, commuting via frequent trains from Grand Central Terminal. In March 1889, a month after his grandmother's death, the *New Rochelle Pioneer*, one of four daily newspapers, noted "extensive alterations and additions" to the Elm Street house, presumably in preparation for bringing home in September his Dutch bride, aspiring artist Harriet Katherine de Vries of Jersey City Heights, New Jersey. Announced in the September 12, 1889, *New York Times*, the wedding was, according to the *New Rochelle Pioneer*, a lavish catered affair in the "large handsome parlors" of the bride's home. Guests were served a "sumptuous supper," there was music and dancing, and the presents were "costly and handsome." The couple honeymooned in the Catskills. In subsequent years the social columns reported many of the Snyders's comings and goings, including the DeVries visits to New Rochelle and the Snyders's trips to Saratoga Springs.

The move to New Rochelle worked well for Snyder on a professional as well as a personal level. By the time his first son, Howard Halsey Snyder, was born in 1890, Charles was a leader in the downtown St. John's Methodist Episcopal Church, the parsonage of which he bought seemingly as investment property. According to the November 22, 1890, *Pioneer*,

Figure 8. Snyder Ad in the *New Rochelle Pioneer* from 1890.

C. B. J. Snyder holds an enviable reputation as an architect, designer, and constructor gained through the uniformly successful carrying out of commissions in various parts of the country. His work in New York City on store, office, and club buildings is so well known as to need no comment, and as he now intends to make a specialty of fine residences and dwelling houses here, we doubt not but that the same success will attend him.[7]

Snyder's first ad appeared in the same issue (fig. 8). It would run weekly for a year, until he joined the New York City Board of Education and one J. Oscar Bunce took over his private practice, according to the November 14, 1891, *Pioneer*. But perhaps the most appealing aspect of New Rochelle was the whole community of artists and architects drawn to the green and quiet of this newly developed suburb—most notably, the artist Frederick Remington, the architectural critic Montgomery Schuyler, and the architect George Palliser, who wrote *Model Homes for the People* and *Late Victorian Architecture* (he also lived on Elm Street). Snyder had many of like mind with whom to socialize and exchange professional ideas.

His portfolio prior to his appointment with the Board of Education, in addition to his family's home at 157 Elm Street and the commercial alterations he did while working for the Demorests, included homes for the well-to-do. For a doctor from one of New Rochelle's old families, Snyder designed a three-story, five-bedroom "modern cottage" that earned the distinction of being pictured and described in the 1895 Building Edition of *Scientific American* (fig. 9). He also designed two more homes on Le Count Place in downtown New Rochelle and two in New Jersey, the four documented in a *Pioneer* article that included this statement: "His practical ideas of house planning meet the hearty approval of the ladies, hence a great measure of his success." Additionally, in 1885 he had designed a four-story townhouse with a first-story bakery on East 58th Street (fig. 10) and,

Figure 9. The Snyder-Designed House Pictured in the 1895 Building Edition of *Scientific American*..

Figure 10. The Snyder Bakery on Fifty-Eighth Street, Manhattan, Demolished. Photo provided by Christopher Gray.

in 1890, a boathouse on the Harlem River for the Lone Star Boat Club, described by the *New York Times* as a "pretty clubhouse" with "the upper floor given up to the ladies." A conspicuous absence from his early experience is schools.

The Move to Public Practice

How did Snyder, a notary, become Snyder, a revolutionary? How did this young man, with only a modest architectural profile, attain the annual salary of $6,000 in the prestigious position of New York City's superintendent of school buildings? Although Snyder didn't have political ambitions himself, he was surrounded by people who did, from his mentor William Bishop to the men he worked for. In the 1890s, on the Prohibition ticket, William Jennings Demorest ran for U.S. president, vice president, and mayor of New York City. Demorest's partner, Joseph J. Little, served in the House of Representatives as a Democrat from 1891 to 1893.

It was Joseph J. Little who seems to provide the answer to how Snyder got the superintendent's position. Like Snyder, Little had come to New York at the age of eighteen from a small town in upstate New York. He advanced from apprentice printer to owner of his own concern on Canal Street. Then, in 1873, a partnership with Demorest escalated his business, with his new partner providing a huge new building for him on Astor Place. Snyder, who worked in Demorest's Fourteenth Street office, would certainly have had frequent dealings with Little.

Joseph Little joined the New York City Board of Education in January 1891. Little was on the Finance Committee and chaired the Committee on Buildings. He may have even mounted an investigation into building fraud that resulted in the July 1, 1891, resignation of George Debevoise, superintendent of school buildings since 1886. That same day the president of the board, John L. Hunt, instructed the Committee on Buildings to present the names of candidates to refill the position for the consideration of the board at the next week's meeting. One week later the minutes of the July 8, 1891, meeting record Chairman Little as saying,

> The Committee on Buildings . . . respectfully report that they have had before them the names of several persons, applicants for the position. Of all the names submitted, your committee has selected that of Mr. CBJ Snyder. Mr. Snyder is an architect in good standing, well qualified to perform the duties of the position, and in the

opinion of your Committee, if elected, will make a very efficient Superintendent of School Buildings. It is recommended that he be appointed.⁸

Snyder was duly elected, winning on the second ballot with twelve out of thirteen votes, having never, as far as is known, worked on a school.

Chapter 2

Auspicious Times for Snyder's Public-School Mandate

The State of the School System

IN 1895, "THREE-QUARTERS of the public school buildings of New York were defective or unsanitary to a greater or lesser degree,"[1] charged a much publicized report by Board of Education commissioner Charles Wehrum, who had personally visited all 132 schools. Here is Wehrum's description of the Allen-Street school, followed by two others:

> Grammar School No. 42, No. 30 Allen street—Tenth Ward—March 21, 1893. Attendance 2,060. Classes 45. Very noisy; elevated road within ten feet from front windows; class-rooms dark; burn gas in a number of them; sixteen class-rooms without desks, girls even in the Grammar Department doing their lessons on their knees, making cripples out of children; in my opinion this is a shameful condition; very poor; closets on boys' side inadequate, only eight seats provided; school crowded and refusing students.[2]

"Shameful conditions" prevailed—overcrowded schools that had to turn away children, dark classrooms requiring gas to be burned with its resulting fumes, classrooms with no desks, and inadequate and filthy bathrooms—conditions causing "sickness" and "cripples." The report listed another ninety-eight schools, using phrases such as "regular tinderbox," "sewer backed up," "exits dark and insufficient," "Babble let loose!" Although Snyder had been working for three and a half years by this time, the devastating 1893 recession had stymied the country, leaving his requests for repair budgets not acted upon.*

In fact, a wide range of other problems beset public schools in this era. For one thing, saloons and brothels were often located within 200 feet of grammar schools. New York's schools in the latter 1800s, one commentator said, took the prize for "sordid, hopeless ugliness."[3] Denunciation of the public schools came from another contemporary activist for better schools, Adele Marie Shaw, who described this scene:

> A room in which 46 little girls live and work five hours in the day contained only one outside window. The miserably flickering gas over their heads consumed the oxygen needed by starved lungs, and yet on the three warm days during which I visited this class I did not once see the window opened more than a few inches. The scourge of New York is consumption; [and] the preventive of consumption is fresh air.[4]

A great crusader for better schools, Jacob Riis, wrote in *The Battle with the Slum*:

> When I think of the old Allen Street school, with its hard and ugly lines, where the gas had to be kept burning even on the brightest days, recitations suspended every half-hour, and the children made to practice calisthenics so that they should not catch cold while the windows were opened to let in fresh air; of the dark playground downstairs, with the rats keeping up such a racket that one could hardly hear himself speak at times . . . I fancy that I can make out both the cause and the cure of the boy's desperation.[5]

Appalling schools were the cause of truancy and failure, reformers insisted; good schools would be the cure.

In addition to the deplorable conditions, the number of schools was insufficient. "Fifty thousand children roamed the streets for whom there was no room in the schools,"[6] Riis wrote. There was a large increase in the

---

*The November 24, 1891, *New York Times* reported that "there were within [200 yards] of Grammar School No. 10, in Wooster Street, twenty-three barrooms, and within the same distance of Grammar School No. 47, in East Twelfth Street, fifteen barrooms and five reputed houses of ill fame. Wooster Street in the neighborhood of the schoolhouse is known to be infested with similar places. . . . Ten barrooms [are found] near a schoolhouse in Twenty-third Street, eighteen in Sixteenth Street, eleven in Twentieth Street, and thirteen in Nineteenth Street, all on the east side." The June 20, 1895, *New York Times* reported 237 saloons within 200 feet of the entrance to a school.

number of schoolchildren at this time because of high immigration, changes in laws, and increases in family size. Snyder's career coincided with the decades of unprecedented numbers of immigrants disembarking in New York City (1890–1920) and with the beginning of the Great Migration of African Americans from the South. Also, because of the 1890s reform efforts, such as better healthcare, that reduced child mortality and the strengthening and enforcing of the Compulsory Education and Child Labor laws, there was a large increase in the number of schoolchildren. From 1890 to 1900, about 80 percent of eligible children enrolled in public schools. But the number actually attending rose from 50 percent in 1890 to 90 percent in 1900. The result was a relentless increase of 25,000 new students per year,[7] requiring additional new school buildings annually simply to accommodate this advancing "army" of children (fig. 11). The replacement of many obsolete and dangerous schools was being demanded by activists and others but could not be addressed. Many schools implemented double sessions but still were faced with not enough "sittings."

A third problem Snyder faced was New York's failure to have stayed abreast of current educational developments. One glaring example: New York was the only major city in the United States with no public high schools. Boston, in contrast, had opened its first public high school in 1821. The city had few mechanical training or physical education classes, the types of progressive offerings appearing in other public schools around the country. Also, the city had no public kindergartens, which had been introduced in St. Louis in 1873.[8] Basically, New York's schools had not changed in thirty years. An academic curriculum was taught by rote, with no specialized spaces to accommodate new teaching methods or pedagogical developments.

How had this dire situation occurred? Eighty-five years earlier, the city's first free public school had opened under the auspices of the Free School Society (of which DeWitt Clinton was the first president) in an 1806 Greek-Revival-style building near the present City Hall Park. That first school building was designed to accommodate a system that had been developed by Joseph Lancaster (1778–1838), a British educator, consisting of one large room surrounded by break-out nooks, which allowed a single teacher to handle 100, even 200 children, by using the older students as "monitors" to hear the recitations of the younger ones.* Because of the economical nature

---

*For two excellent articles on the early schools in this country, see Dell Upton's "Lancastrian Schools, Republican Citizenship, and the Spatial Imagination in Early Nineteenth-Century America," *Journal of the Society of Architectural Historians* (1998): 238–53, and John Rothfork's

Figure 11. Army of 610,000 Children Went to School. *New York World, Evening Edition.* September 11, 1905.

of the Lancastrian system, New York was among the last cities in the United States to move to the more effective method of graded classrooms that had originated in Prussia in the mid-eighteenth century. The Free School Society found itself with outmoded buildings, its government funding threatened by private and parochial schools and a growing awareness that its very name connoted the negative idea of charity. In 1853 it handed over to the newly

---

"Transcendentalism and Henry Barnard's 'School Architecture,'" *Journal of General Education* (1977): 173–87.

established Board of Education seventeen buildings and fifty-three primary schools, many in leased buildings, plus five racially segregated schools.

For the next forty-three years, New York public schools operated on a ward/trustee system. In each of twenty-four wards the schools were overseen by five politically appointed trustees who made all the important decisions for the schools in their ward—curriculum, personnel, repairs, and new building construction. But the funding came, via the Board of Education, from the city Board of Estimate and Apportionment. The twenty-one Board of Education Commissioners financed the ward schools but could not initiate actions; the trustees, who could, didn't control the money to support their initiatives. The resulting red tape, absence of a clear line of responsibility, and lack of city-wide standards or policies compounded the other problems of patronage and inequity. For instance, in 1888 in the Second Ward the average attendance was 66, while in the Nineteenth Ward it was 19,435, yet both had the same five trustees.[9] Similarly absurd, "A man who had been dead a year ago was appointed a school trustee of the Third Ward."[10]

New York's public schools were a microcosm of the ills of society as a whole during the era of Tammany, the notoriously corrupt Democratic machine. Since Boss Tweed's rise to power in the 1850s, Tammany politicians had been siphoning off, by one estimate, as much as 50 percent of city funds. Education had not been a priority. The schools exemplified all "the disgraceful conditions of the average schoolhouse" that Henry Barnard, first United States Commissioner of Education (1867–70), had cited almost fifty years earlier as the impetus for his 1842 "manual on the art of building and equipping schools."*

---

*Henry Barnard, *School Architecture, or Contributions to the Improvement of School-Houses in the United States*, ed. Jean and Robert McClintock (New York: Teachers College Press, 1970), 31–33. Among the "Common Errors in School Architecture," Barnard says the schools are: (1) badly located ("exposed to the noise, dust and danger of the highway"); (2) unattractive inside and out ("built at the least possible expense of material and labor"); (3) too small ("no sufficient space for the convenient seating and necessary movements of the scholars"); (4) badly lighted; (5) not properly ventilated; (6) not properly heated ("The heat is not equally diffused, so that one portion of a school-room is frequently overheated, while another portion, especially the floor, is too cold."); (7) not well furnished ("Seats are too high . . . with no suitable support for the back. Desks are too high for the seats. . . . Desks . . . are . . . attached to the wall on three sides of the room, so that the faces of the scholars are turned from the teacher. . . . Aisles are not so arranged that . . . each scholar can . . . be seen and approached by the teacher, without incommoding any other."); (8) lacking amenities ("Not provided with blackboards, maps, clock, thermometer, and other apparatus and fixtures which are indispensable to a well-regulated and instructed school"); (9) lacking retiring rooms ("for children of either sex, when performing the most private offices of nature"); (10) lacking landscaping ("Deficient in all of those in and out-door arrangements which help to promote habits of order and neatness, and cultivate delicacy of manners and refinement of feeling").

Snyder's immediate predecessor, a Tammany man, hadn't done much to help the situation. George W. Debevoise, the third buildings chief for the New York system following Amnon Macvey (1837–72) and David Stagg (1872–86), did design two schools that have historical designation: PS 35 at Fifty-first Street and First Avenue is on the National Register of Historic Places, and PS 11 in the Bronx is landmarked. He fought in the Civil War. He worked in an iron-manufacturing business, with an investment company, and as president of a railroad. In general, he seems to have had no training in architecture and no real interest in schools—all the while living as part of the establishment in Harlem at 13 East 128th Street just off Fifth Avenue. In 1884, he became a trustee at PS 68 on 128th Street and Lenox Avenue, attended by well-off students and dubbed "the silk-stocking school." This position was presumably his "in" when the position of superintendent of school buildings became open two years later.

Furthermore, Debevoise's tenure as superintendent of school buildings was fraught with questionable ethics. When an inspector said he had found a notice on his desk ordering him to pay no attention to the sanitary work and took it to his boss, Debevoise (only six months on the job) said, "Well, you see what it says, don't you?" Debevoise bullied inspectors to look the other way when encountering substandard work. Another inspector reported that, under direct orders from Debevoise, he had signed off on plumbing and sanitary work that he knew to be deficient. When a third inspector got into a personal altercation with contractors for not "doing their duty," the inspector was removed from his position. Compounding these deficiencies, Debevoise was also snippy, saying once, "I presume that by the time we have finished the work mapped out the public will cease grumbling about its defective school buildings."[11] The building committee concluded that the city had suffered from "gross impositions and fraud."[12] Though never convicted of wrongdoing, Debevoise resigned after four years on the job.

Why in the face of the pervasive shortcomings in the existing schools did this thirty-one-year-old former notary not feel daunted by this challenge? There in fact were manifold reasons that C. B. J. Snyder felt adequate to the task. They all suggest a common denominator: Snyder was in the right place at the right time.

Snyder in the Right Place at the Right Time

To begin with, the very fact that the school system was in crisis made his job clear. He was needed. Despite the magnitude of the system's shortcomings of having failed to provide enough schools, to maintain those schools it did have, or to keep up with the times, Snyder (fig. 12) was hired

Figure 12. Charles B. J. Snyder, from "How New York City Has Solved Some Trying School Building Problems," by Snyder. *School Journal*, 1902, and drawing of same by Hector Janoska.

with the expectation that "the new public school buildings of this city should equal or excel those of any other city in the world."[13] While many would have felt defeated by the prospect of having to reverse years of institutional incompetence, Snyder found the challenge invigorating. He had a mission.

Snyder's personal proclivities were aligned with the times where public sentiment was infused with the Progressive belief "in the perfectibility of the republic," as E. L. Doctorow phrased it.[14] Optimism was in the air. Progressives were confident that social and organizational solutions would correct the disturbing conditions of society and that schools were central to the notions of progress and human betterment. Snyder was bolstered by and then in turn promoted the social activism of the Progressive Era. This historic era's span (1890 to 1920) coincided almost exactly with the years of Snyder's career. His efforts were part of the widespread initiatives intended to ameliorate the difficult life of the disadvantaged—for instance, settlement houses, public health reforms, public baths, public parks, and libraries.

The public schools seemed to be the lynchpin of these attempts to improve society and transform immigrants into model American citizens.

Snyder's mission was part of this groundswell of reform efforts, in New York and in the country as a whole—a response to the desperate poverty spawned by industrialization and massive immigration. In 1891 the New York Society of Parks and Playgrounds was formed, and the first municipal playground opened a year later in Seward Park. In 1893, Lillian Wald, the power behind the playground, also started the "public health nurse" program (which blossomed into the Henry Street Settlement House) and brought social programs to the schools, including special-education classes, free lunches, and school nurses. In 1897 the city started a program for building public bathhouses. In 1902, Jacob Riis wrote about how the myriad reform efforts kept subverting his account of the problems of the slum. He had been "compelled not once but half a dozen times to go back and wipe out what [he] had written because it no longer applied. . . . Yes, ours is the greatest of all times."[15] With all the social activism and reform of the 1890s, Snyder became part of galvanizing forces larger than just himself.

The comradeship and collegiality of this widespread social movement strengthened Snyder. He had a particularly supportive relationship with members of the Board of Education to whom he reported—particularly J. J. Little, who hired him, and longtime Building Committee chairman Robert Maclay, after whom he named his second son, Robert Maclay Snyder. Journalist and educator Adele Marie Shaw remarked about the stupendous energy, skill, and determination of the Board of Education in addressing the city's staggering public-school problem.[16] On the occasion of Snyder's election as superintendent of school buildings for the newly consolidated Greater City in 1898, he wrote in a letter to the *New York Times*,

> Whatever measure of success I may have attained in the administration of the duties of my office, has been possible only through the unswerving confidence and faith reposed in me by every member of the Board of Education from the date of my original appointment in 1891 to the present time.[17]

Snyder's appreciative tone is remarkable and revealing of his strong sense of loyalty to the educational establishment.

Then there was his partnership with William Maxwell, the Progressive first superintendent of schools for Greater New York. Maxwell saw education as involving the whole child, not just the child's brain; he advocated physical and manual training, not just academic subjects. As Riis phrased it, "The 'three H's,' the head, the heart, and the hand—a whole boy—are taking the place too long monopolized by the 'three R's'"[18] The progressive curriculum was expanding beyond narrow, inflexible, authoritarian academics to include teaching techniques that recognized "the sacredness of the child's individuality"[19] and practical, hands-on courses, more in keeping with the life experiences of students. For this expanded curriculum, new types of spaces were needed. Maxwell was the pedagogical architect and Snyder the literal one. About their relationship, a 1903 writer said that once Maxwell had devised the curriculum, a call was "sent to Mr. Snyder to build a home for the school. This he does, fashioning it carefully to meet pedagogical requirements; a year or so later the school begins housekeeping in a new structure handed over by the Building Bureau."[20] The almost twenty-year relationship of Snyder and Maxwell remained synergistic and interdependent, collegial and productive.

Another important relationship was that with journalist, photographer, and consummate reformer of the age Jacob Riis. "Yesterday I went with Superintendent Snyder through some of the new schools he is building . . . in the crowded districts," Riis wrote in *A Ten Years' War*.[21] Riis's settlement house, established in 1892 at 48 Henry Street, would be joined in 1898 by a Snyder school two blocks south at 8 Henry Street. The 1890s were bookended by the publication of Riis's *How the Other Half Lives*, one of the most widely read books of the decade, and its sequel, *The Battle with the Slum*. Particularly in Chapter 13 of *Battle*, "Justice to the Boy," Riis championed Snyder and the new schools. Additionally, Riis worked tirelessly for the schools—for example, lobbying the Board of Education for rooftop playgrounds and for the use of the schools as community centers. His view of education as the common denominator of all the reform efforts made Riis an important ally in furthering Snyder's mission to improve the schools.

New York City mayors were on Snyder's side as well. In 1894, three years after Snyder became superintendent of school buildings, the election of the reform candidate William Strong as mayor broke Tammany's half-century hold on New York City politics. Other reform mayors followed—namely, Seth Low and John Mitchel—though their terms were separated by heavy Tammany backlashes. However, the public schools by this time had been so established in the public's mind as the answer to society's woes that Tammany mayors showed a new interest in quality schools. About Tammany Democrat George McClellan, who in 1904 followed Seth Low, Snyder wrote,

> His Honor the Mayor places the public schools as a matter of paramount importance to the welfare of the Municipality. Almost his first

thought upon taking the oath of office seems to have been devoted to the question of providing the necessary school accommodations to wipe out part-time classes and keep pace with the regular growth in school population.[22]

Even a Tammany figure had begun seeing schools as of paramount importance to the welfare of the municipality.

Financing the public schools also transcended politics. The public now accepted investment in schools as a legitimate use of their tax dollars and as the responsibility of all, not just those whose children would benefit. School budgets, perhaps the single most crucial element in Snyder's success, increased significantly under most Tammany mayors, as well as reform mayors. Starting in 1884, New York had issued schoolhouse bonds of $2,000,000 annually for sites and new buildings. Then in 1895 and 1896, the bond amounts jumped to $5,000,000 each year—at a time when a big school could be built for $200,000. The year 1897 represented an all-time high when, in preparation for the consolidation of the boroughs and New York's prospective status as a premier city, bonds in the amount of $10,000,000 were authorized, with an additional $2,500,000 for high schools. Simultaneously, laws were pushed through that allowed the Board of Education to condemn property for school sites, reducing the acquisition process from twenty-two months to six.[23]

The stars further aligned in support of Snyder's career with the 1898 Consolidation of the Boroughs. Overnight New York City doubled in land mass and population to become the second-largest city in the world, after London. To match its "imperial destiny as the greatest city in the world"[24] (Mayor Hewitt, 1888), the city now aspired to a world-class public education system, and politicians continued to stand behind that desire in deed, not just word.

After the chaos of 1898, when no money was yet available for civic projects while the logistics of the huge new city were being worked out, New York continued to allot unprecedented sums to create a flagship public-school system. Not only did building campaigns receive substantial support, the day-to-day operations budgets of the schools also increased. During the first fifteen years after the consolidation, from 1899 to 1914, while the average attendance almost doubled from about 350,000 to 688,000 and staffing did double from 10,000 to 20,000, city appropriations for running the schools tripled—from $15 million in 1899 to almost $45 million in 1914 (fig. 13).

During that same period, the budgets for new construction amounted to $7,500,000 in 1899, $3,500,000 in 1900, $3,700,000 in 1901 (under Tammany mayor Van Wyck), almost $9,000,000 each year from 1902 to 1904 (under Reform mayor Seth Low), and an average of $6,500,000 annually throughout the next decade from 1905 to 1914 (see the chart in fig. 14). The city was pouring more money into the schools than ever before. No one was more acutely conscious of making the most of the ever-increasing construction budget than Superintendent of School Buildings Charles B. J. Snyder.

	1899	1914
Daily School Attendance	350,000	688,000
Staffing	10,000	20,000
School Appropriations	$15,300,000	$44,600,000

Figure 13. Appropriations for Running the Schools. Arrington table.

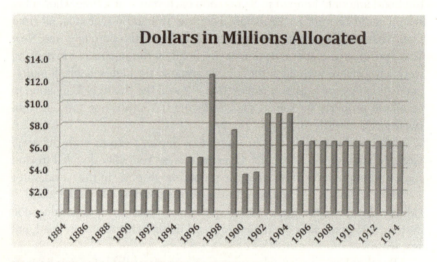

Figure 14. Appropriations for New Buildings. Arrington table.

Adding legitimacy to Snyder's mission, the decade of the 1890s was also a time when children and school systems were preeminent in the media. Newspapers called the twentieth century "the Century of the Child" and "the American Century." In 1890 starting the school day by reciting the Pledge of Allegiance became a routine that persists today in many schools.

Its author, Francis Bellamy, wrote in 1892, "The Public School is the most characteristic product of the four centuries of American life [and] the source of our greatness as a nation."[25] In a similar vein, noted school reformer John Dewey called education America's "fundamental method of social progress and reform."[26] Then in 1896 Nicholas Murray Butler, founder of Columbia University's Teachers College, created the logistics necessary for wholesale change in the schools when he pushed through his bill, which replaced the decentralized Tammany ward/trustee system with the centralized system of university-trained experts we have today. Winning the "second school war," a term coined by school historian Diane Ravitch in her 2000 book *The Great School Wars: A History of the New York City Public Schools*, the city's public schools became for the first time a major political issue. With school systems across the United States becoming consolidated and education the business of university-trained experts, people saw schools as the hope of the nation in dealing with the problems born of urban industrialization. Also, teachers came to command a better salary: "Once hardly thought worthy of a day laborer's hire, [a teacher] ranks to-day with a policeman in pay and privilege."[27]

The first decades of the twentieth century were exciting for a public-school architect, especially since the ideas of John Dewey and Francis Parker seemed to be coming to fruition, necessitating new types of spaces. Graduates of teachers' colleges were full of energy and often possessed a new view of education.[28] Angelo Patri wrote in his 1917 memoir *A Schoolmaster of the Great City: A Progressive Educator's Pioneering Vision for Urban Schools* about the effect that a class at Columbia University, a center for progressive ideas, had on him,

> I realized then that the child must move and not sit still: that he must make mistakes and not merely repeat perfect forms: that he must be himself and not a miniature reproduction of the teacher. The sacredness of the child's individuality must be the moving passion of the teacher. . . .
>
> I went back to the children ready to challenge their intelligence, keen to see them grapple and solve problems set for them, eager to watch them carry into their daily lives the ideas of the school. . . . The God of Discipline was replaced by the God of Watchfulness.[29]

Patri, also a principal of two Snyder schools in the Bronx (PS 4 and then PS 45) and "an important voice for progressive education,"[30] began the fight that is still going on today to replace rote, teacher-centered academic learning with the fresh air of student-centered, relevant, hands-on learning. To accommodate these changes architects were designing new types of spaces such as manual-training rooms and roof playgrounds.

Snyder was in the right place at the right time, in another important way: school architecture itself was coming into its own. About the building of public schools in this country, architectural historian Marta Gutman says, "Imagine the extent of this public works project, as important as any other in shaping a modern nation . . . hundreds of thousands of buildings and manufacture of huge quantities of equipment."[31] As the curriculum expanded beyond academics to include relevant and practical courses, nineteenth-century schoolhouses with just classrooms were being superseded by twentieth-century school buildings with many differentiated spaces such as gymnasiums, auditoriums, manual-training rooms, science laboratories, and libraries, a phenomenon Dale Gyure explores in his 2011 study *The Chicago Schoolhouse, 1856–2006: High School Architecture and Educational Reform*.

The challenge of designing new spaces to accommodate curricular changes sparked the imagination of many architects, and over a relatively short amount of time school design became a prestigious architectural specialty.[32] The new type of architect who specialized in schools included Edmund Wheelwright of Boston, William Ittner of St. Louis, William Mundie and Dwight Perkins of Chicago, and C. B. J. Snyder of New York, to name a few. As a result, wrote educational historian William W. Cutler, "schools have become among the most numerous and easily identifiable public buildings in the United States . . . synonymous with education and a reminder to all of an important time in their lives."[33] These were the glory days of public education.

Further, this era glorified architecture in general, in large part because of a watershed event in urban and architectural history, the 1893 Columbian Exposition, which ushered in the City Beautiful Movement with its belief that beautiful architecture would redeem society (fig. 15).[34] Historian Henry Adams described the exposition this way: America "seemed to have leaped directly from Corinth and Syracuse and Venice, over the heads of London and New York, to impose classical standards on plastic Chicago. . . . The new American world [seemed to have taken a] sharp and conscious twist toward ideals."[35] At the time architect Stanford White, one of the architects of the Columbian Exposition, was as widely and popularly known as any celebrity. Snyder was working in an increasingly prestigious profession.

Finally, Snyder's first decade on the job coincided with one of the greatest building phases of New York City's history. Beginning in the 1890s as

Figure 15. Chicago's 1893 Columbian Exposition. Keene State College, New Hampshire Continuing Education Course.

steel-framed construction became more accepted, great skyscrapers proliferated, primarily in lower Manhattan. Also, grand apartment houses, following the lead of the Dakota on the Upper West Side, offered a new residential possibility for the well-to-do. College campuses emerged in outlying, elevated locations: New York University's new campus on a hill in the Bronx overlooking the Harlem River; Columbia University in Morningside Heights, viewed at the time as the Acropolis of New York City; and City College, on that same ridge but in the Sugar Hill section of Harlem. After the 1898 Consolidation of the Boroughs had catapulted New York overnight into the position of second-largest city in the world, the city wanted to look the part. It chose distinguished architects to design its police precinct houses, fire stations, Carnegie libraries, public bathhouses—and public schools. New York was making itself over in the image of great European cities with imposing civic and cultural institutions. In these years around the turn of the twentieth century, many of the city's iconic buildings arose: the Metropolitan Museum of Art, the Customs House, the Forty-Second-Street Library, Grand Central Terminal, and Penn Station. The phenomenal building feat of the subways linked formerly distant sections of the city. Architectural historian Paul Goldberger comments on how these years of rapid growth "were perhaps the most exhilarating time of all."[36] Snyder participated in a new century like no other, reflected in grand municipal architecture, full of promise and hope, of possibility unhampered by cynicism.

The Right Man

Architecture and education came together at the 1904 St. Louis World's Fair, another of those exciting venues at the time for experiencing far-flung cultures and technologies. Unlike Chicago's White City, the St. Louis World's Fair had a Palace of Education that was spectacularly lit up at night, surrounded by lagoons spanned by ornate bridges. At this world's fair, the subject of the musical and popular song "Meet Me in St. Louis," Snyder was not just a visitor but a participant. The 1904 *Report of the New York State Commission* records "Due acknowledgment . . . to C. B. J. Snyder . . . who prepared the plans for the booth for both the State and city exhibits at no expense to the State," a booth that entailed 3,800 square feet and that won multiple prizes. It had a sixteen-foot façade of "fluted pilasters with ornamental caps" and a dentil cornice; the diagonal arched entranceway at an intersection of the aisles was surmounted by "State of New York" in gold letters. The report continues,

> Mr. Snyder's plans provided for a scheme of installation which, while inexpensive, was both artistic and dignified and admirably adapted for the display of the material to be exhibited. In fact, it was generally conceded that much more effective results had been obtained than by surrounding states which had expended considerably more money.[37]

Those two sentences could as well be describing Snyder's characteristic way of designing schools—at less expense than those of other cities but of high quality, dignified, and admirably functional.*

The following revolutionary events bolstered at least the first two decades and aspects of the third decade of Snyder's career. The optimistic sense of possibility of the Chicago and St. Louis World's Fairs propelled their ideals and classicism to iconic proportions in people's imaginations. Exemplifying and furthering Progressivism, the fairs were contemporaneous with the

---

*No pictures of the booth have survived. Snyder might have also participated in the summer 1901 Pan American Exposition in Buffalo and in the Jamestown, Virginia, Exposition of 1907, others of these frequent popular events that offered a means of celebrating educational and architectural advances.

greatest building program New York City had ever seen and numerous widespread social reforms. But Snyder's huge success lay not just in the ferment and fervor of the times. It also resulted from his personal qualities. In addition to being in the right place at the right time, he was the right man for the job.

Most important was his willingness to tolerate contradiction. He was simultaneously a radical and a bureaucrat. He embraced technologies of commercial architecture that were brand-new in the 1890s, such as steel-framed, curtain-wall construction and forced-air heating and ventilation. Architect Bruce Nelligan calls the book *Modern School-Houses*, published in 1910 and containing pertinent articles by Snyder and contemporaries, a "manifesto for modern schools."[38] Snyder's first high-school building, the Girls Wadleigh High School, an H-Plan design, was unlike any other anywhere. He went against his own tradition, putting auditoriums on the ground floor rather than on an upper one, as had been done in other cities. And he insisted that high-school students not be forced to use side entrances but be allowed to enter by the front door, usually reserved for faculty and visitors. He put primary and secondary students in Collegiate Gothic buildings, a style newly introduced to college campuses in this country but equally suited to all students, in his way of thinking. He was independent and forward-thinking and relished problem-solving.

At the same time, he had bureaucratic skills. He was able to negotiate the morass of state- and municipal-level regulations, all further complicated by the 1898 Consolidation of the Boroughs. He always did his homework: his prose is full of phrases like "after long and careful study," "after much reading and discussion and inspection of other schools," or "after much research and study." He was organized, willing to standardize, and able to run a modern large-scale architectural practice. While he built quality, durable construction for the ages, he employed and highlighted cost-cutting techniques. Noted architect and former dean of Yale's architecture school Robert A. M. Stern writes that "Snyder was a government bureaucrat who got things done while holding on to his ideals."[39]

Like the philosophy of his alma mater, Cooper Union, he was pragmatic yet idealistic. He combined modern functionality with traditional forms. In addition to using the modern construction techniques of steel-framing and mechanical ventilation, Snyder dramatically broadened school functionality from widespread use of classrooms only to include modern facilities such as gymnasiums, auditoriums, science laboratories, and mechanical-training rooms. But these modern functions and technologies existed in buildings dressed in the beautiful garb of traditional Western architecture: Dutch guild halls, Italian palazzi, French chateaux, and cathedral-like Collegiate Gothic buildings (fig. 16). Snyder's pragmatic, modern schools idealistically suggested that all students were worthy and that through education the best of Western civilization was available to them.

He had the courageous, empire-building abilities of a Robert Moses (New York State urban planner and master builder and the impetus behind New York City's highways, housing projects, and pools). At the same time, Snyder was humble, courteous, gracious, personable. He had full confidence that he could solve problems and was fully willing to advertise if not aggrandize his accomplishments. For example, he claimed that the school board was conducting the "most extensive building operations of any firm or corporation in the country."[40] At the same time, he collaborated well with his boss,

Figure 16. Miscellaneous Ornamentation. LaValle photo.

William H. Maxwell (the superintendent of schools, the pedagogical architect), with his employees, and with teachers and principals whose ideas he sought, incorporating those ideas into his designs. He was known for not keeping people waiting. If his one preserved published lecture—to the municipal engineers in 1904—is any indication, he was entertaining and at ease as a lecturer—and willing to be vulnerable. During the questions and answers at the end, he brought the audience back to a question he had posed at the beginning of the lecture about the depth required for the foundation of PS 38. He used the occasion to learn from others, not just dispense knowledge. Throughout his career he was prolific as a leading authority in school design, about which he lectured and published widely (fig. 17).

Snyder's quiet competence and his outspokenness when necessary garnered the affectionate loyalty of those he worked with. Responding in the *New York Times* to a letter that had appeared in the morning edition

Figure 17. Snyder at Desk as Portrayed in the 1898 *Architectural Record.*

criticizing the ventilation systems in the schools, Snyder protested the omission of "any fact whatsoever which would furnish us with a clue sufficient to permit of an investigation and remedying of the troubles, if any."[41] Even as a young man new to the job, he wasn't one to mince words. In his third annual report, he wrote about "how utterly false" was the impression that the Board of Education possessed property for erecting schools. His 1896 *Annual Report* includes an impassioned statement about school upkeep, pointing out that "the law places the power [to make repairs] absolutely in the hands of Trustees, [that he himself cannot] order any work whatsoever done in any building . . . [his] power being limited to recommendations that are entirely disregarded."[42] With wry humor he made his point forcefully.

One additional quality that accounts for his accomplishment bore no contradiction: his integrity kept him from the pitfalls of graft to which both his predecessor and successor succumbed. Each of them lasted only four years on the job. In a position notorious for its opportunities for siphoning-off of funds and substituting low-quality materials for those ordered, Snyder was accused of wrongdoing only twice in his thirty-one-year career and was exonerated both times. At his election to superintendent of school buildings for Greater New York, the Board of Education minutes state that

> The Board of Education hereby expresses its absolute and unshaken confidence in the uprightness, fidelity, and ability of C. B. J. Snyder, and its appreciation of the eminent professional and personal qualities which characterize him.[43]

Of the $34 million spent between 1897 and 1903 on seven high schools and 140 elementary schools, wrote journalist George Wharton, all "this money has gone, all of it, for schools and has not been diverted into the pockets of politicians."[44] William Cutler noted that while Snyder wasn't totally successful at eliminating favoritism, he decreased it significantly.[45] Though occupying the position of a power broker, Snyder remained humble, polite, considerate, and meticulously ethical.

Through the tumultuous years of unrelenting high immigration, two "great school wars,"[46] and the roller coaster of Tammany and reform mayors, Snyder's qualities made him a steady beacon. In contrast to most earlier school architecture, his designs seem to have taken Henry Barnard's principles to heart. With practical common sense, he methodically thought out solutions to problem after problem. He used his "best endeavors to forward and complete" the work that was underway when he took over: he renovated "old buildings [where] the great and immediate need of improvement [was] manifested"[47] and provided new buildings that addressed Barnard's general principles:

> He made sure that new schools were fireproofed.
> He designed huge exterior windows to let in ample light, and interior clerestory windows to light the corridors with borrowed light from the classrooms but also to ventilate the building.
> For dark days and for evening lectures and classes, he brought electricity to the schools, his early buildings having dual systems of gas and electricity.
> He installed mechanical, forced-air ventilation systems.
> He moved bathrooms inside.
> He replaced backless settees with individual adjustable desks.
> He pushed to buy lots around the schools for playgrounds and, when that didn't happen, built roof playgrounds.

His new buildings must have had an enormously positive effect on the experience of students, in part for improving the morale of teachers and thus lessening "the tone of continual exasperation" heard in the old schools.[48] In Snyder's schools, students and teachers benefited from classrooms with huge windows affording light and air, proper ventilation, indoor bathrooms that many didn't have at home, amenities like heated cloakrooms, and the new lights of education: gymnasiums, mechanical-training rooms, and kindergartens. His schools must have seemed that much grander to the many students who lived in tenements with no plumbing, electricity, or central heat. In the process of providing properly for students and teachers, Snyder brought New York City up to date with the rest of the country, transforming the city from laggard to leader in school design.

In the right place in 1891 at age thirty-one, Snyder was right for the job. A 1905 article in the *American Architect and Building News* said,

> Possibly it was not the best, probably it was not the most economical, certainly it was not the most expeditious way to have all the schoolhouses the city stood in such sore need of designed and built by the official architect to the Department of Education. But, since that method had to be followed, it is a matter of wonderful good fortune that the official architect chanced to be such a man as is Mr. C. B. J. Snyder, who not only at the outset showed such distinct capacity for his task, but has proved himself a man able to grow as his opportunities opened before him. Mr. Wheelwright in Boston, Mr. Ittner in St Louis, Mr. Mundie in Chicago, have done excellent service to their

respective cities in the way of building school-houses . . . ; But they have not had to do their work under the same sort of pressure that has been put upon Mr. Snyder, and they have not had to adapt their architectural treatment to as closely restricted sites.[49]

In "sore need" of schoolhouses, the city had the wonderful good fortune to have an architect who, despite the pressures of the job, was to change the face and nature of public schools in New York City. During his three decades as the Board of Education architect, Snyder would fulfill the ideals of progressive reformers: "If there is any place where a citizen may find hope for the solution of an apparently insolvable problem, it is in the new schools of the lower East Side of Manhattan,"[50] wrote Adele Shaw. He would make more changes in school design in his thirty-one years on the job than have occurred in the subsequent century, a phenomenon that architectural historian and writer Dale Gyure documents having occurred in Chicago high schools, as well. Snyder would create "a revolution" and set "a standard for municipal architecture that has proved hard to match."[51]

Chapter 3

The Creative Decade 1891–1900

Making Revolutionary Change

THE FIRST DECADE of Charles Snyder's career was one of startling creativity. In 1891, having assumed the position of superintendent of school buildings for pre-Consolidation New York, which consisted of Manhattan and the western part of what is now the Bronx, Snyder, with the Board of Education, inaugurated a new era in city schools, designing buildings that stood out as oases of hope in poor neighborhoods. His life to this point had paved the way for this accomplishment: his having grown up poor in Saratoga Springs surrounded by grand architecture and the frequent fires that decimated it, the open-mindedness of his Dutch heritage, his having spent six years in the at-once idealistic and practical atmosphere of Cooper Union, his having had early experience as an architect of commercial alterations, and, perhaps most important, his early career having coincided with the progressive spirit and reforms of the 1890s. This background no doubt influenced him to design grand schools, using the most current construction techniques for buildings that, in turn, embodied the most current educational and social-reform theories.

In 1899, toward the end of Snyder's first decade as superintendent of school buildings, Edmund Wheelwright, Boston municipal architect, wrote about the "radical and interesting innovations in schoolhouse architecture [that] have appeared in [New York City]."

A century later, discussing Snyder's entire career, the *New York Times* architectural historian Christopher Gray wrote that Snyder "created a revolution [in school design], setting a standard for municipal architecture that has proved hard to match."[1] These accolades across the twentieth century pay tribute to the fifty new schools and sixteen additions Snyder had built by 1900.*

Twenty-three of these buildings (and only two of the additions) still stand, and of those twenty-five, sixteen or almost two-thirds remain schools. Six have been awarded historical designation. Snyder's first two years were devoted to completing four schools and two additions that his predecessor, George Debevoise, had begun, all in the heavy Romanesque Revival style, while his own designs were going through the labyrinthine approval process. He went on in his first decade to achieve an average of six groundbreaking buildings per year.

On the outside, on the inside, and in construction techniques, Snyder brought the latest good ideas that were being developed in school architecture to New York for the first time. His schools represented a whole new way of thinking. This chapter looks at how, using classical styles, Snyder changed the prevailing metaphor for city schools from factories, even prisons, to palaces. "Literally he found barracks where he is leaving palaces to the people,"[2] wrote social-reformer Jacob Riis. Besides the changed look of the schools, another departure from what had gone before, construction innovations, raised Snyder's schools to a new standard of health and safety. He fireproofed the buildings, put in forced-air heating and ventilation systems, and used steel-frame instead of masonry construction for the first time in a school, allowing for ample light and air through huge windows. The building interiors supported new functions, forsaking the classrooms-only template of earlier schools and offering the kinds of specialized spaces that had been appearing in progressive schools around the country: kindergartens, manual-training rooms, gymnasiums, and rooftop playgrounds.

His thoroughgoing creativity extended to even the smallest details, as shown by the "Public School City of New York" door handles and by the countless ways he made the schools function more smoothly (fig. 18). For

---

*"The American Schoolhouse, XIV," *Brickbuilder* 8, March 1899, 45. At the 1900 opening of the New Hall of Education at 500 Park Avenue, the president of the board, Joseph Little, remarked, "Fortunate it is that in this era of expansion we have at the head of our building department a young and enthusiastic architect, Mr. C. B. J. Snyder, who has by his creative energy brought the school architecture of New York up to the highest standard ever reached anywhere." Even A. E. Palmer's stolid *The New York City Public School: Being a History of Free Education in the City of New York* (New York and London: Macmillan, 1905), reports that from 1890 to 1897 "numerous improvements in the system [were] introduced."

Figure 18. Bushwick High School, 1913: Door Handle. Arrington photo.

modeling-clay classes, for example, he "devised a new attachment . . . whereby the waste clay is . . . prevented from . . . clogging the waste pipes and traps of the fixtures."[3] From major changes in appearance, construction, and makeup down to small problems in the day-to-day operation of the schools, Snyder revolutionized New York City public schools. While he would continue to hone the transformation for two more decades, this first decade was the pinnacle of his sheer creativity.

Innovations in Appearance

Like tenement houses, pre-Snyder city schools were dark, dreary, and depressing. Progressive reformers saw them as "barracks" in the war on poverty, "factories" for turning out American citizens, "warehouses" or "packing boxes" keeping children off the streets while their parents worked, and, most commonly, "prisons" locking children up to master the three Rs. Such attitudes toward schooling had yielded buildings that were massive, soulless, and monotonous. "There is not a public school in New York . . .

which is even a decently creditable piece of architecture," the *Real Estate Record and Guide* had observed in 1884.[4] With few exceptions schools blended in with the blocks of tenement houses, distinguished from them at most by elements such as a short central square tower, a mansarded corner tower, or shallow pediments at each end of the façade. The prevailing style was Romanesque Revival (fig. 19).

Snyder himself started out working in that same style, but with a difference. For some schools, he reached out to the neighborhood's immigrant culture. His oldest surviving building, PS 23, for example, opened in 1893 on the corner of Bayard and Mulberry Streets in what was then the Italian quarter. It had Romanesque Revival round arches at the entranceways, heavy piers, dark red brick, and a rusticated first floor of rough-cut stones, but also an Italianate cornice and dramatic tower. These last features led a turn-of-the-twentieth-century writer to remark,

> The massive building . . . may be called the first expression of the "new thought." One wonders how many homesick Italians, lounging on the benches in the opposite square [Columbus Park] and remembering sadly the blue skies and olive groves of Italy, have looked up at the building and comprehended the gracious, if timid, overture that their adopted home is making to them there. In the wide projecting cornice and square tower, two characteristic features of Italian

Figure 19. PS 2M: Pre-Snyder School with Tenement on Henry Street. Unknown, public domain.

architecture ... it is New York's effort to say a few words of welcome in Italian.[5]

Jacob Riis described the building as the first school that departed from the soulless old tradition, to set beautiful pictures before the child's mind as well as dry figures on the slate.[6]

His PS 67 (1894), located among the social clubs of conservative midtown, constituted a study in the prevailing Romanesque Revival style, but with a more visually complex façade than those of previous schools (fig. 20). The five symmetrically massed recessed and projecting pavilions of the façade were composed of contrasting materials—tan brick, brownstone, rough-cut stone, and wrought iron. Other typical Romanesque Revival motifs included a large round-arched entranceway; complex window patterns, some with round-arched drip moldings; and a roofline with a central tower and pedimented dormers. Then there was the ornamentation—brackets, capitals, and floral friezes of intricately carved stone and terra-cotta. In 1948 this elementary school was reconfigured to become one of the first high schools

Figure 20. PS 67M, 1894: Signed Snyder Drawing. Architecture and Building, 1893.

Figure 21. PS 67M, 1894: then High School of Performing Arts, now Jacqueline Onassis School of International Studies. Landmarked. *NYC BOE AFSR 1906–8*.

of performing arts in the country; it became well-known for its graduates and as the setting for the 1980 movie *Fame* (fig. 21).

Snyder's only other remaining building from 1894, PS 25 on East Fourth Street, stylistically seems light years apart from PS 67. PS 25 had an entirely new look for a public school. Perhaps because he was working on the Lower East Side instead of among the social clubs and mansions of midtown, or perhaps because the building was originally merely an addition to the well-known stand-alone Fifth-Street School, Snyder was more fancy-free in this design. Abandoning the conservative Romanesque Revival style, he chose ornate Dutch Renaissance Revival (fig. 22). He used a light-red brick, further lightened by the visually dominant limestone stringcourses on each floor. The 1894 design consisted of the three eastern bays of the present building, symmetrical with the central bay a quarter again wider than the side bays, its dormer twice as large as the side-bay dormers. When more space was needed a decade later, Snyder added two more bays to the west, a large one and then a smaller one, thus preserving the symmetry of the building.

Figure 22. PS 25M, 1894, now PS 751: Dutch Renaissance Revival. Arrington photo.

The terms most commonly used to describe Snyder's style are "historicist," "eclectic," and "Beaux Arts." His buildings looked to history for their form, hence the term "historicist." He relied on styles from the "old countries" whence our immigrants had come—Italian Palazzo, Dutch or Flemish Renaissance, French Chateau, Baroque, Collegiate Gothic, and Georgian. But Snyder was not a purist; he didn't hesitate to use characteristics of various historical styles on a single building, hence the term "eclectic." Finally, whatever the historicist style or eclectic combination of styles, he approached the buildings of his first decade from the "Beaux Arts" perspective. Incorporating the principles taught at the popular nineteenth-century École des Beaux Arts in Paris, his schools had the monumentality of symmetrical façades, prominent entranceways, and lavish ornamentation and roof features.

For all Snyder's skill in reimagining Romanesque Revival style, he was disposed to practice in the tradition of Chicago's 1893 Columbian Exposition. A four-hundredth-anniversary celebration of Columbus's putative discovery of America, the fair attracted not only Snyder and his wife, Harriet, but, despite a severe recession, almost half the population of the country. A short train or boat ride took people from the dirt, crime, and chaos of downtown

Chicago to gleaming white Beaux Arts buildings amidst parks and waterways. The White City raised hope and possibility for urban life. It occasioned the birth of the City Beautiful movement, with its claim that beautiful architecture had an elevating moral effect on the individual and that such closeness to beauty would redeem society. However, some objected that the grandest civic buildings being built as a result of this movement were located in well-off parts of town not frequented by immigrants and the poor—a major drawback to City Beautiful as a means of transforming society.

Public schools in New York overcame that objection, as did contemporary firehouses, police precinct houses, public baths, and branch libraries. One writer said that Carnegie libraries "advertised literacy, culture, prosperity, and civic bounty."[7] Schools did as well. Architectural historian Robert A. M. Stern deemed them "architecture at the service of democracy."[8] They brought the uplifting effect of beauty to the far reaches of the city for those without the leisure to visit museums or the New York Public Library Main Branch.

In keeping with the City Beautiful precepts, Snyder used ornament to complement the schools' historicist styles—but not without controversy. *The Real Estate Record and Guide* voiced the prevailing view of the day:

> There are those [bureaucrats] who hold that for school buildings no design is called for more pleasing to the eye than that of the factory. . . . They look upon the school-life of a child as a grinding, manufacturing process to which the factory style of building is eminently suitable.[9]

But the editors then went on to assert that ornamentation was

> worth every cent—in the long run the modest and appropriate adornment of schoolhouses will do much more to raise the level of public taste than any amount of money spent on more sumptuous and conspicuous municipal edifices.

And Jacob Riis, of course, was outspoken in his support of handsome schools, especially in poor areas:

> As for the five or ten thousand dollars put in for "the looks" of things where the slum ha[s] trodden every ideal and every atom of beauty into the dirt, I expect to live to see that prove the best investment a city ever made.[10]

By their very existence, the schools modeled ideals and good taste for children and for the public.

Snyder's affinity to the City Beautiful promise embodied in the Columbian Exposition resulted not only from his experience of the fair but also from various environs in his past. The well-off residential neighborhoods of his hometown Saratoga Springs had exhibited a historical spectrum of Western architectural styles. Later, he had lived and worked for eight years near Union Square, an area where great architects of the time, many having been trained at the École des Beaux Arts, were erecting significant historicist buildings.

Then, in New Rochelle, he had socialized and exchanged professional ideas with a whole community of artists and architects, many of them City Beautiful proponents. He had even designed five houses for wealthy patrons, as well as one for his mother and sister. Finally, the house to which he and Harriet moved on St. James Park in the village of Fordham, where he lived from 1895 to 1902, was just twelve blocks north of the emerging Bronx campus of New York University, designed by legendary Beaux Arts architect Stanford White. A short walk from this house would bring him to the spectacular sight of White's Gould Library, which opened in 1899. In fact, en route to his own construction site of the Flemish Renaissance Revival PS 26 two blocks south of the campus, completed the same year as the library, he would have passed White's classical grandeur as it evolved. These various experiences affected the look of Snyder's schools such that they stood out from rather than blended in with the tenement houses in which the majority of public-school students lived, thus participating in the City Beautiful mission of redeeming and uplifting society.

While one might expect a young architect designing his first schools to settle on a single style, Snyder's first ten schools, all of which opened between 1893 and 1894, showed three distinct styles—Romanesque Revival, Italian Renaissance Revival, and Northern European Renaissance Revival. The latter two dominated the style of his large, symmetrical, sometimes four-story but usually five-story buildings. By the end of the decade he had designed approximately an equal number of each type.

For his earliest Italian palazzo-style school, the demolished PS 7, which had opened on Hester Street in 1893, Snyder, not surprisingly, turned to his alma mater for design influence. PS 7, deemed "one of the most magnificent schoolhouse buildings in the city,"[11] resembled the Cooper Union building in that it had a central pavilion with arched third-story windows and a balustrade encircling the roof over a subtle cornice. It and the sober, elegant Italian-Renaissance schools that followed had tripartite vertical organization: a rusticated first floor; relatively plain second, third, and fourth floors; and an ornate fifth floor topped by a balustrade (as on the

Figure 23. PS 158M, 1899: Italian Palazzo-Style. *NYC BOE AFSR 1906–8.*

now-demolished PS 53M) or a heavy overhanging cornice (as seen on PS 42M or 158M, both still standing). Stringcourses and cornices emphasized the building's horizontality and flat roof (fig. 23). Sometimes upper-floor arched windows provided counterpoint to the predominantly square-topped ones; sometimes ornamental carved plaques alternated with the top-story windows, as on PS 42M; often the three-arched entranceway suggested a triumphal arch, as seen in PS 4X and PS 105M. PS 158 on the Upper East Side exhibits much classical ornamentation such as quoins, swags, attic windows with elaborate window surrounds and separating Italian palazzo-style schools opened on the Lower East Side, six on the Upper East Side, and five in the Bronx, as well as PS 69a→b (1893) in midtown and PS 29 (1894) south of Canal Street, for a total of 19.*

---

*The symbol a→b means a building was designed as an addition, but after the original school was demolished became a stand-alone school in its own right. The six Italian palazzo-style schools on the Lower East Side were PS 7 (1893), PS 75a→b (1896), PS 105 (1897), PS 42

Besides Italian (or Southern) Renaissance Revival, the other main Western architectural tradition translated by Snyder was Northern European Renaissance Revival, which combined Gothic characteristics with aspects of Dutch, Flemish, French, and English Renaissance Revival styles. Offering more pizzazz than the elegant but staid Italian Renaissance Revival buildings, schools from this tradition were distinguished by a flamboyant pitched roof, or faux pitched roof, and a picturesque roofline of gables, dormers, cupolas, chimneys, and ornate stonework like those found on Dutch or Flemish guildhalls or French chateaux. After having introduced this tradition in PS 25 (1894) in the East Village, Snyder built another thirteen such schools.* Some, such as PS 1 and PS 2 on the Lower East Side, PS 5 and PS 10 in Harlem, and PS 9 on the Upper West Side, had Dutch or Flemish Renaissance Revival scrolled or stepped gables and prominent chimneys. About PS 9, *New York 1900* says,

> Snyder employed the Dutch Colonial mode popularized by Robert W. Gibson's Collegiate Church in the West End to convey a sense of domesticity that helped elevate the schoolhouse to a level of architectural dignity comparable to that of the house.[12]

On other schools, PS 26X, PS 27X overlooking St. Mary's Park, PS 28X, and PS 157 in Harlem, now apartments, Snyder added a central cupola to the gables and dormers. A few buildings such as PS 6 and PS 103 on the Upper East Side and PS 160 on the Lower East Side had Queen Anne and Gothic elements. These buildings, as well as the three French Renaissance Revival H-plan schools, loudly and dramatically called attention to themselves.

To highlight the richness of Western architectural heritage, Snyder located schools designed in different traditions within a few blocks of one another. Four blocks east of the gabled Dutch Renaissance Revival PS 25M (1894)

(1898), PS 37 (1898, demolished), and PS 20 (1899). The six on the Upper East Side were PS 53 (1894, demolished), PS 57 (1895, demolished), PS 96 (1895, demolished), PS 30 (1896, demolished), PS 151 (1897, demolished in 2008), and PS 158 (1899). The five in the Bronx were PS 4 (1898), PS 8 (1898), PS 25 (1898), PS 29 (1899, with a cupola, demolished), and PS 30 (1900). There were also PS 69a→b (1893) in midtown and PS 29 (1894) south of Canal Street.

*Gothic Northern Renaissance Revival-type schools similar to PS 25 included PS 122 (1895, with Jacobean elements also), PS 1 (1898), PS 2 (1898, demolished), and 160 (1899) on the Lower East Side; PS 5 (1895, demolished), PS 10 (1895, demolished), and PS 157 (1900) in Harlem; PS 6 (1894, demolished) and PS 103 (1896, demolished) on the Upper East Side; PS 9 (1896) and 165 (1900) on the Upper West Side; and PS 26 (1899), PS 27 (1898), and PS 28 (1898) in the Bronx.

on East Fourth Street, Snyder built the flat-roofed, Italian Renaissance Revival PS 105 (1897) with a Roman-style Triumphal arch at its entrance. In the same year, 1898, two very different schools opened within four short blocks of one another on Rivington Street: the grandiloquent Gothic/Dutch Renaissance PS 160 (fig. 24) with a roofline of gables and dormers, and just to the east, the decorous Italian Renaissance Revival, flat-roofed PS 20 (fig. 25).

A year later similarly contrasting schools opened on either side of St. Mary's Park in the Bronx: the flamboyant, ornate Gothic/Flemish Renaissance Revival PS 27X (fig. 26) and the elegant Italian palazzo-style PS 25X (fig. 27). Thus, the "walls where education dwells" allowed public-school students and others to internalize the two dominant European styles. Snyder's school buildings were teachers, as it were, giving their own survey course in aspects of Western architectural history.

Toward the end of the decade Snyder also dared to use for elementary schools the Collegiate Gothic style that, starting with Princeton and Bryn Mawr in 1894, had become the dominant look of American college campuses.[13] Snyder was on the committee that chose George B. Post's Collegiate Gothic design for the new City College campus. Just as Snyder had quickly

Figure 24. PS 160M, 1899: Queen Anne and Gothic Cathedral Elements. *NYC BOE AFSR 1906–8.*

Figure 25. PS 20M, 1899: Italian Palazzo-Style (Pairs with PS 160M). *NYC BOE AFSR 1906–8.*

Figure 26. PS 27X, 1898: Italian Palazzo-Style. *NYC BOE AFSR 1906–8.*

Figure 27. PS 25X, 1898: Gothic/Flemish Renaissance Revival (Pairs with PS 27X). *NYC BOE AFSR 1906–8.*

moved to new technologies such as steel-frame construction and mechanical ventilation systems, as we shall see, he embraced the recently introduced Collegiate Gothic with all its components and connotations. In 1898 he designed six such buildings, five that were almost identical opening in 1900 (PSs 31X [fig. 28], 32X, 40M, 166M, 169M). The sixth (PS 177M) did not open until 1901 because of a shortage of steel. They exhibited many Gothic motifs: stone carvings and sculpture; drip moldings; oriel windows projecting out over the first-floor entrances at either end of the buildings; a central tower with hexagonal corner columns pierced by narrow lancet windows; and chimneys, dormers, and gables. A 1905 article, "Modern Use of the Gothic," asserted

> Mr. C. B. J. Snyder ... deserves great credit. The buildings meet every practical utilitarian requirement, and yet in the successful adaptation of the style are among the most beautiful of the city's possessions.[14]

Significantly, two of Snyder's Collegiate Gothic schools were landmarked (31X and 166M) (fig. 29).

Using Collegiate Gothic for primary and secondary schools, Snyder boldly extended this elite style to a non-elite populace. This grand symbolic gesture told non-English-speaking immigrants that they were worthy of participating in the best of Western cultural, educational traditions. Reacting to PS 31, which sat on an eminence along the Grand Concourse and was fondly known

Figure 28. PS 31X, 1900: Landmarked and Demolished. *NYC BOE AFSR 1906–8.*

Figure 29. PS 166M, 1900: Collegiate Gothic Landmarked. *NYC BOE AFSR 1906–8.*

as the Castle on the Concourse, one modern-day walking-tour participant commented, "It's amazing looking, showing real respect for the children meant to attend." A twenty-year veteran teacher there said, "As soon as you walked in, you had respect for the building—and for education itself." Even though it had been landmarked in 1995, this grand building was demolished in 2015 by the one entity that does not have to abide by the Landmark Commission's rules, New York City itself. Another, PS 169, was demolished in the 1960s. Located across Broadway from Hilltop Stadium, which occupied the site where Columbia Presbyterian Hospital is now, it stood out, larger and whiter than anything else around. A person who grew up to be an architect said that as a child in the 1960s walking past her Collegiate Gothic school, PS 166 on West Eighty-Ninth Street, with friends who went to private schools, she felt quite proud. The similarly designed PS 40 on East Twentieth Street and PS 32, tucked into the Little Italy of the Bronx, have retained more of their original interiors. Instead of the dramatic white limestone and cream brick of the others, PS 32 is dark red brick. The very different Collegiate Gothic PS 177 on the Lower East Side, which Jacob Riis called "the biggest of them all, and the finest,"[15] was the only Snyder school with a corner entrance on a diagonal; it perhaps inspired the entrance to William Martin's dramatic 1929 Herman Ritter Junior High School public-school students by putting them in buildings that evoked the prestigious settings of Oxford and Cambridge.

Finally, in 1898, Snyder introduced a new design: the H-Plan School. "I cannot see how it is possible to come nearer perfection in the building of a public school," Jacob Riis said about it. Snyder himself, writing in *Educational Review*, one of the leading journals in the field, described his H-plan as "a radical departure from the established order of things."[16] The cover of the issue pictured the school's floor plan. Significantly, at the end of Snyder's career, in a *New York Times* interview, he described this school type as "the most important" of his innovations.[17] A completely new concept in New York City schools, the H-plan was designed to occupy a midblock location with courtyards opening onto each of the two side streets; all classrooms faced the courtyards and were thus guaranteed light and air, regardless of what type of building went up adjacent to the school (figs. 30, 31).

By the end of his first decade, Snyder had completed three H-plan schools. The first, PS 147, it turned out, was not in a midblock location. Situated on the Lower East Side, it filled the whole of one of the irregular blocks just north of where the Manhattan Bridge would open a decade later. The austere

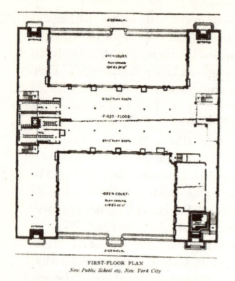 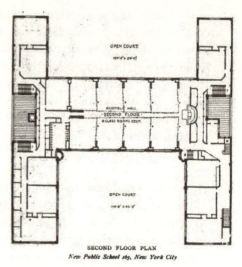

Figure 30. PS 165M, 1900: First Extant H-Plan Design, First Floor Plan. *Educational Review*, 1898.

Figure 31. PS 165M, 1900: Second Floor Plan. *Educational Review*, 1898.

1899 school had medieval-type walled-in courtyards and a two-story crenellated entranceway.

A year later, in 1900, Snyder's oldest surviving H-plan school, PS 165, opened a few blocks from St. John the Divine, where the first services had taken place that same year. A French Renaissance Revival, Loire Valley chateau-type school, it had twenty-two dormers topped by acute-triangle pediments emerging from a steep-pitched roof with a round spire in the middle and chimneys at each end. Molded in terra-cotta within the dormers punctuating the skyline were stars and stripes, the symbol of America, indicating that the school promoted the Americanization of immigrants. Girls had the two-bay-deep 108th Street side (fig. 32), boys the slightly larger and more ornate 109th Street side (three bays deep) (fig. 33)—Snyder clearly wanted children to enter a realm grander and more exotic than the city streets they inhabited.

PS 159 also opened in 1900 in the Chateaux style, a block from the recently erected Romanesque Revival Harlem Court House on East 121st Street. Upon completion the school was sufficiently grand to become the home of the New York Training School for Teachers, which had been established in 1898. Snyder would go on to build fifty more H-Plan schools, the vast majority in the second decade of his tenure.

Figure 32. PS 165M, 1900: 108th Street Façade. NYC BOE AFSR 1906–8.

Figure 33. PS 165M, 1900: 109th Street Façade. NYC BOE AFSR 1906–8.

When Snyder had been on the job for less than a year, the *New York Tribune* quoted him as saying, "We seek to make the school building itself quite as much a factor in education as the textbooks."[18] In this statement he seemed to echo British architect E. R. Robson, hired in 1870 after the passage of the Education Act to create the London Board Schools. Robson called his schools "sermons in stone." Through them, he said, "a glimpse of nobler things will have been brought under the daily ken, and to the very door, of the working man."[19] Snyder shared Robson's passion. Even his early Romanesque Revival schools were designed to "set beautiful pictures" before children's minds, to showcase civic bounty as well as the comfortable amenities, and to make immigrants feel ennobled in their new country. Snyder went on to create a primer of architectural styles by placing schools from different Renaissance Revival traditions in close proximity to one another. Then his Collegiate Gothic buildings suggested that elementary school was as important and prestigious as elite colleges. What else did the buildings teach?

For one thing, the three standard horizontal registers of the building moving from the ground plane to the roof conveyed the idea that education was uplifting. The tripartite façade design was a standard of many Snyder schools. The students' experience in the school paralleled the architectural sequence of the façade, which itself mirrored the base/shaft/capital composition of the classical column: the "uncultivated" kindergarteners had special classrooms on the rusticated first floor (base); moving through the grade levels, students ascended the second, third, and fourth stories (shaft); finally, the graduating fifth- or eighth-graders, now "cultivated and educated," spent school days up among the console brackets, elaborate band courses, and sophisticated roof treatments (capita). The building itself was thus emblematic of the students' progress through the school.

The façades suggested other positive aspects of education—namely, the idea that schools offered balance, enlightenment, and refuge. The symmetry of the buildings said that education, with its ordered, planned curriculum, wasn't random or chaotic but brought balance to one's life. The huge windows said that education was enlightening. The façades, in general, conveyed the idea that school was healthy and expansive rather than depressing, freeing rather than imprisoning, inviting rather than forbidding—a place where a student would want to be. In *Bronx Accents*, Lloyd Ultan and Barbara Unger write, "For most Bronx immigrant children, the New York City public school was the center of existence."[20]

Further, by dominating the streetscape the grandiose buildings proclaimed the worthiness of students and education. They said to students who entered, "You matter, and your education matters." Snyder rendered schools important-seeming not just through size, but through color and deployment of the flag. After a fact-finding trip to England and France in 1896, he reported that all French public schools flew the French flag; that same year the Board of Education placed flagpoles on the roofs of all New York's schools.[21] Augmenting the flag in drawing the eye to the buildings was their color. Snyder's colleague, the architect John Beverley Robinson, wrote, "The coloring of the newer schools is most happily confined to the grays and brown, and sometimes to the cream tints of stone or modern brick." Given "the interminable red brick of a city, the eye welcomes a quieter color."[22] About schools on the Lower East Side, another contemporary wrote, "The great new grey-brick buildings stand, rising impressively out of the surrounding squalor, and carrying the stars and stripes proudly and protectingly above it all."[23] Finally, while the sheer size of many of Snyder's schools could be intimidating, especially for younger children to whom the buildings appeared even larger, it instilled in many a feeling of privilege and importance. About PS 160 on Rivington Street, architectural historian Francis Morrone has written, "Snyder showed a lighthandedness that kept the often . . . gigantic buildings from ever feeling oppressive."[24]

Snyder buildings showed that the best of Western civilization was available to students. Former *New York Times* Streetscapes columnist Christopher Gray has written that they were "created to bring not simply instruction but also an uplifting cultural influence to New York City's poor and working-class sections." They stood out "like beacons of gentility in their tenement neighborhoods."²⁵ Like an English manor house surveying its realms, the Bronx's PS 27 looks out over St. Mary's Park, as do PS 4 and PS 61 over Crotona Park. The seals of the Board of Education and the City of New York, prominent on the fronts of the schools, were like the coats-of-arms of an aristocratic family. The size and intricacy of those carvings varied, depending largely on what stone cutters were available for hire. PS 27, located near the home and shops of the renowned stone cutters, the Piccirilli brothers at 467 East 142nd Street in the Bronx, has the largest, most elaborate seal of all (fig. 34). It shows

> the rising sun of the Bronx and the familiar windmill of New York (Manhattan), surrounded by a globe, a ship, books, and scales of justice, as well as a quill pen, protractor, mallet, and palette. Above this ensemble glows the lamp of knowledge and below is a cornucopia suggesting the fruits of knowledge.²⁶

The windmill was an allusion to New York's Dutch past; Excelsior, meaning "still higher," is the motto of the state of New York. An impressive building asserted that students deserved grandeur, whimsy, heritage, and aspiration—

Figure 34. PS 27X, 1898: Combined. Board of Education and the City of New York Seals. Arrington photo.

a building that drew attention to itself the way palaces and cathedrals do. Schools were now people's palaces that held out the promise of living the life of the established and the learned.

Finally and most importantly, Snyder's schools reflected his democratic ideals. Working within the budgetary restrictions imposed by the Board of Education, he designed the same types of schools for poor neighborhoods as he did for well-off neighborhoods. This practice conveyed that education, ideals, and beauty were not just the province of the privileged; everyone was equally worthy, regardless of income or social class. In democratic America, public schools are, Snyder said, "for the children of the rich and poor, who are taught in the same class room, which fact alone always causes comment among foreigners who visit us."[27] Snyder's egalitarian ideals were reflected in his use of standardized designs, which also improved efficiency in erecting numerous large schools quickly. Snyder practiced standardization in school construction twenty years before it became common practice.[28]

Snyder created schools for poor children on the densely populated Lower East Side the equal of any in better-off sections of the city. PS 1, just east of Chatham Square, and PS 160, on Rivington and Suffolk, were basically the same design as PS 6 at Madison Avenue and Eighty-Fifth Street, three blocks from the Metropolitan Museum of Art and the academically prestigious private St. Regis High School. The two Italian-palazzo-design schools on York Avenue at Seventy-Seventh Street and at Eighty-First Street echoed one of his earliest buildings, PS 7, which sat among the pushcarts of Hester Street (fig. 35). Like the buildings of City College on a ridge above Harlem, which suggested that poor immigrants received as good an education as people who could afford Harvard or Yale, Snyder's public-school buildings conveyed the sense that the disadvantaged were provided the same education as the well-off.

Jacob Riis saw Snyder as heroically leading New York City out of the wasteland of dark, dank, unwholesome, unsafe schools and into the promised land of handsome and inspiring buildings. His 1902 *The Battle with the Slum* included a photograph of Snyder with the caption, "Superintendent C. B. J. Snyder, who builds our Beautiful Schools" (fig. 36). He wrote that

> Snyder does that which no other architect before his time ever did or tried: he builds them beautiful. In him New York has one of those rare men who open windows for the soul of their times. Literally, he found barracks where he is leaving palaces to the people.[29]

Figure 35. PS 7M, 1893: Italian Palazzo-Style. *NYC BOE AFSR 1906–8.*

Snyder schools, embodying the progressive agenda of improving the plight of the poor, incarnated the "soul" of the times, Riis claimed. His palace metaphor—which replaced the previous images of schools as barracks, factories, warehouses, and prisons, all stressing unpleasant monotony—offered a new level of hope, echoed and intensified by later writers' descriptions of Snyder schools as "cathedrals of culture."[30] Standing in front of a Snyder school, one twenty-first-century walking-tour participant commented, "Anybody'd be proud to go to a school like that." Another remarked, "You go through those portals. How can you not learn?" In just eight years—the period that culminated with the advent of the twentieth century—this young architect had adorned the city with new and varied buildings that, like the residential architecture of his native Saratoga Springs, touched on much of the best of the Western architectural tradition. He was indeed the man "who builds our Beautiful Schools."[31]

Figure 36. "Superintendent C. B. J. Snyder, who builds our Beautiful Schools." Picture and caption from Riis's *The Battle with the Slum*, 1902, Chapter XIII.

Construction and Mechanical Innovations for Health and Safety

In 1893, novelist Stephen Crane wrote in *Maggie, A Girl of the Streets* of the Lower East Side tenement house where Maggie Johnson lived as "a dark region," "a careening building" with "dark stairways and . . . cold, gloomy halls [in which people] floundered," a building that "quivered and creaked from the weight of humanity stamping about in its bowels."[32] In buildings such as the one Crane described, each of the four three-room apartments per floor had only one window to the outside. Often as many as twelve adults slept in one room, using outhouses downstairs, one toilet per twenty people, and lugging up the stairs—as many as seven stories—water for cooking, bathing, and laundry. Deferred maintenance was the rule. The infant death rate was one in ten. Two-thirds of New York's population were living in such conditions in 1900. The percentage was no doubt higher for those in public school. The majority of the children who attended one of the forty-nine new buildings Snyder had erected by the end of his first decade walked from dark, gloomy, harsh living conditions like Maggie's through dirty streets into an airy, gleaming, clean centrally heated school with indoor plumbing and electricity. While children who were assigned to pre-Snyder schools entered a familiar world, those who were fortunate enough to come a few years later experienced a wholly new world of modern amenities and comfort. Snyder's new schools constituted in brick and mortar the Progressive promise of improving the lot of the poor by means of light, air, good sanitation, and education.

The new schools were so different from the tenements because, despite their historicist appearance, Snyder used modern construction techniques for buildings with modern functions. Those were the elements that he wrote about in his articles and annual reports, rarely mentioning style. Snyder's construction and mechanical innovations—his modernism—created safe, sanitary, well-lit schools.

Those innovations demonstrated the architect's priorities and qualities. They showed his willingness to use cutting-edge techniques and his orientation toward solutions, ones that grew out of study and careful thought; he had even titled a 1902 article in the *School Journal* "How New York City Has Solved Some Trying School Building Problems." And they showed his emphasis on quality and frugality, accomplished by repeatedly formulating his own products rather than relying on patented, marketed ones, which were prohibitively expensive when it came to outfitting the country's largest school system. His method effected, he wrote, "a great saving of expense to the city."[33] Ultimately, it was his progressive, public-servant vision and commitment that led him to embrace modernism.

Snyder transformed schools that were gloomy and deficient to ones that were safely conducive to learning. He brought to the New York Public School System the following construction innovations:

Steel-frame construction
Fireproofing using noncombustible materials such as terra-cotta and steel and double stairs (scissor or interlocking) for egress
Indoor bathrooms to replace outhouses, with better urinals and water closets
Electrification
Large double-hung windows
Mechanical "plenum" ventilation and heating systems
Classroom amenities such as adjustable desks and cloakrooms
Other improvements like shades, bulletin boards and snow-melting equipment

In addition, he worked to bring up to standard the hundred or so existing schools that had been deemed defective or unsanitary.

In the early 1890s, before steel-frame construction had become commonplace, Snyder dared to use this new technology on public schools. He had attended Cooper Union, one of the first buildings using rolled-iron I-beams for structural support.[34] The leap to steel-frame construction made sense. It allowed first-floor walls to be less thick—sixteen inches for a five-story building versus the thirty-six inches required for an equivalent masonry building—and thus opened up more usable space. It also reduced construction time. Snyder explained that the shorter construction time balanced out the higher cost of steel as a building material. Most important, the steel framework made possible fireproofing and banks of large windows. In the 1898 *Educational Review,* Snyder wrote,

> In the first and most essential particular, the new buildings are fireproof throughout, of steel skeleton construction, with . . . an abundance of light and air.[35]

Notice how Snyder's sentence yokes three disparate elements—steel construction, fireproofing, and the abundance of light and air—as "the first and most essential particular."

Fireproofing was a current and crucial issue. Snyder's article continued:

> New York [is] in the enviable position of not having erected any but fireproof public-school buildings since the year 1892. . . . Ours is the only city, thus far, that has made provision for housing the helpless little children in structures of this character. Boston is preparing to follow the example thus set, but shrinks from the task.[36]

Growing up in Saratoga Springs and having witnessed the devastating fires of enormous wooden hotels, Snyder was insistent upon fireproofing schools. He felt that all new school construction should incorporate the most advanced fireproofing techniques possible and that all older buildings be retrofitted to get as close to this ideal as practicable. He was adhering to and superseding the requirements of the 1892 law New York City had enacted that required all structures over thirty-five feet to be constructed of fireproof, or incombustible, material.

Snyder had learned important lessons, as did all architects, from fireproofing techniques developed in the aftermath of Chicago's Great Fire of 1871. He made the ground floors of his schools asphalt, installed asphalt treads on stair steps, inserted terra-cotta boxes between floors and rooms, wrapped the steel beams in brick, and placed metal fire doors at crucial points—always between the rest of the building and the boiler room in the cellar, which had masonry floors, walls, and ceiling. Corridors, without lockers or wardrobes, were wide enough to avoid congestion: twelve to fourteen feet for main corridors and at least eight to ten feet for side corridors. The director of the City Island Historical Society, located in the former PS 102 (1898), renumbered to PS 17 (1903), on the highest point of the island, marveled at how a 1998 fire did so little damage. Pointing out that all the electrical wires and water conduits were surrounded by terra-cotta, the best insulation available in 1901, she credited Snyder's design for averting tragedy.

But perhaps Snyder's greatest contribution in the realm of fire safety was his devising, after "long and careful study," the double stairs (scissor or interlocking), memorialized in Bel Kaufman's popular 1960s book and movie *Up the Down Staircase* (fig. 37).[37] Two staircases were placed within each stairwell—an arrangement that saved space but, more importantly, allowed the building to be emptied twice as fast. One staircase was for ascending and one for descending under normal circumstances, but in the case of an emergency both became the down staircase (fig. 38). He insisted upon enough staircases with doors on each floor opening in and exit doors opening out so that everyone could exit the building within a maximum of three to three and one-half minutes—in an effort to have the building empty before the arrival of any fire-fighting apparatus.[38] He further specified that each staircase was to be four feet wide to prevent children's getting hurt. He wrote,

> The limitation in width [of the stairs] is fixed so as to provide for only two lines of children on a stair each with its continuous line of handrails, thus not permitting the introduction of a third line . . . [which] is liable to slip and fall, causing confusion and panic.[39]

Such stairs became standard in urban schools of four stories or more.

The technique of wrapping the steel columns with bricks to minimize damage in case of fire contributed as well to the longevity of the buildings. They were built for the ages. After an 1896 trip to view European schools, Snyder wrote about those in England, "All of the buildings are of a most substantial character, everything being designed so as to obtain the utmost durability."[40] Clearly, he wanted the school buildings to emulate England's.

Snyder buildings were anything but a discredit to New York. He disdained stopgap measures. In 2008, the custodian/fireman who had taken care of PS 25 in the East Village for seventeen years said, "These buildings were made to last forever. The Board of Education was going to tear out the stairwell and put in an elevator. If they had, I'd have been sheet-rocking all day." While modern sheet-rocked walls succumb to student kicks and

74 · THE CREATIVE DECADE 1891–1900

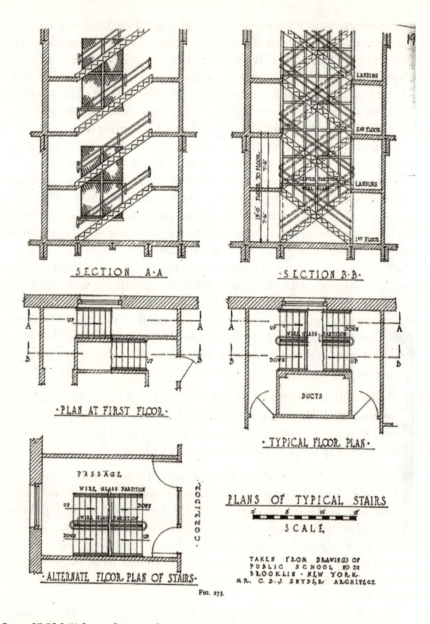

Figure 37. PS 24K: Scissor Stairways Drawings. John J. Donovan, *School Architecture: Principles and Practices*. Norwood, Mass: Norwood Press, 1921.

Figure 38. Stairway Pictured in Riis's *The Battle with the Slum*. https://www.gutenberg.org/files/28228/28228-h/28228-h.htm#page341.

punches, Snyder's walls were indestructible. In 2010, when Harlem's PS 90 (1907) was renovated as condominiums after having sat open to the elements for forty years, the 100-year-old steel was all in good condition (fig. 39). Donald Friedman, the façade engineer, said,

> Snyder schools are overbuilt either because Snyder was a naturally conservative designer or because he was compensating for sketchy maintenance. He built very resilient buildings that were able to take a lot of punishment for a long time.[41]

Nearby PS 186 (1903 [fig. 40]) was also allowed to sit and deteriorate for forty years. Even though trees grew out of the roof, the niched statue of Minerva, Roman goddess of wisdom, still presided over 145th Street (fig. 41). About its walls, Friedman said that they "still stand plumb." In 2014, the Harlem Boys and Girls Club renovated it into a community center and low-income housing. PS 125 in Brownsville, Brooklyn, after languishing empty and decrepit for several decades, has recently been reborn as a medical facility. One other school stands abandoned and derelict: landmarked PS 64

Figure 39. PS 90M, 1907. From *School Architecture*, 1910.

Figure 40. PS 186M, 1903: H-Plan. *NYC BOE AFSR 1906–8*.

Figure 41. PS 186M: Minerva Statue. Mike Janoska photo.

in the East Village. Another, PS 31 across the 145th Street Bridge on the Grand Concourse in the Bronx, which had been landmarked but unused for twenty years, was demolished in 2015. Continued community diligence and involvement are needed to ensure that the rest of Snyder's buildings remain a vital part of New York City's heritage.

Steel-frame construction that improved fireproofing and longevity also made possible walls that were as much as 60 percent windows—almost double the window area possible in masonry buildings. During this era when skyscrapers were creating the dark canyons of lower Manhattan, when the average tenement-house apartment had only one window, and when tuberculosis had not yet been controlled by antibiotics, light and air were top priorities, associated with cleanliness and health, morality and optimism. In the early years of Snyder's career, before he had convinced the board that indoor bathrooms were more economical, he had designed skylights even for the "closet" buildings (a.k.a. outhouses), in order, he said, "to avoid dark corners and consequent uncleanliness; for darkness and uncleanliness go hand in hand—in fact they are inseparable."[42] In his earliest extant building, PS 23, which opened in 1893 in the Five Points area, a classroom still exists with two skylights and their shades in the pressed-tin ceiling. At PS 25 in the East Village, skylights brighten the main staircase, parts of the cellar, and those classrooms up in the smaller stepped-gabled dormers, suggesting that Snyder was as concerned about students in small top-floor classrooms and custodians shoveling coal as about faculty and visitors to the school. The *Architectural Record* reported in 1898, "The playrooms, which constitute the first story in all New York schools, have been built with high ceilings and large windows, making them light and cheerful as well as healthful."[43]

An apt symbol of enlightenment, windows probably more than any other single feature characterize Snyder's buildings. In the twenty-five-foot bay created by the steel frame, double, triple, quadruple, sometimes even quintuple windows could be installed. They were typically ten feet tall and sixteen feet wide, typically double-hung nine-over-nine or twelve-over-twelve panes, topped by a transom. The exterior transom windows above the standard double-hung ones further contributed to the complex patterns that enlivened the buildings' façades. At PS 122, for example, the transoms consisted of seven narrow pointed panes creating a Gothic ensemble at the top of every window. Although they were replaced when the building was renovated, they can be seen in the movie *Fame* (1980), as can the transoms on the original DeWitt-Clinton High School; both buildings were used as sets.[44] In Robert A. M. Stern's *New York 1900*, the writer puts it this way:

> His designs were easily distinguished from earlier New York City schools by the enormous double-hung windows used to give every classroom plenty of light and ventilation. . . . Placed in façades that had less wall surface than window area, [the over-scaled windows] helped to produce geometric compositions that Snyder easily manipulated for Gothic, Jacobean, Colonial, and Modern French designs with a minimum of detail.[45]

In 1903, Adele Marie Shaw, English Department chair at Newtown High School in Queens, described visiting schools where "sunshine—warmth and light—pervaded the place and the work. If there is any place where a citizen may find hope for the solution of an apparently insoluble problem it is in the new schools of the lower East Side of Manhattan."[46] Shaw is echoing Riis, who proclaimed, "The windows of the school-house have been thrown open, and life let in with the sunlight.... The way to fight the slum in the children's lives is with sunlight and flowers and play, which their child hearts crave, if their eyes have never seen them."[47]

Snyder's classrooms were designed to rely entirely on natural light during the day; artificial lighting systems were installed only, or primarily, to extend the building's usefulness for evening activities. Snyder wrote,

> Children attending day sessions in public schools are entitled to daylight, and not gas or electric light, or, what is worse, a dim or twilight, in which to attempt to pursue their studies.[48]

In keeping with his respect for children generally, Snyder saw them as "entitled" to light and health; to that end, he established standards and developed an instrument to enforce the standards. One standard involved room size. Conforming to the characteristics of Class A office space as defined by the real-estate market, Snyder made classrooms twenty-two by twenty-eight feet, such that no desk was more than fifteen feet away from the windows.

He also felt the urgency of retrofitting many of the masonry schools he had inherited that were only 25 to 30 percent windows. His 1894 Annual Report included this impassioned logic:

> No man erects a manufactory or office building with a proportion of wall to window spaces 3 or 4 to 1, and yet that is what exists in many of the old school buildings. Does a silk mill or office building need more light than a school room? Is the work more important? You will answer "no" to both questions. Then let us, when the old school buildings are well situated and worth retaining, have the funds to purchase the property which adjoins the school, if it in any way interferes with the light and air thereof, and alter the old building into one that will not be a menace to the eyesight and health of the pupils and teachers, and a reproach to the system.[49]

To increase light in the many dark classrooms of the older school buildings, he also looked at a new kind of "ribbed or prismatic glass now upon the market."[50]

Clerestory windows lining the top of the corridor wall of classrooms meant that, during the day, corridors also were lit naturally (fig. 42). It is worth noting that Snyder did not provide artificial lighting in the halls. Many of the clerestory windows have now been removed or covered over to conform with fire-department regulations or, as a holdover from the Cold War

Figure 42. PS 11R: Clerestory Windows. LaValle photo.

era when the school corridors were used as air-raid shelters, to protect the children from shattered glass. Originally often both the exterior transom and interior clerestory windows were on toggles, making possible marvelous cross-ventilation.

Custom-Designed and Built Machinery and Fixtures

But Snyder wasn't satisfied with relying only on cross-ventilation to bring fresh air to the classrooms, the method of earlier school buildings. It did not "keep the children from being poisoned by foul air."[51] Demonstrating his forward-thinking willingness to embrace new technologies, he joined the American Society of Heating and Ventilating Engineers (ASHVE) in 1895, the year it was founded; he later served on its Board of Governors and in 1907 became its president.* The prevailing ventilation technology in the

---

*Its 1895 founding president said, "We need to look backward but a very few years to find that our profession was unknown. The rapid strides of modern civilization have created many new professions, and ours among them."

1890s wasn't practical for schools. Because of the confines of the building site, Snyder was unable to incorporate the ventilating shafts that were the standard way of heating in the 1890s.

Thus, after reading about the ventilation practices around the world and "an inspection of the methods employed in the Boston schools," Snyder developed a *plenum* system of heat and ventilation, a technology that involved sucking air through the building (fig. 43). By 1900, Snyder's solution was "believed to be the best in use anywhere"; namely, "a volume of fresh air, heated to a certain temperature, is poured into the classrooms at the ceiling, and the vitiated air is drawn out at the floor level."[52] Whereas Switzerland called for six to nine cubic feet of fresh air per pupil per minute (CFM) and Italy seven to twelve CFM per pupil, New York schools provided thirty CFM per pupil and could, if required, increase the supply.[53] That number was the standard recommended by the ASHVE (fig. 44). Someone who taught for many years in Snyder schools made this observation: "The volume of air moved is so large that when the system turns on, it's silent—unlike newer systems where you can hear and feel it when the blowers turn on." Snyder's ventilation systems, supplemented by the volume of light and air from large windows, were so successful that New York City schools remained open

Figure 43. PS 11R: Plenum Ventilation. LaValle photo.

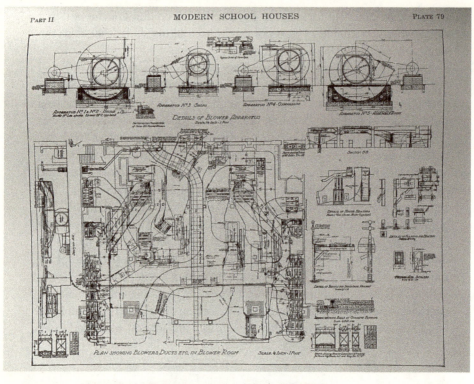

Figure 44. Bushwick High School: Details of Blower Apparatus. *Modern School Houses*, Part II, 1915.

throughout the 1918 flu pandemic, while most U.S. cities closed their schools. That schools were able to stay open then is in stark contrast to the city's response to the 2020 Covid-19 pandemic.[54]

Faced with the "difficult problem" of ventilating the schools, as with other problems, Snyder didn't depend on patented, marketed products but, after studying practices in school systems worldwide, developed his own solution "to equal in effectiveness the high-priced patented systems at a greatly reduced price."[55] He kept costs down by creating his own ventilating machine parameters and contracting out, rather than purchasing prohibitively expensive name-brand equivalents. Plenum ventilators are working to this day in a number of Snyder's schools, even though finding skilled workmen to repair the wide leather belts has become challenging.

He would do this for a range of problems—from adjustable desks to flushing mechanisms, from water fountains to snow-removal equipment. He reported in 1895 on two small plumbing improvements he designed to large effect, including

A fresh air inlet which the boys cannot fill up with refuse, and a yard or cesspool catch basin or grating . . . which will drain the yards as fast as the water falls.[56]

On numerous fronts he made progress toward devising solutions that allowed for "great savings" and smoother functioning of the schools. Snyder's ready eye for glitches in the smooth operating of a school and his penchant for solving problems are encapsulated in other minor improvements:

> Easily adjusted shades [have] been substituted for Venetian blinds.
> [To solve the problem of teachers' putting thumbtacks in walls], there has been devised the idea of covering the wall surface above the blackboard for a distance of three feet in length with a strip of cork carpet in natural finish, secured to the walls with a plastic cement.[57]
> Drinking facilities are furnished so that from fifty to sixty children can obtain water at the same time, the troughs to receive the waste being so designed that the clothing of the children, either large or small, is not wet from the spattering of the water.[58]

Enlarged drinking facilities, wrote a contemporary, "must simplify matters wonderfully when at recess the stampede for a drink begins."[59] All of these small changes show a large concern for the people using the building.

In furnishing classrooms, Snyder used the same strategy of self-sufficiency, designing his own desks rather than purchasing them ready-made. In his earliest annual report, he recognized the effect proper seating has on the learning process, writing that "comfortable seating tends greatly to check the nervous restlessness of a child."[60]

The seating, of course, had not been proper—often backless benches—as Jacob Riis had made memorably clear:

> In New York we put boys in foul, dark class-rooms where they grow crooked for want of proper desks; we bid them play in gloomy caverns which the sun never enters . . . and in the same breath illogically threaten them with the Jail if they do not come.[61]

A New York physician voiced his opinion that "ninety-nine out of a hundred girls are deformed by the schoolroom postures before they reach the high school; curvature of the spine is one of the commonest effects of schoolroom chairs."[62] Worse, as Commissioner Wehrum had reported, numerous classrooms had no desks. To remedy the situation, Snyder proposed to make

> a sample desk and seat peculiar to the needs of our schools [and] procure bids in that style and that alone. We would then avoid the trouble which now ensues from the competing furniture firms submitting their

own style of desks, leaving this Board to determine whether the figures of the lowest bidder means inferior style, workmanship and materials.[63]

By 1898, he was able to write, "The children are seated with single desks and seats of the adjustable pattern, with aisles between each row."[64] This accomplishment was, however, only a partial victory for good schooling. While desks had been introduced and while kindergarten classrooms had the flexibility of movable desks, those in primary and secondary classrooms were bolted to the floor in rows. Thus, regimentation and discipline were privileged over the progressive ideals of creativity and intellectual exploration. Class size told a similar story. From a design perspective, Snyder had managed to reduce it from sixty-five in 1891 to forty-five in 1898, but after that one golden year, the New York City public-school formula became established at fifty "sittings" per class. With classes then basically double or even triple the size of twenty-first-century classes, teachers were hard-pressed to address each child's individual potential. While Snyder schools had made many dreams reality, on these two counts, budget and practicality won out over vision and ideals.

Snyder also focused his attention on classroom quality-of-life issues, providing not just cloakrooms, but heated cloakrooms. He explained that he efficiently heated them

> by means of an exhaust flue placed in the upper part connected to our forced ventilation system, the air being drawn in along the bottom of the wardrobe, thence up through the clothing, passing off through the vent flues and into the outer air. The proof of its effectiveness is the entire absence of odor in the class-room or wardrobe, although the clothing may be damp and be the property of those children whose garments as such, or in fact at any time, to say the least, have a very perceptible smell. In addition, some of the later plans provided for each wardrobe being fitted with heating pipes, so that the clothing can be dried when damp.[65]

Later he eliminated the need for heating coils:

> This scheme [placing out-take screens in wardrobes] obviates the need of steam coils in wardrobes, as the vitiated air is sufficient to thoroughly dry ["and warm"][66] the clothing even in wet weather, and overheating of classrooms by coils in wardrobes is thus also prevented.[67]

"Ventilated wardrobes have taken the place of the usual upright boxes into which wet wraps are packed to ferment in seclusion,"[68] Shaw reported from her visits to the schools. Heated cloakrooms must have seemed like an amazing luxury.

In the 1890s electricity and indoor bathrooms were replacing gas and outhouses in commercial and residential buildings—and in the schools. Even in most of Snyder's earliest buildings he installed electrical systems as well as gas, sometimes even providing the school with its own dynamo for generating electricity. As for bathrooms, he inherited outhouses behind the schools, many wooden "and consequently filthy through absorption, to a disgusting and dangerous degree."[69] Then when an 1892 law required that outhouses be built of brick, Snyder moved the facilities indoors, arguing for this improvement on economic grounds:

> We could make the money granted us for the installation of new sanitary appliances go very much further, if we were not obliged in nearly every instance to provide a building in which to place them . . . of brick, with foundation at least 4 feet deep.[70]

"On a more liberal allowance per capita than elsewhere," he installed sanitary accommodations that, he wrote, "designed after much research and study, are accepted as the standard, save by those who control patented articles."[71] In his annual reports between 1892 and 1895, he stressed the critical necessity of good sanitary conditions in schools. "I am fully of the opinion that no part of a school building is of such vital importance as the sanitary work," wrote Snyder in 1892. In his discussion of "this most vital though vexatious problem," he reveals his concern with every imaginable aspect, from the siphons and urinal waste pipes to the sinks, the number of toilets to students, and the making of toilets that didn't overflow. His reports show us his repeated devising of new parts when those he had didn't work, his concern about eliminating "source[s] of annoyance and uncleanliness," and his awareness of both his immediate and larger clients, which are the school's occupants and the city. The school's occupants were naturally concerned about quality, the city about "saving of expense" and improvements that "will not again be a charge against the city for many years to come." Snyder satisfied both.

Generally, Snyder schools received the kind of intelligent concern that had not previously been accorded schools. "Space fails to describe the innumerable evidences of careful thought that are observable everywhere,"[72] John Beverley Robinson proclaimed in *Architectural Record* in 1898. The evidence ranges from small amenities to improvements in classroom comfort (huge windows, adjustable desks, heated cloakrooms) to the building-wide issues of fireproofing and mechanical heating and ventilation. In contrast to his predecessor, Snyder used cutting-edge techniques such as steel-framing to fulfill the progressive vision and to transform the three main adjectives describing New York City's schools from dark, dank, and unsafe to healthy, pleasant, and safe. A. E. Palmer wrote, "In fact a new era in school architecture may truthfully be said to have been inaugurated."*

Greater Functionality in Response to Educational/Pedagogical Innovations

Toward the end of the nineteenth century, as Progressive educational reformers and psychologists such as John Dewey, G. Stanley Hall, and William James broadened knowledge of how the mind functions, schools came to be seen as needing to provide more than just classrooms geared to exercising the mind in isolation.

According to reformer John Dewey:

> Give the pupils something to do, not something to learn; and the doing is of such a nature as to demand thinking; learning naturally results.
>
> Were all instructors to realize that the quality of mental process, not the production of correct answers, is the measure of educative growth something hardly less than a revolution in teaching would be worked.[73]

They needed a broader curriculum that would develop and strengthen students' fine and gross motor skills and their sense of community, belonging, fair play, teamwork, and aesthetics. In response, progressive schools around the country started providing specialized facilities such as physical and manual-training rooms and assembly halls. Snyder, too, "to keep pace with the new lights that have blazed for us in these latter days in educational matters,"[74] added to New York schools manual-training rooms for activities such as cooking, sewing, drawing, clay modeling, and carpentry; physical

---

*Palmer continues that during 1890–97 "great improvements in the designing and erection of school buildings were made. The steel skeleton system of construction was employed, saving time in the erection and, by reducing the thickness of the enclosing walls, securing more light and air; five-story buildings were built, the fifth story furnishing accommodation for physical and manual training; more ornate structures were planned, with more artistic treatment of materials; the so-called 'H' style of building, giving abundant light to all classrooms with no possibility of its being cut off by the erection of adjacent buildings, was adopted for sections of the city where sites were very costly; mechanical ventilation for classrooms and adjustable seats and desks were introduced"; *The New York City Public School: Being a History of the Free Education in the City of New York* (New York: Macmillan, 1905), 191.

education facilities—gymnasiums and roof playgrounds; kindergarten rooms; and assembly space for both school use and community use after school hours.

Before Snyder's time, New York public schools had done little to keep abreast of educational developments in the rest of the country. No high school buildings existed in pre-Consolidation New York; the typical primary school consisted of only classrooms and the principal's office, with the occasional assembly room, and for the most part New York teachers followed a strictly academic curriculum, which they taught by rote. However, the Board of Education had initiated some advances. As early as 1866 the first evening high school had been established, with three more in the late 1880s—alternatives to the crowded city college and normal school, both of which accepted advanced eighth-graders. In 1885, the board had asked Snyder's predecessor, George Debevoise, to provide manual- and physical-training rooms. By 1890, 20,000 students—7 percent of the 307,809 enrolled in public school—took such classes.[75] In a third advance, in 1888, the board had embarked upon an evening lecture series designed to involve the whole family in education, parents using school assembly rooms in the evening, children during the day. Snyder took over these fledgling efforts and expanded them in alignment with progressive educational reforms.

In keeping with Dewey's vision that students learn to think by doing, Snyder designed spaces for the kind of new broader curriculum that was already being offered in progressive schools around the country. One of his first actions was to propose adding a fifth floor for specialized physical- and manual-training rooms. About PS 23 (1893) in Chinatown (fig. 45), the plans for which were approved October 5, 1891, just three months after he became superintendent, he wrote,

> The Committee on Buildings . . . approved of the construction of an attic under the pitched roof of a sufficient size for a gymnasium, which I demonstrated could be built for a very slight additional cost. . . . All their hopes have been more than realized. The attic story of that building has been made into a complete gymnasium and Manual-Training rooms for cooking, clay modeling and carpenter work. (fig. 46)[76]

Snyder's "new departure" immediately became standard, allowing for physical education and for practical, hands-on subjects. Almost all the schools from Snyder's early period included this new type of specialized facility "now deemed requisite and necessary in every well-equipped school building."[77] Reporting on the fifth floor of PS 20M (1899), educator Adele Marie

Figure 45. PS 23M: Drawing with Four Floors and an Attic. *Real Estate Record and Guide*, 1892.

Figure 46. PS 23M: Renovated to Five Full Floors. LaValle photo.

Shaw enumerated the new types of spaces: "reading-room, library, sewing-room, cooking-room, girls' gymnasium, boys' gymnasium, modeling-room, draughting-room and carpentry room."[78]

Although manual training has been all but eliminated from academic programs today in the interest of enhancing the possibility for all students to reach their potential, not just the privileged, it was at the time a new, exciting area of study. William Maxwell, the first superintendent of schools for Greater New York, put it this way: "It is as essential to train the hand to express thought by 'action' as it is to train the power of speech."[79] The 1881 Cooper Union trustees went further, seeing mechanical/vocational training as the answer to urban blight. The vision was that technical training could eliminate poverty by creating workers skilled in numerous blue-collar professions. It could transform, in a single generation, entrenched paupers into self-sufficient citizens. In 1897 a "radical change" in the mechanical-training curriculum was made by the Board of Education Committee on Instruction to offer art-related courses such as drawing, color design, and modeling. Prospective teachers were required to pass an exam documenting their proficiency in drawing with charcoal, watercolor drawing from still life, the theory of color, and clay modeling. New courses were introduced in the schools, in accordance with this plan. The assumption was that the new

Figure 47. PS 38M, 1906 (Later Became West Side Vocational High School). *NYC BOE AFSR 1906–8.*

Figure 48. West Side Vocational High School. Principal Laffin Family Archives.

methods would arouse the pupils' interest in learning.[80] Under Snyder's tenure many vocational schools were needed, hence various elementary schools were reconfigured to become vocational schools, including PS 38M, which became West Side Vocational High School (figs. 47, 48).

Snyder began a tradition of art in the schools that remains strong today, as evidenced by Michelle Cohen's 2009 book *Public Art in Public Schools*. As education during the Progressive Era (1890–1920) was transitioning from the realm of training the children of the elite to educating the masses, the arts were valued for their potential for active learning. The standard curriculum did not include highbrow painting and sculpture but had the more practical focus of preparing students with the skills burgeoning industries required. Manual-training classes such as woodworking, metalworking, sewing, and technical and mechanical drawing were added in rooms double or half again as large as the standard classroom. By 1900 the number of students taking these mechanical-training classes had increased fivefold, to 100,000. In this era when beautiful architecture was thought to be uplifting to society as a whole, Snyder designed beautiful and impressive school buildings inside and out. His buildings were art on display for all to see, for passersby as well as students and staff.

Progressivism also championed physical education, and thus Snyder faced the challenge of designing yet another new type of space in public schools. In the latter nineteenth century, the view of play as the devil's work was replaced by the idea that play contributed to a child's physical development and moral sense. Julia Richman, New York City's first female district superintendent of schools, argued that "obeying the rules of a game in a sportsmanlike manner . . . was the most important part of the athletic lesson."[81] Yet at the same time much of the play space in neighborhoods had been eliminated as residential New York became more densely built up in the change from one-family houses occupying half a lot to tenement houses that laid claim to whole lots. In reaction to this lack of play space, Lillian Wald established the first public playground in New York City, in Seward Park, to which 20,000 children came, despite rain, on the October day in 1903 that it opened. And, for the public schools, Charles Snyder improved the design of first-floor playrooms ("indoor yards"), designed gymnasiums and rooftop playgrounds, and urged the purchase of land to improve or create playgrounds around existing and proposed schools.

Snyder raised the quality of the schools' first floors, which traditionally in New York had been left as open space for "indoor yards." Steel frames, which allowed for better fireproofing and larger windows, also reduced the number of columns required, making this large, open first-floor room less obstructed. In addition, Snyder heightened the ceilings to create a sense of spaciousness,[82] finished first-floor play spaces in hard white plaster, and lined the walls, up to six feet, with glazed light-colored tiles, which were durable and attractive and reflected light.[83] In 2016, a security guard in one of Snyder's third-decade schools—the 1913 PS 61 on East Twelfth Street—pointed out an original retractable basketball hoop and the low benches around the perimeter of the playroom for little children to sit on, commenting, "These schools were built with love of the children"

To complement the first-floor indoor yard, gymnasiums were installed in almost all the first-decade schools, often the largest space in the school, and usually on the fifth floor (fig. 49). Those gymnasiums are still being used in schools such as PS 166 (1900) on the Upper West Side, PS 158 (1899) on the Upper East Side, and PS 32 (1900) in the Bronx. In other schools, such as PS 27 in the Bronx, the gymnasium was a two-classroom-sized space on the fourth floor. In the H-plan schools, also on the fourth floor, it filled the end of one of the sides of the H. In 1898, Snyder commented that Boston "marvels how we introduce gymnasiums and many other features in our elementary-school buildings, while there they are found only in the high schools."[84]

Rooftop playgrounds were probably the most celebrated innovation implemented by Snyder and his department. They had existed in the city—the one that opened at architects Brunner & Tryon's 1891 Educational Alliance on the Lower East Side is still being used today—but had not previously been available to public-school children. Although Jacob Riis had

Figure 49. PS 166M, 1900: Fifth-Floor Gymnasium. Arrington photo.

been the one who actually proposed the idea of roof playgrounds to the Board of Education,[85] Snyder was ebullient, explaining in his 1896 Annual Report how advances he'd made in "the art" of designing school buildings had "led up to the grand feature of this year's work, which was the introduction of *roof playgrounds for the school children* [italics his]."[86] Again, it was the children he wanted the best for. He faced the problem that when sites were expensive and land at a premium, little space could be given up for a playground. He wrote,

> A happy solution of the difficulty was found by providing, in addition to the indoor playroom on the first story and the outside playground at the rear of the building, a roof playground, which, located high above the adjoining houses, has better light and air than the others, and is more enjoyable in every way. Care is taken to inclose [*sic*] both the roof and sides with wire netting to prevent accidents, while sanitary accommodations are provided on the floor next to the roof.[87]

The "enjoyable" rooftop playgrounds with better "light and air" became standard for the big schools being erected all over the Lower East Side, "where the streets are narrow and crowded and facilities for children's pastimes are scant."[88] That same year *Outlook* magazine celebrated how rooftop playgrounds provided

> a good deal of sunshine and fresh air to children whose lives are spent in narrow streets swarming with life and reeking with bad odors. Seventy-five thousand square feet of space, with nothing in sight but the sky! Who can calculate the influence that these playgrounds will have?[89]

Rooftop playgrounds appeared on almost every new school in the area. Thus it can be said that, in the realm of student's healthful activities, Snyder had been behind but soon pulled out ahead. He was designing more complex buildings to support increasingly varied functions. According to an 1899 article in the *Real Estate Record and Guide*,

> It is a matter of local pride to know that the school architecture of New York, as developed by Mr. Snyder, is being copied not only in other American cities but abroad. . . . His success as a designer is largely due to his readiness to accept suggestions from the teaching staff.[90]

Snyder's responsiveness to the Board of Education and to the teaching staff helped him move New York from public-school laggard to leader in record time. Already New York schools had become a model, a far cry from the outdated facilities consisting of classrooms alone that Snyder had inherited only seven years earlier.

Another new type of space Snyder was called upon to provide was kindergarten classrooms. Friedrich Frobel in 1837 had pioneered the idea that children should be taken care of and nourished in "children's gardens." The first kindergarten in this country opened in Boston in 1860. Though St. Louis offered kindergarten through the public schools in 1873, most cities, including New York, did not start to move kindergartens from private to public schools until the 1890s. In 1893, the New York City Board of Education established seven kindergarten classes. By 1896 that number had doubled, and a supervisor of kindergartens was appointed. Two years later there were forty-eight kindergartens; soon thereafter kindergarten had "become a recognized and indispensable part of the educational work."[91] Snyder put kindergarten classrooms on the first floor, so that kindergartners didn't have to climb stairs and were separated from the other elementary students. In contrast to the standard classroom, kindergartens had movable furniture, their own bathrooms, and, in some schools such as PS 21 (1904), even their own playground.

One additional design challenge was the assembly room or auditorium. This was particularly important in New York for its symbolic role of bringing together diverse cultures, since some schools had a student body that spoke as many as twenty languages. But with real estate expensive, having an auditorium to be used only for morning meetings and special events was too inefficient a use of space. Instead, Snyder utilized assembly rooms—a double-loaded corridor with a stage at one end and three or four classrooms on each side separated by moving partitions (fig. 50). After the morning meeting of inspirational words and songs, the assembly space was converted back into classrooms. Almost all of Snyder's first-decade schools had assembly rooms of this type, some with stained-glass windows, an ornate podium area for the principal, and inspirational inscriptions. No working partitions have survived.

The schools Snyder designed have been called an "intelligent translation of new educational theories into bricks and mortar." He summed up the challenge this way:

> All [the architect's] efforts are . . . directed towards planning a building without one square inch of waste [*sic*] space, and which shall provide for the maximum number of [class] rooms . . . with individual, adjustable desks and seats arranged with proper aisles, also manual and physical training, kindergartens, library, bath, and other rooms now deemed requisite and necessary in every well-equipped school

Figure 50. PS 8X, 1898: Assembly Rooms with Partitions. Unknown, public domain.

building, all laid out with reference to a proper and sufficient number of stairways.⁹²

PS 147M (1899) exemplified what Snyder was doing in all the first-decade schools: Its floor plan included an "indoor yard" on the ground floor divided into separate boys' and girls' sections, each with indoor bathrooms. On the second and fourth floors, in addition to traditional classrooms, an assembly room could be opened up in the crossbar of the H with the stage at one end of the corridor and moving partitions that allowed the three classrooms on either side to become a large open space. Traditional classrooms filled the third floor. The fifth floor had boys' and girls' gymnasiums and mechanical training rooms for sewing, cooking, carpentry, and clay modeling (figs. 51, 52). PS 147M also had a rooftop playground and a swimming pool!

Once schools had assembly spaces and gymnasiums, they began to function as community centers, a role in keeping with their imposing architectural presence. An 1898 law forwarded that trend, providing that schools be used not only for educational purposes but, after hours, also for "recreational and other public uses." The law confirmed the idea "that the schools belong to the people, and are primarily for the children and their parents; not mere vehicles of ward patronage."⁹³ Prior to Snyder, many of those involved in the building of the schools had gotten or attempted to get their cut. Thus, despite the opposition of janitors and teachers, who were asked to work longer hours without additional pay, the school-as-community-center idea became reality.

Figure 51. Girls in Cooking Class. Unknown, public domain.

Figure 52. Boys in Design Class. Unknown, public domain.

One particular after-hours activity that Snyder schools housed was the Board of Education's evening lecture program, which turned into what school archivist David Ment has called a people's university.* In 1891 eight schools were used for evening lectures, with a total attendance of almost 80,000 for the year. By the end of the decade the number had risen around tenfold: 713,955 people attended 2,306 lectures in eighty-eight centers. In some schools, instead of the assembly room, Snyder made the first floor functional for evening uses. For example, he recommended that the first floor of PS 23 be configured so that it

> could be used for a drill room or Evening Lectures, without damage or detriment to the balance of the building, and with absolute confidence of the inability of the crowd to injure this first story lecture room, or have any trouble in case of a panic, as there would be eight or nine outlets directly into the street, with only two or three steps intervening.†

For easy egress of large audiences, all of Snyder's larger first-decade schools had seven to ten doors to the street. Later, when the public had developed more faith in the efficacy of fireproofing techniques, schools started having fewer entrances.

Another after-hours function of schools was to offer settlement-house-type services. The settlement house idea that university students and

---

*"A people's university emerged in the form of a program of Public Evening Lectures conducted from 1888 to 1917, offering hundreds of evening courses throughout the city in science, literature, art, music, and history, taught in English, Yiddish, and Italian"; *Encyclopedia of New York City*, ed. Kenneth Jackson (New Haven, Conn.: Yale University Press, 1995), 958.

†The passage in full reads, "Careful attention has been paid to making the first or ground floor of all the new school buildings suitable for Evening Lectures. [For PS 23], the Committee carried out the recommendations I made to them . . . which were: (a) The changing of the construction of the building so that the girders heretofore showing below the first story ceiling be concealed; (b) that the story be increased somewhat in height; (c) that the first floor be of fireproof construction, iron beams, brick arches and paved with asphalt; (d) that instead of the usual stationary partitions between the boys' and girls' playgrounds, there be substituted sliding doors with wire work in the upper panels for ventilation; (e) and that this first floor when so constructed could be used for a drill room or Evening Lectures, without damage or detriment to the balance of the building, and with absolute confidence of the inability of the crowd to injure this first story lecture room, or have any trouble in case of a panic, as there would be eight or nine outlets directly into the street, with only two or three steps intervening"; Snyder, "Annual Report of the Superintendent of School Buildings" (1894), 218.

philanthropists should "settle" in poor neighborhoods in order to provide services and bridge the gap between rich and poor had originated among British social activists, the founders of London's Toynbee Hall in particular. In New York, University Settlement House, the first in the United States, opened in 1886 and Lillian Wald's Henry Street Settlement House in 1893, both preceding Jane Addams's famous 1899 Hull House in Chicago. Both, on the Lower East Side, still function today. Because school buildings were larger than settlement houses, more activities could be offered—for instance, opening classrooms "to the citizens of the neighborhood for purposes of reading and quiet amusement"[94] Moving doctors, nurses, and clinics from the settlement houses to the schools, Jacob Riis argued, was the most efficient way to make them broadly available.

The schools also functioned as recreation centers. The public didn't, however, at first take to rooftop playgrounds. Although the first rooftop playground, at PS 75 located in what is now Seward Park, was only one floor up (on top of a one-story indoor-playroom addition with which Snyder had upgraded the 1875 building), it wasn't used. But Snyder persisted, sustained by Jacob Riis's unflagging promotion of the idea. Snyder wrote,

> Not discouraged, I designed a second one for the roof of PS 1, at Henry and Oliver Streets, where the cost of the plot had been very great and the demand for school accommodations so urgent that it was necessary to utilize almost the entire plot for the building.[95]

Again the Board of Education gave its approval, with the addition of a brick elevator shaft to be used in the future, should it be found wise to do so. [The Cooper Union building also had had a forward-thinking elevator shaft.] This school and most of the others required a six-story climb, which the public was finally brought around to accepting.

Another innovation was the so-called vacation schools, which benefitted not just the neighborhood children but curriculum development as well. William Maxwell wrote about the collateral benefit of vacation schools as "experiment stations that will supply valuable suggestions to work in the regular school."[96] Riis reported that by 1902 there were seventeen vacation schools in which the boys are taught basketry, weaving, chair-caning, sloyd [practical handicrafts], fret-sawing, and how to work in leather and iron, while the girls learn sewing, millinery, embroidering, knitting, and the domestic arts, nature.[97] Except for the hint that girls shared in the boys' work where they could, the new manual-training curriculum in vacation schools, like such classes during the regular school year, followed traditional gender lines. In these temperance days, rooftop playgrounds were seen as keeping boys out of the saloon.

Evening lectures, settlement-house activities, recreation centers, vacation schools—Snyder's first-decade schools were used well more than for just the regular school day. Snyder described their community function in this way:

> The idea that public school buildings should be thrown open for use under proper restrictions for all hours, even Sundays, when not in use for school purposes is one that is rapidly growing in favor and should be encouraged in every way possible. . . . The summer or vacation schools have gained such popularity during the few years they have been in existence that this bureau cannot find the buildings sufficiently long unoccupied to make the needed repairs.[98]

In just this one decade, Snyder had made numerous functional changes in what constituted a public-school building. One commentary at the time called him a magician:

> The transition from the old buildings, with their depressing exterior and, in many cases, dark rooms and bad sanitary conditions, to the light and airy buildings of to-day, with their ventilating plants, roof playgrounds, fine sanitation, and conveniences of all sorts, has been quick enough to savor of magic.[99]

Snyder had graduated from an outdated high school housed on the third floor of elementary school #4. Six years later, in 1884, Saratoga Springs had built a new high school, "the latest word in construction," with science laboratories, boys' and girls' gymnasiums, an auditorium, and a library.[100] The irony that Snyder's small hometown was at least a decade ahead of New York perhaps had further prompted his creativity and sense of urgency in providing the city with better schools.

A letter to Snyder from departing Board of Education president Hubbell in 1898, when Snyder was unanimously named superintendent of school buildings for the Greater City of New York, voiced Hubbell's unqualified admiration: "The beautiful buildings that have arisen under your inspiration will ever be a monument to your skill and genius in your profession." Hubbell praised Snyder's "skill and genius" that had made him, in just seven short years "head of the department of scholastic architecture in

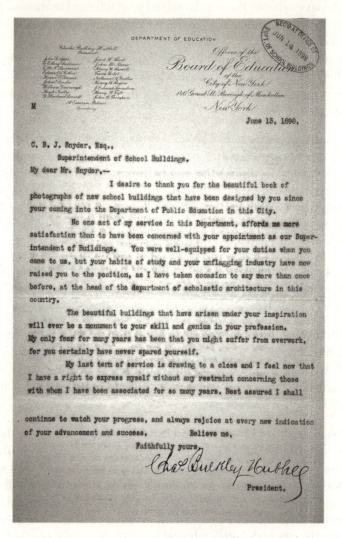

Figure 53. Letter from President Hubbell. Snyder Family Archives.

the country" (fig. 53). In two particularly conservative fields, architecture and education, Snyder relished new ways of doing things. Because of his responsiveness to the ideas of educators, he made dreams reality and, in the process, became a major contributor to the creation of the modern school, with the kinds of classrooms and extracurricular facilities that have become standard today.

Chapter 4

The Prolific Decade 1901–1910

Building a World-Class Public-School System

"YES, OURS IS the greatest of all times,"[1] Jacob Riis proclaimed in *The Battle with the Slum* (1902), and indeed the first decade of the new century bore out his excitement about the many reforms that were being enacted. The spirit of the time was embodied in the charismatic Teddy Roosevelt, whose two terms as president spanned the decade, proposed radical reforms and put in place a domestic policy that offered ordinary citizens a "Square Deal." Prosperity prevailed: it was "the high noon of capitalism in America,"[2] wrote historian Edward Robb Ellis. Except for a few far-flung exceptions, peace reigned throughout the world—Roosevelt won the Nobel Peace Prize and made the populace feel secure with his slogan, "Speak softly and carry a big stick." During this period of stability, however, tremendous change occurred. The car began to supplant the horse. The Wright brothers demonstrated that humans could defy gravity and fly. The Panama Canal was established, yoking the Atlantic and Pacific Oceans.

New York City experienced the best and the worst of the decade. Although the United States was still a rural nation with only 40 percent of the population living in cities, and although within the five boroughs there were still more than 2,000 working farms, New York nevertheless became the first city of skyscrapers, growing up while other cities grew out. On October 27, 1904, the first nine miles of the subway opened, allowing New Yorkers to move at the astonishing speed of forty-five miles per hour. Immigration during the first five years of the new century more than doubled to a million people a year, the greatest number of immigrants ever to come to the United

States. Eighty-five percent of the city's population was foreign-born or of foreign parentage, asserted a 1903 article in *World's Work*.[3] And therein lay the dark side of this prosperous decade, defying Riis's optimism. More than a million and a half New Yorkers lived in tenements and slums. There were hundreds, if not thousands, of homeless children in the city. The customary workday stretched from 5 a.m. to 9 p.m. "New York's poor lived under worse conditions and paid more rent than the inhabitants of any other big city on earth."[4] Only 13,700 of the 500,000 pupils enrolled in the elementary schools graduated from eighth grade—that is, fewer than 3 percent—and women teachers could still be fired for marrying. Against this background of dynamic social transformation shadowed by human deprivation, Snyder carried out his second decade on the job.

If the first decade of his career involved startling creativity, the second was marked by sheer volume and size. This is not to say that the creativity stopped: Snyder continued responding to changing conditions and challenges with additional innovations in the schools' appearance, construction, and functionality as reflected in Snyder's 1908 four-part article, "Public School Buildings in the City of New York," in *American Architect and Building News* (fig. 54). But the seminal event defining the nature of this decade, the 1898 Consolidation of the Boroughs, meant that Snyder was working on an unprecedented scale. When a unanimous vote made him superintendent of school buildings for Greater New York, his responsibilities expanded from Manhattan and the North Side (the western sections of the Bronx) to include Brooklyn (the third-largest city in the United States at that time) and the thirty-four villages and townships of Queens, as well as the ten villages and townships of Richmond County (Staten Island). His one potential competitor for the position, James Naughton, twenty-year superintendent of school buildings for the City of Brooklyn, had died the year of the Consolidation. Snyder was now dealing with double the landmass and population of his first decade. But unlike his first decade of finding his way in the new terrain of schoolhouses, he now had the confidence born of extensive experience and many accolades.

He was now responsible for the largest school system in the country—indeed, larger than those of the next five largest cities in the United States combined (Boston, Philadelphia, Chicago, Cleveland, and St. Louis). The number of New York City schoolchildren, reported the *New York Tribune*, was "nearly twice the size of the standing army of Austria-Hungary." A single schoolhouse, PS 188 at the eastern end of Houston Street, accommodated "as many as attend all the schools in the entire State of Nevada."[5] Snyder had noted in his 1902 annual report that "contracts for the year amounted

Figure 54. Four-Part Snyder Article, Part I. *1908 American Architect and Building News* (AABN).

to $6,492,394.82, the largest in the history of the City,"[6] and two years later that the Board of Education was conducting "the most extensive building operations of any firm or corporation in the country."[7] The number of new schools he completed more than tripled, from fifty in the first decade to 176, and the number of additions more than doubled from fifteen to thirty-six, not including additions smaller than six classrooms or additions to his own schools.

He accomplished unprecedented volume despite the more numerous challenges faced by a public-school architect than by an architect in private practice. To begin with, a new school went through a lengthy and involved approval process. During the first decade of his career, Snyder had worked successfully to reduce from several years to four months the time required for getting a site vested. However, even if the site sat ready, the school plans had to be approved by six separate city agencies: the art commission and the departments of building, of highways, of finance, of fire, and of water supply, gas, and electricity. Then, the Board of Estimate and Apportionment had to authorize the funds. That entire process required on average four and a half months. Another challenge was the perennial problem of money: Snyder wrote about experiencing "exasperating delays" because qualified draftsmen were "coaxed away" by higher salaries elsewhere.[8] Also, the Board of Education was required by law to use whichever contractor gave the lowest bid, regardless of quality. While certain contractors such as P. J. Walsh and P. Gallagher built as many as twenty schools each, more generally a contractor built only one or a few schools. Thus, Snyder was working with multiple contractors, many of them not the best qualified.

There were other challenges. The Building Bureau often dealt with less desirable sites than did architects in the private sector. In addition, stringent materials requirements led to higher costs. Another challenge arose from the fact that the school year had to go on: if an old school existed on a site, it couldn't be torn down until at least half of the new building was ready to accommodate classes. New schools, therefore, often had to be built in two sections.

Despite the lengthy approval process, numerous contractors, demanding sites and conditions, stringent materials requirements, and intense accountability, Snyder pushed ahead undaunted. He showed his concern for fire safety by, for several months in 1908 and 1909, serving as chairman of a committee consisting of engineers from the five Building Bureaus and a deputy chief from the New York City Fire Department. Their objective was to produce a more comprehensive set of standards and rules for fire prevention and safety in public schools. He said,

> While it is true that in the City of New York we for many years prior to 1908 erected all our new school buildings of the standard fireproof type, in accordance with our building regulations, yet there were many points upon which there were no rules or data, especially as to stairway and exit.[9]

To support his ambitious agenda, Snyder needed a school bureaucracy responsive to his needs. The Building Bureau of the Board of Education had become a large modern architectural practice on a scale not unlike that of the Columbian Exposition organizer Daniel Burnham or even that of the prominent contemporary architects McKim, Mead, & White. From a staff of forty, soon more than 300 employees were required to handle the bureau's work. Snyder's 1904 annual report laid out the situation:

> In order to carry out [the vast scale of our building operations], there has been developed an organization of men trained in the various professions of architecture, mechanical, electrical and sanitary engineering, each with his special phase of the work.
>
> [It is crucial to have] all of these divisions under one responsible head, whose suggestions for improvement can be incorporated in the work day by day, instead of spasmodically.[10]

For greater efficiency, Snyder reorganized the bureau so that a deputy superintendent for each borough, sometimes two for Brooklyn, reported to him. There were assistants in charge of six aspects of the building process: design and planning; heating and ventilation; electricity, plumbing, and drainage; furniture; inspections; and records. All were supported by draftsmen, clerks, stenographers, and office boys. Even as the reorganization of the Department of Education as a whole was accomplished "without any undue delay or friction,"[11] so too was the reorganization of the Building Bureau.

Spanning the whole of Snyder's second decade was his collaboration with the legendary William Maxwell, Greater New York's first superintendent of schools.[12] Snyder provided, according to a 1903 article in *School Review*, "the architectural vestment to fit the measurements of the body scholastic,"[13] as defined by Maxwell. Snyder himself emphasized the cordiality of his working relationship with Maxwell:

> The endeavor has been to study each problem with reference to the needs as laid down by the City Superintendent, who has shown great readiness and courtesy in modifying his requirements when the lack of ground space or other physical difficulties to the carrying out of his recommendations presented themselves.[14]

This fecund collaboration produced many advances that earned recognition from contemporary as well as modern commentators. A 1905 *New York Times* article said,

> The paraphernalia of the new style education would certainly astonish a New Yorker of even fifty years ago if he could return to earth

and visit one of the modern up-to-date school palaces such as are being put in operation one after another as fast as money is forthcoming for their erection.[15]

That view is confirmed in the 1983 canonical publication *New York 1900*:

> The expansion of the city's school system between 1890 and 1915 mirrored, and in some cases pioneered, the most advanced theories of public education popular in the United States, introducing specialized facilities like laboratories, auditoriums, gymnasiums and playgrounds.[16]

Even as Maxwell "made a new educational New York, full of instruction for every other city in the land,"[17] so too Snyder's buildings attracted the attention of architects and educators from all over the country, even the world.

Snyder's most prolific decade, with an average of eighteen new schools a year—that is, a new school every twenty-three days—recorded other benchmarks as well. Innovations in schools in this decade included a new institutional Italian palazzo-style look; construction refinements; new types of differentiated spaces, the most important being the auditorium proper; and new types of facilities such as open-air classrooms and a residential school for truants. Perhaps most significantly, New York got a new type of school—its first public high schools. The traditional academic high schools were quickly joined by specialized vocational, commercial, and teacher-training high schools. In addition, the H-Plan, initiated in the late 1890s, came into its own as a school type and by the end of the decade had passed through four stylistic phases. Overall, Snyder's second decade saw New York's schools again undergo major revamping and expansion.

Innovations in Appearance

By the beginning of the new century, City Beautiful no longer held the stylistic cachet that it had in the 1890s. Though New York's two iconic train stations, the Forty-Second-Street Library, and many of the public bathhouses and fire and police stations still exemplified the classical style, tastes were changing. Society rejected Victorian clutter in favor of a sparer, simpler, more modern look as typified by Scotland's Charles Rennie Mackintosh and Chicago's Louis Sullivan. When Snyder became responsible for the borough of Brooklyn, he honored and perpetuated a style reminiscent of that of longtime Superintendent of School Buildings James Naughton. But in his second decade, for economical as well as aesthetic reasons, he moved away from palaces and pitched roofs to a style more in keeping with a more modern look.

Italian palazzo-style came to prevail in all the boroughs—not the Italian palazzo of the first decade, but in the style of the original classroom buildings on the Columbia University campus. Its architect, Charles McKim, at the turn of the twentieth century on, created "the first monumental urban ensemble designed in America following the World's Columbian Exposition," which included classroom buildings that were, according to architectural historian Andrew Dolkart, "an innovative hybrid" combining "Italian Renaissance massing and ornamental detail with Colonial-inspired brickwork." The rectilinear, symmetrically massed buildings were composed of red brick with Italian palazzo-style details such as quoins, ground-floor rustication, window enframements, and cornices. This Italian palazzo-style/Colonial combination "established a new mode of design that influenced other architects in New York—Babb, Cook, Flagg."[18] And Snyder. Versions of this type of building dominated Snyder's second decade (figs. 55 and 56).

Based on sheer numbers, Brooklyn claimed the bulk of Snyder's attention in the second decade. There he erected a total of eighty-one new schools and additions, as opposed to sixty-one in Manhattan and eighteen to thirty-four in the smaller boroughs. Of those eighty-one, almost half resembled the Columbia classroom buildings in being rectangular, symmetrically massed, primarily red-brick, five-story buildings with one or more elements of Classical ornamentation: a rusticated limestone base, window dressing, terra-cotta sculptural decoration, and a heavy cornice. The earliest school in this style still standing is PS 132 (1902) in Williamsburg, a four-story,

Figure 55. PS 132K, 1902: Institutional Italian Palazzo-Style. NYC BOE AFSR 1906–8.

Figure 56. PS 132K 1902 Close-up Views of Front and Side. Arrington photo.

quietly elegant building with a dentil cornice and central roof ornament over a round-arched entranceway approached by steps coming up from both sides. PS 130 (1903), just southwest of Prospect Park, is one of five schools in the borough with a round-arched, heavily ornamented entranceway, topped by a lion's head (figs. 57, 58, 59).

Recently renovated PS 159 (1908) in East New York is a wonderful example of the architect choosing to restore two cornices that had been removed in an earlier renovation. The customary practice of removing cornices happens because it is less troublesome and cheaper, but the building is left with a denuded look. The other Brooklyn schools from this decade included three one-of-a-kind Collegiate Gothic buildings that seemed a throwback to Snyder's first decade, twelve Brooklyn-style elementary schools, ten H-Plans, five high schools, one small school (PS 120 on Barren Island), and eleven additions. He was responsible also for 131 Livingston Street, the Brooklyn headquarters of the Board of Education.

During Snyder's first two years of designing new schools for Brooklyn, he produced a series of thirteen buildings unlike any that he built anywhere else or at any other time. These particular schools consist of seven look-alike

Figure 57. PS 130K, 1903: Institutional Italian Palazzo-Style, Marion's School. Arrington photo.

THE PROLIFIC DECADE 1901–1910 · 107

Figure 58. PS 130K: Entrance. Arrington photo.

Figure 59. PS 130K: Interior Entrance Foyer. Arrington photo.

three-story buildings (one is in Queens) and six four-story versions in the same style. Except for the demolished PS 64K and the formerly abandoned PS 125K, all still function as schools. None of them has been landmarked. They stand out for having pitched roofs like many of Snyder's first-decade schools at a time when, in general, he had moved to the more economical flat roof. Because of their visual echoes of the schools James Naughton had designed for Brooklyn, they might be called Brooklyn-Style or Naughton-Tribute.

James Naughton (1840–98) held the position of superintendent of school buildings and repairs for the twenty years leading up to the 1898 Consolidation, coincidentally the year of his death. He left Brooklyn a legacy of 100 distinguished school buildings, ten of which have been landmarked. Twenty years Snyder's senior, Naughton had come with his family from Ireland to Brooklyn at age eight and later studied architecture at the University of Wisconsin and then Cooper Union. He worked for the Brooklyn Board of Education for thirty years, during his last decade collaborating with William Maxwell, who would move on from having been Brooklyn's superintendent of schools for eleven years to become the first Superintendent of Schools for Greater New York. Naughton's schools were Romanesque Revival with French Second Empire elements: four-story symmetrical buildings characterized by a raised basement, a façade of projecting and receding pavilions with an interplay of arched and square-topped windows, and an elaborate pitched roof complicated by chimneys, gables, hooded dormers, and broken cornices, as epitomized by PS 108K (fig. 60). Given the architectural richness of Naughton's Brooklyn schools, it is not surprising that Snyder would respect and, to some extent emulate, his work (fig. 61).

The close similarity of Snyder's thirteen Naughton-tribute schools was unusual at this point in his career. Each sported nine arched windows along the third floor, topped by a frieze with medallions, a dentil cornice, and hipped roof, flanked by a receding pavilion on each side. On the side pavilions, third-floor rectangular windows are set between ornamental terra-cotta cartouches. Entrance stairs lead up over a raised basement to a heavy round-arched doorway set within a pedimented temple front. A wide horizontal stringcourse over the raised basement gives the pavilions unity; prominent quoins contribute to the verticality and plasticity of the buildings. Inside, after a small foyer with a built-in bench on each side, twenty classrooms are located throughout the three floors, a gymnasium spans a two-classroom length along the front of the second floor, and an auditorium occupies the central section of the third floor. Of the seven sister schools, PS 125 sat derelict in Brownsville from the 1960s until the early 2020s, and PS 79 in

Figure 60. PS 108K, 1894: James Naughton School. *NYC BOE AFSR 1906–8*.

Figure 61. PS 102K, 1901: Three-Story Naughton Tribute School. *NYC BOE AFSR 1906–8*.

Whitestone, Queens, has been altered beyond recognition. The rest remain well-preserved and functioning as public schools, all on the Brooklyn plain south of Prospect Park and Greenwood Cemetery.

The six four-story Naughton-tribute schools all show the same basic layout as the first seven do for the entrance lobby, auditorium, and gymnasium. But in the case of PS 136, PS 137, and PS 123, the pedimented entranceway stretches up two stories instead of just one; a heavy cornice around the top of the third floor sets off the top-floor windows, all rectangular, the central window of each grouping having a dormer-like pediment; and to add to the complex skyline, two large ventilators sit astride the peaked roof, like those on the Second Empire Castle of Cheverny (fig. 62).

PS 122M and PS 126K (fig. 63) have arched windows on the top floor; roof playgrounds on each of the side pavilions; a rusticated first floor, both it and the third floor topped by an unbroken stringcourse; an entranceway that extends up three stories; and a single-pedimented side entrance at each end. PS 64K, the first to be built and the only one to have been demolished, had the same basic design but with a flat roof, a balustrade around the side

Figure 62 PS 136K, 1902: Four-Story Naughton Tribute School with Ventilators on Roof. Arrington photo.

Figure 63. PS 126K, 1902: Four-Story Naughton Tribute School. *NYC BOE AFSR 1906–8.*

pavilions, and two rectangular ventilators on either side of the roof flagpole. To it and PS 123K, Snyder almost immediately added a side wing that doubled the school's capacity—the wing basically a classroom-only version of the original building.

These Naughton-tribute schools celebrate the fact that Brooklyn itself in the late nineteenth century already had "one of the most comprehensive and extensive public education systems of any city in the United States."[19] And, they constitute an appropriate tribute to Naughton himself by celebrating his vision and accomplishments.

Of the sixty-one schools that opened in Manhattan during Snyder's second decade, as in Brooklyn, the Italian Renaissance-style design accounts for almost half, but with far more variety than their Brooklyn counterparts. There are four strikingly Columbia-University-like rectilinear buildings with red brick and Classical detailing, PS 183 and PS 190 on the Upper East Side and PS 24M and PS 39M (demolished) in Harlem, all having a heavy lion-topped, Roman-arched entrance. At these and many other Snyder schools, one ascends one flight, either an outdoor staircase or an inside one, often flanked by stained-glass windows, to the second floor or piano nobile in a

Figure 64. PS 85M, 1906: Institutional Italian Palazzo-Style, East Harlem. *NYC BOE AFSR 1906–8.*

true Italian palazzo, establishing a psychological distance between the realm of the street and that of the school. PS 132 in northern Manhattan, PS 85 in East Harlem (fig. 64), and PS 4 on Rivington Street are all quintessential institutional Italian palazzo-style. To PS 66 and PS 101 on the Upper East Side, Snyder added a rooftop pergola. Manhattan was also graced with another eighteen Italianate schools, many of which hearken back to the greater complexity of Snyder's first-decade designs.

PS 110 is highly sculptural and ornate, edging toward Baroque. Its two dressed façades have a rusticated second instead of first floor, pediments surmount round-arched doors, deep stringcourses surround every floor, and, between the Dutch gables, a string of sculpted owls lines the roof, most easily visible as the eastbound J/M/Z train approaches the Williamsburg Bridge. Also having two exposed façades of limestone and buff brick, PS 38 is one of Snyder's few schools with a corner entrance; on its façades ornamental shield-like cartouches crown the piers under the dentil cornice.

Overlooking Seward Park (in which two years earlier the first municipally funded playground had opened) and designed in conjunction with its principal Julia Richman, PS 62 had a low-pitched roof that, hiding its sixth floor, contributed to its quiet, neo-Classical elegance (fig. 65). Among Snyder's largest schools, it opened in 1905 for seventh- and eighth-graders, an early forerunner of junior high schools, but was demolished in 1929 for the East Broadway stop on the IND subway. The school lasted only twenty-four years. A few blocks north, PS 12 (now apartments) was another huge school with a partial sixth floor (PS 62 had eighty-seven classrooms and PS 12 sixty-three, when the average school had thirty); across its ten bays runs a heavy stringcourse separating the rusticated first two stories from the plainer floors three through five. As for the other Manhattan schools during Snyder's second decade, he designed two Collegiate Gothic throwbacks to his first decade (PS 177 and an addition to PS 68); four high schools; nineteen H-Plan schools, almost twice the number in Brooklyn; eight additions; and, under the approach to the Williamsburg Bridge, several temporary schools, an answer to shifting populations.

In Queens Snyder got off to a slow start after the Consolidation, as he had to complete eleven buildings that were already in process when he took over. Two of those had been designed by Boring & Tilton, architects of the

Figure 65. PS 62M, 1905: For 7th & 8th Graders, Institutional Italian Palazzo-Style. *NYC BOE AFSR 1906–8.*

main building on Ellis Island, PS 14 (later Newtown High School, now demolished), and PS 34, which still operates as a public school. As in Brooklyn and Manhattan, in Queens half of Snyder's thirty-four new buildings and additions were Italian palazzo-style. Some were particularly lush and ornate reminders of Columbia classroom buildings, especially Queens PS numbers 81 through 85. PS 84 sits back from the street with steps ascending a terraced rise to a building with prominent quoins, top-floor arched windows with elaborate surrounds, and a grand entranceway consisting of a double staircase and temple front set off by two oval windows on the third floor, the overall design influenced by the Brooklyn-style schools. Snyder's only red-brick Italian palazzo-style high school in the tradition of Columbia classroom buildings was the home he designed for Long Island City High School. PS 88 and PS 16, both overlooking a park, have shallow pediments at each end of the front façade. A renovation job on PS 88 replaced its cornice, restored the building to its original glory. Three of Snyder's new buildings in Queens carried on the historicist, Beaux Arts look of schools he had been building in Manhattan, with elaborate hipped rooflines of gables, cupolas, ventilators, and chimneys (PS 5, PS 78, PS 80). Of those, only PS 80Q still exists, now the City View Inn (fig. 66). He did one H-Plan (PS 90Q) and one Brooklyn-style school outside Brooklyn, the now radically redesigned PS 79Q. An unusually large percentage of his efforts in Queens, almost one-third, were additions. He also designed the Spanish-Mission-style Parental School that is now part of Queens College.

Figure 66. Former PS 80Q, 1903: City View Inn. Mike Janoska photo.

Figure 67. PS 32R, 1902: Two Entrances. Arrington photo.

Staten Island followed the 50 percent pattern with nine of its eighteen new structures Italian palazzo-style: fourteen elementary schools, three additions, and, on a hill overlooking St. George, Curtis High School (1904), a smaller version of the Bronx's Morris High School. On Staten Island, Snyder faced a situation antithetical to high-density, expensive urban sites. Seven of the elementary schools he built there in his second decade ranged from two to eight classrooms and looked residential (fig. 67).* The smallest, PS 33, was wooden. The step-gabled PS 31, with an average attendance of thirty pupils, Snyder described as

> a modern up-to-date two-room structure, plain but substantial, the cost of which, because of its isolation and distance from all lines of travel or transportation, is much in excess per classroom than that of buildings in the Borough of Manhattan.

---

*They were PS 3 a→b, PS 6, PS 28, PS 31, PS 32, PS 33, and PS 34, all demolished except PS 32 and PS 28, now part of Historic Richmond Town. Only City Island and Woodlawn in the Bronx and Barren Island in Brooklyn had similarly small schools.

He continued that the two-room building presents "the most difficult problem in schoolhouse design."[20] Two were Italian palazzo-style: PS 6 and PS 34 were most sophisticated with elaborate dentil cornices, balustrades around the roof, and pediments. The proportions of PS 34 are based on Paris's Petit Trianon, according to *New York 1900*.[21] The other seven elementary schools from the decade were institutional Italian palazzo-style buildings, each with window embellishments and a heavy, dentil cornice. Three of them were four-story (PS 1R, PS 16R, PS 13R) and four two-story (PS 26R, PS 23R, PS 21R, PS 30R). All were entered on the lengthwise axis, an unusual arrangement for Snyder. One characteristic found exclusively among Staten Island schools, small and large alike, was placing two entranceways symmetrically on either side of the façade. As with his Brooklyn-style schools, this dual-entrance configuration may be a tribute to and continuation of the Staten Island school design that preceded him, by architects such as Edward A. Sergeant.

As in the other boroughs, the Italian palazzo-style building also prevailed in the Bronx. In fact, except for the two H-Plan schools and the Collegiate Gothic Morris High School, all eleven new schools there were a version of Columbia-classroom-building Italian palazzo-style. For this new, modern borough, there were no throwbacks. PS 35, like its sister-school PS 36, had particularly ornate terra-cotta quoins and window surrounds, and a dentil cornice over the fourth floor set off the attic floor (fig. 68). The ornate PS 6 sits up on a hill overlooking Tremont Avenue with shield-like cartouches at the tops of pillars and medallion-type decorations spaced out along the top cornice (fig. 69). Longwood's PS 39 was constructed of cream instead of red brick. A 1950s graduate, George L. Colon, wrote,

> But the center of this early world, no, of the universe, was P. S. 39. . . .
> The front stairs . . . on Longwood Avenue between Beck and Kelly Streets seemed like the steps of Olympus and the main entrance, the portals of heaven.[22]

A 1912 article in the *Real Estate Record and Guide* pictured several of the new Bronx schools, the first five from Snyder's first decade, the last three from his second (fig. 70). A 1904 *New York Times* article, in its celebration of a century of free education in New York, pictured Morris High School.

As early as 1906, a few of the Italian palazzo-style buildings evolved into Simplified Collegiate Gothic, retaining the heavy, overhanging cornice but

Figure 68. PS 35X, 1902: Institutional Italian Palazzo-Style. *NYC BOE AFSR 1906–8.*

Figure 69. PS 6X, 1904: Institutional Italian Palazzo-Style. *NYC BOE AFSR 1906–8.*

Figure 70. *Real Estate Record and Guide,* June 1912.

with shallow Tudor arches outlining the top-floor windows.* Instead of the single Tudor arch, PS 121M (1908) and PS 114M (1909) had little Tudor arches over each unit of the fourfold top-floor windows. Then, by the last year of the decade in Brooklyn, six schools had become fully Simplified Collegiate Gothic style, having in addition to top-floor Tudor-arched windows a crenellated roofline rather than an overhanging cornice—the style that would dominate Snyder's third decade not just in Brooklyn, but also in Queens and the Bronx.

During his second decade Snyder started explicitly addressing standardization. He wrote in his 1902 annual report,

> Early in the year an earnest attempt was made, through a conference with the City Superintendent of Schools and his Associates, to set some standard of uniformity in the planning of school buildings for the various Boroughs constituting the Greater City.[23]

In 1906 he found he had been able "to duplicate the types in all but thirteen of the buildings turned out from the draughting rooms."[24] In those pre-copying machine days, duplication raised the question of which was less expensive: to start over from scratch creating a new set of blueprints or using plasters (overlays) on an existing set of blueprints to make all the changes necessary in fitting the building to its particular site. Here's a description of just one set of blueprints:

> Public School 152, Brooklyn, required 29 sheets general drawings, 75 sheets details [sic] and 30 sheets for heating, ventilating and electrical work, a total of 134 sheets, averaging about 15 square feet each, a total of 2,010 square feet.[25]

Sometimes adapting that many "sheets" to another site required so many plasters that it was easier to begin anew.

Securing funds for the grand, imposing, recognizable look Snyder had developed for New York schools was a perennial issue. After the spike in funding around the years of the Consolidation, appropriations for construction leveled off. By 1906 it was reported that

> Mr. C. B. J. Snyder . . . says a school building must not have the appearance of an office building, a hotel or an apartment house. It must look like a school house, and as such it's exterior should be cast,

---

*Namely, PS 151 (1906), PS 94 (1908), and PS 155 (1908), in Brooklyn; PS 40 (1906), PS 42 (1907), and PS 43 (1908), in the Bronx; PS 85 (1908) and PS 89 (1908) in Queens; and PS 59 (1908, demolished) and PS 91 (1908) in Manhattan.

as far as this may be expedient, in classic lines expressive of some definite style of architecture.[26]

In 1909 Snyder protested that scant appropriations were making schoolhouses

> more and more like factories, for while there is improvement in exterior and interior design and decoration, yet they are almost wholly without . . . any features which would represent the dignity that should be part of an educational building.[27]

Despite his concerns and despite the fact that, with a few exceptions, his second-decade buildings did not continue the complex Renaissance Revival and Collegiate Gothic designs of his first decade, most of them did have a dignified Italian palazzo-style presence, not unlike that of Columbia University's classroom buildings. These financial constraints were exacerbated by the new construction reality that, as electricity supplanted gas and people generally expected brighter lighting, the interiors of some Snyder schools, finished in dark brown wood, came to seem dim and gloomy.

Innovations in Construction

Snyder rethought at least one of his earlier innovations for health and safety. After his dramatic introduction of steel-frame construction in New York City schools, a scarcity of steel around the turn of the century meant that PS 33X and many others were "delayed owing to the great difficulty in getting steel work, etc."[28] This experience, coupled with better fireproofing techniques and changes in building laws that reduced required bottom-floor column thickness, caused Snyder to return to load-bearing walls in some buildings: PS 40X he describes as of "fireproof construction throughout, all walls being laid up in cement mortar, with floor system of steel beams and brick arches."[29] While all first-decade schools had had steel skeletons as would all high schools, in his second decade Snyder would choose, based on cost and time considerations, to use either steel-skeleton or load-bearing construction.[30]

As to fireproofing, one small change he made involved using only metal or wood-covered-with-metal bookcases and wardrobes because "the majority of the fires . . . that have occurred in our schools, seem to have originated in either the wardrobes or bookcases."[31] *Fireproof Magazine* reported that in Snyder schools, "stairs are constructed of iron and are inclosed [sic] in fireproof shafts, with automatic doors held open by fusible links."[32] The article also commented,

> As one may easily surmise it costs a good deal of money to erect a model fireproof school building in New York to seat several thousand scholars, and the line of least resistance would be to put up cheaper affairs at less cost to satisfy political pressure.[33]

That is one expedient to which Snyder never resorted.

He also faced fireproofing the older buildings. At the time of the Consolidation only one school in Brooklyn and none in Queens or Staten Island were fireproofed. Despite the urgent need, he routinely received less than half the funds he requested for repairs and alterations to bring older buildings up to code.

In order not to have to depend on expensive and sometimes unreliable commercial sources, Snyder continued to develop his own materials. For instance, in the move from gas to electric lighting when problems arose with poor-quality electric wire and misleading company claims, Snyder reacted this way:

> We therefore determined to set up our own testing apparatus, the same as we have done for other materials.
>
> The Building Committee granted us funds for the purpose, and we expect that very shortly we shall be able to present a specification based upon chemical analysis and other scientific data, which will enable us to do away with the use of trade names entirely, the same as in our use of cement in building operations. [The Portland cement requirement had been lifted.]
>
> We will then be assured of good results and of receiving the goods we know will give us the greatest service.[34]

Even as he had devised an instrument for measuring light and a portable apparatus to measure the percentage of carbonic acid gas (carbon dioxide) in classrooms and thus check on his ventilation systems, similarly now he was determined to set up his own testing apparatus for electric wiring in order to guarantee getting "goods we know will give us the greatest service."

The ventilation systems themselves occasioned criticism in 1906, but Snyder had met with harsh criticism and worse before. There had been graft charges in 1897, from which he was thoroughly exonerated, and accusations in 1902 of failing to follow proper procedures, against which he had successfully defended himself. But criticisms of his ventilation systems were more recalcitrant. Although in 1904 he reported,

> Heating and ventilating engineers who have examined our plants are practically unanimous in the opinion that the system upon which our heating and ventilating plans are laid out is correct, both from the practical and the economical standpoint.

Still, he recommended moving to a higher-quality machine, arguing that the slightly higher cost is more than offset by an "almost absolute immunity from stoppages for repairs."[35]

By 1906 a headline read, "344 school buildings badly ventilated."[36] The number 344 was actually Snyder's own estimate, calculated on the basis of the 324 schools he had inherited that hadn't yet been upgraded plus the first twenty of his own 200 buildings with the *plenum* systems he had designed. The *plenum* technology was so new and fluid that the systems installed early on had now become outdated. Another problem was providing custodians sufficient training to handle the machines effectively. The criticisms of the massive, complex, and numerous ventilating machines could not be summarily dealt with.

Innovations in Functionality

As the curriculum was becoming more and more inclusive of subjects beyond academics and schools were functioning more and more as neighborhood centers, Snyder wrote, "Certain it is that every year adds to [the school building's] already complicated requirements."[37] During his second decade, he added specialized spaces for medical suites, showers, and, most notably, auditoriums while also enhancing the existing specialized spaces for kindergarten, mechanical training, and athletics.

One major expansion involved the number of kindergarten classes. With the kindergarten movement in full swing by the 1890s, in 1893 Snyder had started providing kindergarten rooms on the lower floors, each with its own bathroom, with movable instead of fixed seating and often with a separate entrance. By his second decade, he significantly increased the number of kindergartens as well as the quality of their accommodations. "The kindergarten [at PS 21] has two terraces for its own use and for growing plants and flowers," the *New York Times* reported.[38] That was just one of the touches that caused educator/reformer Adele Marie Shaw to exclaim, "I have pored literally hours over the plans for the new [PS 21], realizing in them dreams that have been often scoffed at as 'impossible.'"[39] During Snyder and

Maxwell's tenure, the number of kindergarten classes increased dramatically: they almost quintupled from 101 in 1899 to 478 in 1904, accommodating 16,008 children, and then more than doubled to 913 by 1914.[40]

As mentioned earlier, this was the era when manual training seemed the panacea for urban blight brought on by industrialization. Cooper Union's 1881 annual report included a rousing endorsement of vocational classes.[41] Superintendent of Schools William Maxwell saw mechanical-training classes in the same idealistic vein, as improving students' "observation, practical judgment, . . . and manual dexterity,"[42] thus preparing them for medical school or a scientific career. John Donovan, on the other hand, in his 1921 treatise *School Architecture* (MacMillan) voiced the pragmatic view of mechanical training as accommodating "a course of studies [that] has become more and more extended to meet the requirements of the industrial, commercial, and social life of the nation."[43] Whether out of practical or idealistic impulses, manual training became more and more ubiquitous in the curriculum.

Snyder, as a result, designed spaces for disciplines that were "unknown half a century or even a decade ago"[44]—a foundry and a construction and milling lab at Stuyvesant High School, for example, and at Manual Training High School, a steam and dynamo laboratory, electric testing laboratory, pattern-making laboratory, and dressmaking room.[45] All new co-ed PSs had at least one manual-training room for boys and one for girls, usually on the top floor; when possible, Snyder reconfigured old school buildings to include such facilities, as, for example, at PS 16 in Manhattan. About PS 62, designed in collaboration with its principal, Julia Richman, Snyder wrote, "Visitors from many parts of the world came to observe this model school. . . . An educator from Japan read a glowing account of the school while traveling in Germany and later came to New York to see for himself."[46] Visitors' particular interest was the "sixth story with its splendidly lighted spaces by means of the peculiar roof construction, which does not show from the front . . . utilized for classrooms, gymnasiums, manual training and domestic science rooms."[47]

In the elementary-school curriculum that Maxwell instituted in 1902, such vocational subjects were supplemented by the introduction of music, drawing, and nature study, demanding of Snyder additional specialized spaces. For high schools, besides music and art rooms, he designed new types of facilities such as science laboratories, faculty offices, libraries, lunchrooms, and study halls.

Snyder also devoted time and energy to improving athletic facilities, for the progressive view of education held that athletics was essential in a child's development, not a frill. As the schools started more and more to fill the role of community center, Snyder moved the gymnasiums from the upper floors (as in earlier schools such as PS 158M, PS 47M, PS 166M, and PS 25X) to the first floor or the raised basement to "be readily accessible from the street without throwing open the balance of the school premises."[48] He encircled many high-school gymnasiums at the second-floor level with banked running tracks, which are still being used in schools such as the original Stuyvesant High School, the Brooklyn Teacher Training School/PS 138, and Manual Training School in Park Slope, where his older son Howard ran track. About refinements to roof playgrounds, Snyder wrote,

> In our earlier schools ... light trusses with intermediate supports rest[ed] on the columns below. Later, as the playgrounds were really appreciated, other forms of trusses were devised so as to permit a clear span for the sixty odd feet of the width of the building, but at no greater expense.[49]

Rooftop playgrounds were designed for all eight schools that opened on the Lower East Side during Snyder's second decade, raising the total to sixteen with the eight from his first decade. (fig. 71): On the Upper East

Figure 71. PS 126K, 1904: Girls' Playground on the Roof. *Proceedings of the Municipal Engineers of the City of New York,* 1904.

Side, PS 66 (1908) and PS 101 (1910) had rooftop pagodas. Third-decade schools PS 130 (1922) in Chinatown and PS 11 (1924) in Chelsea to this day depend on roof playgrounds as their primary outdoor play space, as do post-Snyder Seward Park and Brooklyn Tech High Schools, among others.

When the rooftop playgrounds were opened up for neighborhood after-hours use, even though Jacob Riis saw them as "under the electric lamps, a veritable fairyland of delight,"[50] people were at first unwilling to climb the six flights of stairs. It was even debated whether the climb was "a stimulant or gave rise to heart strain."[51] To encourage community use of the rooftops and make a success of this "attempt on the part of the municipality to get the boys off the street and out of the reach of the saloon,"[52] Riis suggested providing entertainment. Accordingly, in 1902 the city earmarked $25,000 for "bands of music to be engaged for a number of rooftop playgrounds, which greatly increased public interest."[53] The following anecdote from Riis's *The Battle with the Slum* (1902) gains poignancy if one reads it while standing on the corner of Eldridge and Rivington Streets, between the University Settlement House (1901) and the former PS 20M (1899):

> I was at dinner with friends at the University Settlement, directly across from which, on the other corner, is one of the great new schools, No. 20, I think. We had got to the salad when through the open window there came a yell of exultation and triumph that made me fairly jump in my chair. Below in the street a mighty mob of children and mothers had been for half an hour besieging the door of the schoolhouse. The yell signaled the opening of it by the policeman in charge. Up the stairs surged the multitude. We could see them racing, climbing, toiling, according to their years, for the goal above where the band was tuning up. One little fellow with a trousers leg and a half, and a pair of suspenders and an undershirt as his only other garments, labored up the long flight carrying his baby brother on his back. I watched them go clear up, catching glimpses of them at every turn, and then I went up after.
>
>   I found them in a corner, propped against the wall, a look of the serenest bliss on their faces as they drank it all in. It was *their* show at last. The band was playing "Alabama," and fifteen hundred boys and girls were dancing, hopping, prancing to the tune, circling about and about while they sang and kept time to the music. When the chorus was reached, every voice was raised to its shrillest pitch: "Way—down—yonder—in—the—cornfield." And for once in my life the suggestion of the fields and the woods did not seem hopelessly out of

place in the Tenth Ward crowds. The baby in its tired mother's lap looked on wide-eyed, out of the sweep of the human current.

The band ceased playing, and the boys took up some game, dodging hither and thither in pursuit of a ball. How they did it will ever be a mystery to me. There did not seem to be room for another child, but they managed as if they had it all to themselves. There was no disorder; no one was hurt or even knocked down, unless in the game, and that was the game, so it was as it should be. Right in the middle of it, the strains of "Sunday Afternoon," all East Side children's favorite, burst forth, and out of the seeming confusion came rhythmic order as the whole body of children moved, singing along the floor.

Down below, the deserted street—deserted for once in the day—had grown strangely still. The policemen nodded contentedly: "good business, indeed." This was a kind of roof patrol he could appreciate. Nothing to do; less for tomorrow, for here they were not planning raids on the grocer's stock. They were happy, and when children are happy, they are safe, and so are the rest of us. It is the policeman's philosophy, and it is worth taking serious note of.

A warning blast on a trumpet and the "Star-spangled Banner" floated out over the house-tops. The children ceased dancing; every boy's cap came off, and the chorus swelled loud and clear: "in triumph shall wave/O'er the land of the free and the home of the brave." The light shone upon the thousand upturned faces. Scarce one in a hundred of them all that did not bear silent witness to persecution which had driven a whole people over the sea, without home, without flag. And now—my eyes fill with tears. I said it: I am getting old and silly.[54]

Since boys were playing on the buildings' roofs instead of committing petty crimes in the streets, the schools were literally reducing crime in the slums, as progressive visionaries had claimed they would.

For decades, children growing up in the city, especially poor children, used city streets and sidewalks for play areas, and city schools did not have playgrounds. In this era when progressives had deemed play crucial to a child's moral and social development, Snyder also lobbied for more traditional outside play space for the schools. In 1895 the state had "made it law that a playground should go with every public school,"[55] though without specifying size. After Snyder's 1896 fact-finding trip to Europe, he reported that British law required thirty square feet of play space per child, recognizing however that with New York's much larger schools, such liberal proportions were unfeasible.[56] Snyder's 1902 annual report recommended five square feet per pupil in the already densely built-up areas of Manhattan and Brooklyn; ten square feet per pupil in the less densely built-up areas of Manhattan, Brooklyn, Bronx, and Long Island City; and fifteen square feet per pupil everywhere else.[57] Not until after World War I and especially in the second half of the twentieth century would the city start seriously providing playground space for every school. Ironically, at some schools now, that hard-won space sits empty or is used for staff parking.

Another "revolutionary . . . path" in the early years of the twentieth century that required an entirely new type of space was "the field of social service, . . . medical inspection, appointment of school nurses, [and] a school lunch program." All of these innovations responded to the recognition that if children are "sick, hungry or emotionally disturbed, they can't learn."[58] Snyder fashioned clinics, classrooms for the handicapped, showers, and sometimes even public bathrooms. Under Mayor Seth Low, "a vigorous immunization program was initiated in the public school system."[59] According to the *Sun*, PS 165 was "the first school building to be designed in which provision is made for the medical inspection of the pupils by the officials of the Board of Health."[60] During his second decade Snyder put a medical inspector's room in many schools on the first floor near the principal's office, as was the case at PS 84 in Long Island City.[61] Many small clinic rooms on the lower floors are still used by school nurses today. Educator Adele Marie Shaw reported that, since illness exacerbated the truant habit, "wherever trained nurses supplement the labors of the medical inspectors, truancy is practically wiped out."[62]

On the heels of the movement that opened fifteen public baths in New York City in the first decade of the twentieth century followed the idea of baths in the public schools (fig. 72). In addition to showers in many of the boys' and girls' locker rooms, Snyder outfitted some of the first-floor large bathrooms with showers as well as toilets. As early as 1901, a thousand free baths a week were taken at PS 21 on Elizabeth and Spring,[63] and in 1905, the *New York Times* reported that, at PS 188 at the eastern end of Houston Street, "in a single afternoon 1500 children have been given baths."[64] Both schools were situated among Lower East Side tenement houses in which one study found only one bathtub per seventy-nine families. E. L. Doctorow, in *World's Fair*, wrote about how, as late as the Great Depression, some students at his Bronx elementary school saw water only the one time a week they were assigned to showers. Avery Corman, author of the novel *Kramer*

Figure 72. PS 102K, 1901: Bathing. Unknown, public domain.

Versus Kramer, attending a junior high school in the 1950s in the building that had been the original Evander Childs High School, had showers on his schedule. He wrote,

> We thought it might have been a Board of Education-mandated subject from the time when poor children might have taken showers they didn't have at home. We didn't shower during showers; it became an additional gym period.[65]

The most dramatic functional expansion of schools was the move from the partitioned assembly room to an auditorium proper. The auditorium/assembly room was important symbolically: "In a nation as diverse and fragmented as the United States," it was viewed as "engender[ing] respect for American institutions . . . instilling civic virtue and achieving cultural uplift."[66] Though certainly the use of sliding partitions to make classrooms into an assembly room had represented an efficient use of space, no one liked the arrangement except the boys chosen to do the actual pushing. Teachers complained particularly about the lack of soundproofing in the classrooms, and the classroom furniture was too small for adults coming for evening lectures.

Snyder pondered the problem for several years. As early as 1899, an article in the journal *School* reported,

> In view of the fact that public lectures are to be introduced in the schools in Brooklyn, the question as to the best location for the assembly rooms has been much discussed, and Mr. Snyder's proposition to have them on the ground floor is fast being accepted, as most convenient for such assemblages and safest on all occasions.[67]

Flying in the face of his own first-decade experience of locating auditoriums on upper floors where the light was better and structural columns unnecessary,[68] Snyder started putting them on the first floor or in the basement. Even in physical details, one can feel the influence of his years at Cooper Union (fig. 73). In its underground Great Hall where Abraham Lincoln's 1858 speech had catapulted him to national prominence, Snyder had probably attended in 1884 "The Architecture of the Renaissance" and "New York City, Old and New," both illustrated, two of the Saturday-night lectures that drew huge audiences. Locating auditoriums at street level made sense from the points of view of audience safety and convenience. The auditoriums were readily accessible for evening lectures, could be emptied quickly in case of fire, and had the further advantage that the rest of the school need not be opened.

Figure 73. Great Hall at Cooper Union. Courtesy of Cooper Union.

It was for H-Plan buildings that Snyder first figured out the logistics of an auditorium proper. Writing in his 1902 annual report about PS 21 (1904) in Soho, now demolished, he said,

> This year's work has as a part of its record certain radical improvements in schoolhouse planning and construction.
> ... In the endeavor to form an assembly room which would seat one thousand or more ... and at the same time not to encroach in any way upon the yard or recreation space, which is, at the best, none too large, I set out to turn to account the difference in grades which almost invariably exists in the levels of the two streets upon which a school building faces when running through the block ... raising the playground pavement [on the higher side] and forming the assembly room beneath it.[69]

His "radical improvements" enabled him to proclaim about what had seemed a necessary evil, "There is not a sliding partition in the whole building [the H-Plan PS 21]—a thing heretofore deemed impossible."[70]

Then in 1904, addressing the municipal engineers, he described how he had planned the auditorium at the H-Plan PS 37 (1905) in the Bronx, now apartments.

> The number of column foundations is due to a change made in planning, in order to avoid the criticism, which, for a number of years, has been leveled at the public school buildings of this city because of the formation of assembly rooms by the use of movable partitions between several of the classrooms, it being considered impossible to properly conduct exercises in these classrooms because of the readiness with which sound passes from room to room. In the [H-Plan schools], occupying spaces, as they do, between the avenues and extending through from street to street, I have utilized the basement beneath the surface of the play yard for an assembly room, it being readily accessible from the street for the use of lecture purposes, also from the school building, the outdoor play yard overhead being supported by columns passing through the auditorium or assembly room.[71]

He continued that PS 65M on the Lower East Side would "have two auditoriums in the basement, thus making use of every inch of the property, which will cost in the neighborhood of $400,000."[72] PS 65M opened in 1908, the only H-Plan school with six floors and two auditoriums. It was demolished in the 1960s for a more modern school and community center. Cooper Union's Great Hall had become a prototype for underground auditoriums.

Snyder continued the same under-the-courtyard configuration in all subsequent H-Plan buildings. With the assembly rooms on the second and fourth floors in the center of the H no longer needed, the movable partitions could become permanent and soundproofed.

After having solved the problem of adding auditoriums to H-Plan buildings, Snyder turned his attention to the traditional rectangular school. About the plans for the 1905 PS 62M, another six-story school on the Lower East Side, this one built to accommodate 5,000 seventh- and eighth-graders, he said (still addressing the municipal engineers), "It was decided that the best place for the auditorium would be in the basement, occupying what otherwise would be waste [sic] space."[73] By a year later he had figured out a better way to bring to rectangular schools the "radical improvement" of an auditorium proper. It came in the form of a new footprint, the E-Plan, explained in his 1906 annual report as an arrangement such that the auditorium extended back into unused space between the two shallow wings at each end of the rectangle:

> Under the old plan there would be three classrooms along the rest of the corridor on the first floor, this, however, we do away with and move the wall back so that we get a clear space of about 50 feet by a length of 90 feet, encumbered by only two columns placed near the center and used to support the rear of the building above where the usual three classrooms appear at the rear of the corridor on each floor.
>
> We thus form an assembly hall seating about six hundred and fifty, lighted by large skylights above and four windows at the rear, the platform being placed next to the corridor so that the children or the audience do not face the light.
>
> Entrance is had through corridors while special means of exit are provided by two doorways at the rear of the hall opening upon short flights of steps leading directly to the outdoor yards.[74]

Starting with PS 42 (1907) in the Bronx, Snyder used this floor plan, which put the auditorium directly behind the main entrance. It became standard for hundreds of schools built in the first half of the twentieth century.

The vast majority of his auditoriums had skylights (fig. 74). His inspiration may have come from those he would have seen as a young man wandering in dry goods emporia on Fourteenth Street between where he lived and where he worked. All also had shades for darkening the room. The skylights, which tended to be high-maintenance, have now been removed or covered over—with the one exception of PS 61 on Crotona Park in the Bronx.

Figure 74. Stuyvesant High School, 1908: Auditorium with Skylights. *NYC BOE AFSR 1906–8.*

High school auditoriums, often five times the size of those in elementary schools, were proportionately grander, including a complex pattern of skylights, full-sized pipe organs, and space for public art. The one in Wadleigh High School (1902) was the earliest, occupying the north courtyard of the H-Plan building (rather than located beneath it). Morris High School's auditorium is a hexagonal Elizabethan space with a clerestory and Gothic tracery; a mural on the proscenium was added after World War 1. The DeWitt Clinton auditorium, reported a 1905 *New York Times* article, "will be the largest yet provided in any school building, having seats for 1000 persons. . . . Light comes from the roof. To the right and left of the commodious stage, space has been left for mural paintings and provision has also been made for a pipe organ" (fig. 75).[75] The Erasmus auditorium looks like an Elizabethan banqueting hall. About one of its stained-glass windows, Michele Cohen comments,

> In this shrine to learning, we encounter the "Triumph of Education" as personified in the life of secularized "saint" Erasmus. Instead of the Virgin Mary or scenes from the life of a saint, this window celebrates a scholar, metamorphosing the rays of spiritualism into the

Figure 75. Former DeWitt Clinton High School, 1906: Auditorium and Stage. *NYC BOE AFSR 1906–8.*

rays of enlightenment. Here Snyder has achieved the apotheosis of secular education.[76]

The Erasmus organ was renovated in 2008. The difficulty now is in finding anyone able to play it. The grandeur of these auditoriums echoes the one in Shepard Hall at City College with its Edwin Blashfield mural—familiar to Snyder, since he had been on the committee that had determined the architect and design of City College. During this period, he started lobbying and arranging for art—stained-glass windows, murals, statuary—first in the high schools, but then in elementary schools, as well. The tradition he started has continued.[77]

The auditoriums made it possible for the Board of Education, for twenty years, to run what amounted to a people's university.[78] The school system offered single lectures and series of lectures on topics such as great composers, the value of vaccinations, the development of Japan as a nation, and New York architecture, complete with lantern slides. In 1903 alone, one million working men and women attended 3,300 lectures, the majority held in public schools. In 1905, the *New York Times* reported that "at least eighty-five of the school buildings are used for evening school purposes."[79] By

1908–9, evening-lecture attendance had risen to 1,213,116 persons, according to philanthropist C. A. Perry, "and what a cosmopolitan multitude they were! Croatian, Greek, Russian, Hebrew, Sicilian, Lithuanian, Yankee, Magyar, Pole." In 1910, 119 of the 610 Board of Education schools were used as lecture centers for a staff of 600 lecturers from every walk of life: "In one particular center weekly lectures on science were given for years, like a college education,"[80] Perry continued. Through World War I public-school auditoriums hosted the evening lectures for schoolchildren's parents and other working men and women—all financed by the Board of Education.

Auditoriums contributed to making the schools into neighborhood centers for all ages. Jacob Riis's ideal, fast becoming a reality, was that the school could "develop a social spirit and an enthusiasm among young and old" that would make it "truly the neighborhood house and soul."[81] Clarence Perry wrote that, in addition to the evening lectures, the New York City Board of Education conducted

> the most highly elaborated and efficiently organized recreation centers in this country . . . for boys and girls who're no longer in school. . . . The school house has become a place . . . where youths can continue an interrupted education and shop girls enjoy exhilarating physical exercises after the day's grind; where neighbors may gossip and mothers come together to learn how they can supplement the teacher's work in their own homes.[82]

In his autobiography, *The Right Time*, Harry Golden wrote about how the classrooms of PS 20 on Rivington Street were kept "open until midnight to give immigrants a place to argue" and how that "lent the school an air of intellectual ferment and vitality that carried over into the classes I attended next day."[83] Snyder schools were intergenerational, offering community activities far beyond the 8:00 a.m. to 3:00 p.m. school day, activities that in turn informed the school day. Many cities followed New York's lead in using schools as after-hours community centers.

During his second decade, Snyder developed not just new differentiated spaces but also new facilities, including open-air classrooms and a parental school and farm for truants. Open-air classrooms, part of an international movement that had originated in Germany in the years before World War I, were designed to serve tubercular and anemic children (fig. 76). Since the urban setting did not allow for outdoor classrooms in the woods, Snyder did what he could by creating rooms with walls that were almost 100 percent louvered windows, located on upper floors of the school building where the air was thought to be cleaner. Sometimes he added a balcony so children

Figure 76. PS 135M, 1895: Open-Air Classroom with Balcony. Unknown, public domain.

Figure 77. PS 102M Annex, Jefferson Park: Open-Air Class in Warmth-Providing Bags. Unknown, public domain.

could literally be outside. Each child had a chaise-lounge-like chair and individual sleeping-bag-type protection from the cold (fig. 77). One can still look up at the south façade of the former PS 135, now condominiums, and see on the fifth floor an area of oversized windows, which had been altered into an open-air classroom with a balcony.

One would be hard-pressed to find in the history of school design another such period to rival the volume and ingenuity of this first decade of the new century in New York. The total number of schools in the system increased by 50 percent, from 400 to 600, and they spread out into all areas of the city. Their makeup confirmed the change from the simple nineteenth-century schoolhouse consisting of basically only classrooms to the complex twentieth-century school building with numerous differentiated spaces. New spaces such as gymnasiums and auditoriums both broadened school-day activities and encouraged after-hours use of the schools. As community centers and neighborhood anchors, the large school buildings often provided the types of services that the smaller settlement houses could not accommodate. Economy, convenience, and concern about faculty, student, and community needs—these were the hallmarks of Snyder's vision.

The New York H-Plan

Additionally, Snyder amplified the idiosyncratic New York H-Plan during this period, a design contribution that made him extremely proud at the end of his career. Dramatically different from any other public school, it solved various problems of school design, especially within New York City.

It is widely assumed that the idea for the H-Plan had come to Snyder in 1896 while he was standing in front of Hotel de Cluny in Paris on a Board of Education trip to study school architecture in Europe. He himself gave credence to this notion when he wrote,

> Dealing as we do, day after day, with the rush and stress of the work in the effort to accomplish as much as possible with the time and means at our disposal, we lack the opportunity to get away and study the situation, as it were, in perspective.[84]

He implied that sometimes simply getting away from the daily grind sparked clear, creative thinking, and Snyder's job was nothing if not stressful. However, an article in *School* in October 1896 makes clear that he had already submitted the H-Plan design before he ever went to Europe.* Certainly here in New York, he could have seen pictures of the Hotel de Cluny; furthermore, he could have stood, and probably did, in front of Richard Morris Hunt's 1875 Lenox Library (on Fifth Avenue and East Seventieth Street) or McKim, Mead, and White's 1884 Villard houses on Madison Avenue behind St. Patrick's Cathedral and seen a building wrapping itself around three sides of an oasis of space. Christopher Gray suggests that he must have been inspired by the infirmary of the Immaculate Conception Church (1896) at 414 East Fourteenth Street, which "bears a strong similarity to the H-Plan schools."[85]

The H-Plan would come to provide the structural basis for numerous skyscrapers as well, for architects were seeking to maximize light and air. As early as 1880, George Post's Mills Building in Lower Manhattan, "with its six-story wings above the base two floors, forming a significantly larger than usual light court in the shape of a U, or half of an H, was considered the forerunner of the skyscraper H-Plan that came into use in 1907,"[86] Sarah Landau wrote in *The Rise of the New York Skyscraper*. Others consider Raymond F. Almirall's 1912 Emigrant Industrial Savings Bank Building on Chambers Street "the first to be laid out on an H-Plan, providing light and air to almost all office spaces."[87]

---

*"To Improve City Schools," *School*, October 22, 1896. The article opens, "An article in *The Evening Sun* recently stated that the Committee on Sites and Buildings of the Board of Education had accepted a design submitted to them by the Superintendent of School Buildings, Mr. Charles B. J. Snyder. The plan is in the form of the letter H, a suggestion from the style of the Musee Cluny in Paris."

Snyder's H-footprint buildings, unique in school design, came to be known at the time as the New York Plan, though to locals they were always the H-Plan schools. Three years after Snyder had returned from Europe, having seen the actual Hotel de Cluny and one year after New York City's consolidation of the boroughs, the first H-Plan building opened on the Lower East Side. By the end of his career, he was to complete another fifty-one of these buildings.

From the beginning of his tenure Snyder had been struggling with the problems that the H-Plan building was to solve. They were twofold: the proliferation of tenement houses and the particular geography of upper Manhattan. In all his early annual reports, Snyder discussed how the typically three- or four-story schools he had inherited were "hemmed in by towering tenement houses shutting out light and air" and how "these same enclosing walls darken the class-rooms of the schools, many of which are rendered unfit for use by this reason alone."[88] The 1895 Wehrum report, which had found three-fourths of the public schools defective or unsanitary, said about one, for example, "A large flat is being erected on Eighty-eighth street which will further impair the light."[89] At issue, as Snyder defined it, was the fact that the schools had not been built "self-contained as to light and air."[90] They were victims, he repeated a year later, of "the steady march of progress [that] is transforming [New York's] old-fashioned, two- and three-story dwellings into five-story tenements and factory buildings, thereby cutting off light and air from the school buildings, rendering them, in several instances, entirely unfit for school purposes."[91] Snyder argued that schools needed to be independent of the surrounding buildings such that, whatever was subsequently built on either side, they would retain their access to light and air.

A second challenge that sparked the H-Plan idea was the problem that the north end of Manhattan Island narrows, leaving only a few broad avenues with their ample light and air, long considered prime sites for schools. Snyder was not stymied. He wrote,

> Being a believer in the theory that there is a practical solution of all practical difficulties, I applied myself to the task of solving this one, with a result that was a pleasant surprise, for, instead of being obliged to extol the merits of the design, it did the work itself without my help.[92]

Snyder's prose conveys his good-natured confidence that a practical solution is just a matter of thinking the problem through. His fix for this particular dilemma was, upon a plot "running through the block from street to street," to build a school "in the form of a capital letter H."[93] The spacious courtyards flanking the main section of the building—the crossbar of the H, parallel to the streets on either side—would provide ample efficient and cost-effective space.

In an address to the Municipal Engineers in 1904, he recapped:

> [It] occurred to me that the erection of school buildings on avenue corners was unwise, not only on account of the cost, but also of the incessant noise of the up and down town traffic. . . . I therefore designed what has become known as the "H" school building, to be erected upon a plot in the middle of the block away from the avenues, extending through from street to street, the side walls on the party lines being entirely blank, the only break being a recess in the center of the line of the plot, with stairways placed at this point. The light and air of the school building was taken almost wholly from a central court.[94]

Snyder's explanation is as elegant and functional as his buildings themselves.

The H-Plan building had numerous advantages. To begin with, it solved the problem large-city schools faced when twentieth-century technology created taller buildings with larger footprints, thus leaving the schools cramped and dark: the H-Plan school was self-contained with regard to light and air, unaffected by the buildings around it. Nearly all classrooms faced one of the courtyards, leaving their large windows unthreatened by any obstruction. Another advantage was that midblock real estate was not only less expensive than the more desirable corner locations, but there was less noise from elevated trains or vehicles rattling over cobblestones. (Once New York had started using asphalt to surface streets, Snyder argued that all blocks around schools should be paved.) The courtyards, moreover, guaranteed two areas of outdoor play space, "protected from sweeping, driving winds and . . . accessible directly from the street," Snyder wrote. Finally, the school created not just one but two handsome streetscapes, or as he phrased it, "the opportunity for architectural effect is not wanting."[95] A 1908 observer wrote that the courtyards "may be beautified, and the view is unobstructed by unsightly shops, smoky chimneys, and tenement houses."[96] With all these advantages, no wonder Snyder was not obliged to extol the merits of the design. Not exercising similar restraint, Jacob Riis in his 1902 *Battle with the Slum* wrote:

> I cannot see how it is possible to come nearer perfection in the building of a public school. There is not a dark corner in the whole structure,

from the splendid gymnasium under the red tiled roof to the indoor playground on the street floor, which, when thrown into one with the two yards that lie enclosed in the arms of the H, give the children nearly an acre of asphalted floor to romp on from street to street; for the building sets right through the block, with just such a front on the other street as it shows on this one.[97]

The second decade of Charles Snyder's career as superintendent of school buildings in New York saw the proliferation of this new and singular H-Plan design celebrated by Riis. In 1922, at the end of his thirty-one-year career, Snyder viewed them as the single most important of his many contributions to school architecture. Although he had been the first to fireproof and ventilate New York City schools, the first to put gymnasiums and auditoriums in the elementary schools, and the first to provide New York City with public high schools, nevertheless, in a retirement interview, the H-Plan was what came to his mind as most significant.[98]

A 1906 *World's Work* article pronounced them "a step in the public-school progress of the world." The writer said that this "model school house" had "caused a 30 per cent improvement in the general health and in the vision of the New York school children." He saw the schools as applying "American genius to the very problem [Europe] has created in America's chief city through a flood of immigrants of school age."[99]

In addition to their many other advantages, H-Plan schools addressed the crucial overcrowding problem Snyder perennially faced in that they almost doubled the capacity of his early rectangular schools. The beginning of each school year was a race to provide enough "sittings" for the number of children—a race Snyder never won. Even though he built an average of thirteen schools and additions a year for a career total of over 400—more than any other single architect has constructed in any other single city in the United States—still the front-page news every September was how many children had been turned away or forced to attend school in shifts. The typical H-Plan school had fifty classrooms, accommodating 2,500 students, whereas his earlier schools had averaged twenty-five to thirty classrooms. Fifty students per classroom was the norm at that time.

The three H-Plan schools from Snyder's first decade paved the way for another forty-nine. Symmetrically massed of red or buff brick having five or sometimes four stories, these buildings used the floor plans of the original three as a template. Of the fifty-two total H-Plan schools, a total of forty of them were built in Snyder's second decade. Forty-two were located in Manhattan. All in historicist styles, forty-three were elementary schools and nine were high schools. As of 2021, forty still stand, and of those, thirty-two still function as public schools. Three have been landmarked, and one is on the National Register of Historic Places.*

Most of the H-Plan schools fall roughly into five architectural eras in Snyder's career—Chateau, Italian palazzo-style, Baroque, Collegiate Gothic, and Simplified Collegiate Gothic—all proclaiming schools to be important civic monuments. Each era except the Simplified Collegiate Gothic was epitomized by a high school that took the elementary schools' architectural characteristics to a higher, grander level.

PS 165 on the Upper West Side from Snyder's first decade, his oldest surviving H-Plan school, ushered in the Chateau era, which culminated in Manhattan's first high school. All have the type of tall, delicate Gothic pediments over dormers in steep-pitched roofs found on Loire Valley chateaux. A present-day neighbor commented that when he overlooks the school first thing in the mornings, he feels as if he is in the south of France. Following PS 165, the next two-year period saw another eight chateau-style H-Plan buildings in northern Manhattan, half of them on the west side to accommodate the population shift occasioned by the 1904 opening of the subway up to 145th Street. After the first two (PS 165 and PS 159, now demolished), Snyder simplified the roofline from hipped to gabled. PS 170 was built just above the northeast corner of Central Park on a site that the Polo Grounds had vacated in 1888, such that the school overlooked the park and was a grand sight from the park (fig. 78). Only seven blocks south sits PS 171 in all its renovated glory, directly behind the Museum of the City of New York. PS 179 on the Upper West Side carries the unfortunate distinction of being the most recent H-Plan building to have been demolished, in 1995 (fig. 79). PS 109 on the Upper East Side escaped that fate when it was reincarnated as an arts center after having spent the first decade of the

---

*The nine high schools are Wadleigh, High School of Commerce, the original DeWitt Clinton, Commercial, Eastern Division, Brooklyn's Teacher Training, the original Stuyvesant, Bushwick, and the original Evander Childs. Six have the courtyards facing within the block instead of onto side streets (High School of Com-M, T Trg Sch-K, Stuyvesant-M, PS 28K, PS 72 Annex-M, PS 47M). Ten occupy a full block (PS 147M, PS 146K, PS 147K, PS 149K, PS 158K, DeWitt Clinton High School-M, Commercial High School, Eastern District High School, Bushwick High School). Four are only half H's (PS 188M, PS 115M, PS 72 Annex-M, Bushwick High School). The H-Plan buildings that no longer function as schools are an arts complex (PS 109M), a health facility (PS 168M), the home of the Harlem Boys and Girls Club/ affordable housing (PS 186M), apartments (PS 37X), a Jewish private school (the original Eastern District High School), a CUNY branch (the original DeWitt Clinton High School), and condominiums (PS 90M). One sits derelict (PS 64M). PS 64M, Wadleigh High School, and the original Stuyvesant High School have been landmarked. PS 109M is on the National Register of Historic Places.

Figure 78. PS 170M, 1901, Drawing: Chateau-Type H-Plan above NE Corner of Central Park. Architecture and Building, 1898.

Figure 79. PS 179M, 1901: Chateau-Type H-Plan. *NYC BOE AFSR 1906–8.*

twenty-first century boarded up because of a stand-off between developers and community activists who wanted the building used for its original purpose. A few blocks away, PS 168 is now a health facility. "Streetscapes" columnist Christopher Gray wrote that the chateau-era H-Plan schools

> remain startling mid-block surprises wherever they appear. They elbow apart long rows of dark tenements and flats with their tall, peaked roofs and big courtyards.[100]

The apogee of the chateau-type H-Plan schools was the French Renaissance Revival Wadleigh High School for Girls, which opened in 1902, showing the progressive concern for the education of women (fig. 80). Although Snyder had studied the design of high schools in this country and abroad, Manhattan's first high school was unlike any other anywhere. Wadleigh gave Harlem its own version of the Chateau de Blois, having just completed nine chateau-style schools. Snyder nearly doubled the size of the elementary-school H-Plans and added a 125-foot tower to the keyed quoins and window surrounds and to the limestone-clad gabled dormers. While the elementary schools had partitioned assembly rooms, at Wadleigh an auditorium proper sat in the north courtyard, with independent entrances

Figure 80. Wadleigh High School for Girls, 1902. Mike Janoska photo.

off 115th Street that made it easily available for community events. The stars and stripes that ornamented the pediments, like those on PS 165M, showed that this school promoted the Americanization of immigrants. Snyder would return to the chateau style one final time in 1916 for the original Evander Childs High School in the Bronx, now a primary and middle school.

In 1902 Snyder moved to a new style of H-Plan school that allowed for the greater cost- and space-efficiency of a flat rather than a pitched roof. These Italian palazzo-style schools were marked by a tripartite façade—a rusticated first floor, a relatively plain second through fourth floors, and fifth-story attic with small windows, topped by an overhanging dentil cornice. Each section was set off by a stringcourse. In the case of the distinctive first two in Harlem, PS 186 (1903) and PS 184 (1904), Snyder used arched windows on the first and fourth floors instead of the rectangular windows of the chateau-style buildings, and a bust of Minerva, goddess of wisdom, presided over the main entrance of both. Snyder referred to PS 188 (1903) at the eastern end of Houston Street as an H-Plan building, although it consisted of only the bottom half of the H (as would be true for later PSs 115M, 72M Annex, and Bushwick High School); its courtyard was covered by a huge "indoor yard" entered through a seven-arch arcade. (It was enclosed during the Depression to prevent people from sleeping there.) With seventy-two classrooms, it was the largest H-Plan at the time. A year later PS 21 opened on Elizabeth Street south of Houston; the *New York Times* reported, "Along the street extends a beautiful colonnade with iron grillwork between the pillars. The ornamental portico is one of the most handsome features of the new school."[101] In the next four years, Snyder would design another seven Italian palazzo-style elementary H-Plan schools. Brooklyn's Commercial High School (1906) carried on this style in grander form.

After the first four Italian palazzo-style schools, Snyder essentially moved on to the Baroque, yet he would also keep going back to Italian palazzo-style. Perhaps he thought that while the simple elegance of the Italian palazzo-style appealed to the social elite and to those tutored in architectural history, it could be mistaken for plainness by the students actually using the buildings. The dramatic nature of Baroque made a more obviously forceful statement about the importance of education. It more clearly asserted that all children, poor as well as rich, were worthy of buildings that draw attention to themselves; it more forcefully suggested to students the opulence available to the educated and the possibility that they too could be part of the elite. The major characteristics of the Baroque phase are (1) a balustrade around the flat roof, (2) an imposing central pavilion flanked by Doric columns on each side of the second floor, Ionic on the third, Corinthian on the fourth, the whole topped by a false frontispiece and urns, and (3) the same curlicued frontispiece repeated four more times, at each end of the H. Manhattan's PS 63M (1906) (fig. 81) and PS 150M (1905) are sister schools, though their auditoriums are located differently. In this phase, from 1905 to 1908, there were for the first time more H-Plans in Brooklyn than in Manhattan. Snyder said about PS 146K that it was "designed in adaptation of the Jacobean."[102] In this Baroque era a new development in elementary-school auditoriums occurred: rather than partitioned assembly rooms, Snyder designed actual auditoriums. While the earlier chateau- and Italian palazzo-style era elementary schools had been built for a little less than $300,000, the addition of an auditorium raised the per school cost of Baroque-era schools by $40,000 to $60,000. But the increased cost was considered worth it, and auditoriums became standard. A *World's Work* 1905 article described the auditorium in the Lower East Side PS 21 as

> easily accessible from the street, that with its toilet rooms and special approaches can be shut off from the upper building. Weary mothers that would never have climbed four flights of stairs will slip in here to free evening lectures and rest worn eyes on stereopticon

Figure 81. PS 63M, 1906: Baroque. Arrington photo.

views of lake and country, sometimes the valleys and mountains of their native land.[103]

The crowning achievement of this phase was not one but two dramatic high schools. Like Wadleigh, the original DeWitt Clinton, which opened in 1906, more than doubled the size of the typical H-Plan elementary school, its 100 classrooms housed in five stories, an attic, a basement, and a sub-basement (fig. 82). "Without doubt, it is the largest secondary school in the world,"[104] Snyder wrote in his 1904 annual report, regretting that the site for such a building wasn't double the area. Because the projected size and site had kept changing—at first the school was to occupy the present site of the original Stuyvesant High School—it was the fourth set of plans that "finally crystallized into a building contract."[105] "Designed somewhat after the style of the Flemish Renaissance, with large gables and dormers on the various fronts covered by high pitched roofs,"[106] the building is limestone to the level of the second-story window sills, above red brick trimmed with terra-cotta. Approached by a large loggia with Guastivino vaulting, the main entrance leads to an eight-door entryway to the main foyer, "finished in marble, with ornamental plaster ceilings."[107] Snyder said, "Every room will have direct outside light, and in no case be provided with less than 150 square feet of window openings" and "Every effort has been made to provide

Figure 82. Former DeWitt Clinton High School, 1906. *NYC BOE AFSR 1906–8.*

for the comfort and convenience of both teachers and pupils."[108] Beautifully lit at night with its ornate loggia opening onto 10th Avenue, the building is one of the grand sights of the city—created not for judges, politicians, or wealthy individuals, but for public-school students.

The other high school capping the Baroque phase was the former Stuyvesant, which has interior courtyards and therefore side-street façades. The Sixteenth Street façade, the side with all the shops and vocational classrooms, is factory-like red brick, while the Fifteenth Street façade for the academic side is limestone and buff brick with an extravagantly handsome four-story entrance pavilion composed of terra-cotta ornamentation.* Snyder placed the science laboratories and mechanical-training rooms at the ends of the H so the academic classrooms would be protected from the noise of the laboratories and so that they would get light on three sides. Perhaps this intelligent plan and the grand nature of the building were factors in Stuyvesant's becoming one of the most prestigious public high schools, not just in the city but in the country.

The Gothic/Collegiate Gothic era that followed in 1907–8 went a step further in proclaiming the worthiness of students by associating public schools with great universities—Oxford and Cambridge, Bryn Mawr and Princeton, University of Chicago, University of Pennsylvania, and West Point. The Collegiate Gothic style also eliminated the expense of a heavy cornice and balustrade. The identifying characteristics are a central tower with Gothic stonework on top; a crenellated instead of corniced roof; Tudor-arches, especially on the first and fourth floors; and drip moldings. Though PS 90M (1907) has recently been converted to condominiums, for almost seventy years its proud bearing elevated the feelings and aspirations of Harlem schoolchildren (fig. 83). Its sister school, PS 150K (1908), still fulfills that role for Brownsville students. The Gothic complexity of Brooklyn's PS 157K (1909) also still says to young students who enter that the world cares enough to give them a school that feels like a palace or cathedral; near Pratt Institute, PS 157K has won two prizes for its renovation, which involved replacing 6,000 pieces of terra-cotta.† This phase is capped by Bushwick

---

*In the *Designation Report for the Landmarks Preservation Commission*, Jay Shockley notes its "colossal pilasters with capitals ornamented by large, festooned cartouches surmounted by female heads set within shells and colossal tassel-like foliate moldings. The large segmental window grouping on the fifth floor is surmounted by a cartouche amidst palm leaves and flanked by pairs of stylized pilasters. A pediment with a modillioned metal cornice enframes [the school's name], Stuyvesant, flanked by a pair of cornucopia."

†The Lucy G. Moses Preservation Award for 2001 from the Landmarks Conservancy and the Excellence in Historic Preservation Award from the Preservation League of New York State.

Figure 83. PS 90M, 1907: Drawing by Brandon Phillips, Unfinished.

High School (1913). With its auditorium filling what would have been its front courtyard, it has complex layers of crenellated surfaces receding in space such that students enter an environment distinct from everyday ordinary life.

The final H-Plan phase occurs in Snyder's final decade (1911–22) as did the former Evander Childs High School and Bushwick High School (fig. 84). As happened in his career as a whole and in keeping with the ahistorical, unornamented nature of international modernism, Snyder streamlined his H-Plan schools, preserving however a few Gothic elements to make clear the schools' place in the great Western educational tradition. Simplified Collegiate Gothic dominated the last decade of his career. Each building had one or more Gothic attributes—a two-story medieval crenellated or towered entrance; Tudor-arched windows, especially on the top floor; drip moldings; decorative stonework—enough to convey the idea of Gothic but without the complex, rich ornamentation of the earlier Collegiate Gothic phase. Since high schools were by definition highly ornate, this phase is the only one without a high school.

Figure 84. Bushwick High School, Brooklyn, 1913. *Modern School Houses*, Part II, 1915.

In conclusion, the H-Plan design generated much excitement at the time, as shown by Jacob Riis's exuberance. That same year Snyder himself referred to "the now famous H schools,"[109] and the *Evening World* reported, "The indenting of portions of the front elevations give light to every room and a larger measure of light than any other method. The plan has been adopted by school architects all over the country who speak of it as 'the New York idea.'"[110] The *World Work*'s 1906 article "The Model School House" has this rousing finale:

> So impressive is [the H-Plan school] that almost every nation in whose economy the public school has a place, has sent a representative to New York to study school buildings and educational methods. The H-Plan is, therefore, not simply a local achievement in New York City. It is a step in the public school progress of the world.[111]

But the excitement was merely that. It didn't materialize. Indeed, some California schools did use its footprint, but they were only one story, not five. St. Louis school architect William Ittner labeled one type of his schools as H-Plan, but the term had a different meaning for him. The truth is that the H-Plan was ideal only for big-city, high-density, expensive-real-estate locations—namely, New York City. Even Chicago neighborhoods had more space, allowing schools to be more expansive, not shoehorned into a midblock tight space. Also, five-story, non-elevator buildings were not something other cities were eager to have. For New Yorkers who, to this day, still climb an average of fifteen floors a day, according to one estimate, just going about their routine business in and out of the subway, the stairs aren't daunting—although one security guard did say that the fifth-floor teachers go to their classrooms, order out lunch, and don't descend till dismissal time. The lack of handicapped accessibility was another drawback that has become more of an issue since the 1990s. An additional obstacle to the proliferation of H-Plan schools was that they could not be enlarged. The ingenuity of their design proved to be a double-edged sword. The H-Plan was inflexible. In New York, the plan did continue to be used by Snyder's successors, particularly for the huge high schools of the 1920s and 1930s, but despite enthusiastic claims early on, it did not spread to other cities.

So the H-Plan for schools is a New York phenomenon unseen anywhere else in the country. These unique schools, part of the exhilaration of the early days of the consolidated city, constitute an important contribution to the city's heritage.

High Schools for the Elite

In 1891, when Snyder took over the building department of the Board of Education, as previous chapters have shown, New York City schools were generally behind the times, having few of the features that were appearing in progressive schools around the country, such as manual-training rooms, gymnasiums, kindergartens, auditoriums. But probably the most glaring example of New York's failure to stay abreast of the times was the fact that it had no public high schools. Although during Snyder's first decade he had brought schools up to date in many aspects, he hadn't addressed high schools. William Maxwell, the first superintendent of schools for Greater New York, wrote in his first annual report (1898–99) that New York "was later than any other city in the Union in establishing high schools."[112]

Starting in 1821 with Boston's High School of English and Classical Studies, for the next hundred years high school buildings across the country were something like cathedrals in medieval Europe—a sign of a community's enlightenment and a source of pride. This was a period in history when a high school had the kind of prestige and influence a college does today: teachers were called professors, some science teachers had private research laboratories, and a high-school diploma pretty much guaranteed a white-collar, well-paid job. The buildings that housed these institutions were concomitantly grand. By the 1880s, public high schools had become standard in every major American city, except New York. By 1890 they numbered 2,526, and by 1900, 6,005,[113] including Flushing High School (1875) in Queens (fig. 85) and in Brooklyn Girls' (1886) and Boys' High Schools (1891).

In the 1890s, New York, the largest city in the United States, needed, most immediately, to keep up with the third-largest, her sister city, Brooklyn. When Girls' High School had opened there in 1886, it was called by the *New York Times* "Brooklyn's most creditable achievement." The building housed sixty-six classrooms "in every portion open to the light and air," three laboratories, two 500-seat lecture rooms, and "a handsome Assembly Hall,

Figure 85. Flushing High School, Queens, 1915. *Modern School Houses*, Part II, 1915.

which had a seating capacity of 1,800 persons." The article continued, "There is not a meeting hall in Brooklyn or New York City that is its superior either in acoustic properties or in its furnishings."[114] A distinguished faculty of seventy—accomplished graduates of prestigious colleges, some having won distinction by original work—taught 2,200 students. James Naughton's grand new Romanesque Revival building for Girls' High School thoroughly looked the part, eclipsed only perhaps by his Boys' High School, also Romanesque Revival, which would open five years later only a few blocks away.

While old New York did offer Evening High School classes, not until 1897 were the first day high schools even organized, thanks to the efforts of the first Reform mayor, William Strong. They were located like stepchildren in elementary schools; some came to have annexes in as many as five different locations around the city. That same year, to get New York on the educational bandwagon, a $2.5 million bond was issued for the construction of four high schools—in Manhattan, one for boys, one for girls, and one for vocational training and, in the Bronx, a mixed (co-ed) high school. After the 1898 Consolidation made New York the second-largest city in the world, the status symbol that high schools then constituted became all the more crucial for the city.

As exciting as the assignment to design New York City's first high schools must have been for Snyder, it did not accord with one of his deeply felt beliefs. He was a thoroughgoing progressive, Democrat, and champion of the working class. In his 1904 Address to the Municipal Engineers, he explained his philosophy:

> We are unanimous in our belief that to the establishment and development of our peculiar system of free public schools is due, in a very large measure, the phenomenal absorbing and welding power of our country, taking, as it does, all peoples of the earth and transforming them into citizens; citizens who hold the country of their adoption in such high esteem as to be willing to make any sacrifice therefore that may be expected of one native born.
>
> ... "Peculiar" ... [in that the schools] are for the children of the rich and poor, who are taught in the same class room, which fact alone always causes comment among foreigners who visit us.
>
> On another point we are also unanimous—that the advanced position held by our country to-day among the nations of the world, and which is causing some of them to turn uneasily toward us in a spirit of irritated inquiry, is due, in a large measure, to this same system of compulsory, though free, education for every boy and girl in the country.[115]

Snyder saw free, compulsory education "for every boy and girl in the country . . . for children in every social class" as the source of "the phenomenal absorbing . . . power of our country," which in turn accounted for our "advanced position . . . among the nations of the world." He went on to describe a British "party of experts" who concluded that

> the supremacy of this country in commercial or other lines is due to our system of free public education. . . . More than once [they] mention . . . the amalgamative or welding effect of our free school system in making successful citizens of the almost incredible horde of immigrants which has poured into this country, one boldly saying that "it is the one thing which has stood between the country and dissolution through anarchy."[116]

While a British sense of superiority to immigrants can be felt in a phrase like "incredible horde," Snyder avoided any hint of social superiority on his own part, celebrating the non-elitist nature of New York City's public schools as "our safety and salvation," as what made the country politically stable and commercially successful.

Snyder elementary schools were thoroughly democratic. Whatever the neighborhood, they were equally grand and offered the same amenities—in contrast, for instance, to the classist nature of Philadelphia's public schools as noted by George Thomas.[117] In fact, if anything, Snyder's sympathies lay with the immigrant and working class rather than the well-off. The immigrant Lower East Side came to have by far the highest concentration of his schools of any neighborhood, being of course the most densely populated, but it also had the unusual ones—the first and one of the few elementary schools with a swimming pool (PS 147M, 1899, demolished); the only school at the time designed for seventh- and eighth-graders, having six stories and elevators (PS 62M, 1905, demolished); the only H-Plan building with two auditoriums (PS 65M, 1908, demolished). "Here is architecture in the service of democracy," Yale University's Robert A. M. Stern said about Snyder's schools in his *New York Times* article from 2000.[118]

High schools, however, forced Snyder for the first time to go against his own inclusive philosophy and build schools that served primarily the well-to-do. Compulsory education laws extended only to age fourteen, at which point children of working-class families typically went to work. Going to high school was a luxury—theoretically available to all, in reality available only to those whose families did not depend on their children's earnings. In 1890, only 3.5 percent of fourteen- through seventeen-year-olds in the United States graduated from high school, with the percentage in New York City's limited high-school program slightly lower. By 1920, that number had jumped to

16.8 percent. But not until 1940 did the country reach 50 percent, and since the high of 77.1 percent in 1970, the rate hovered in the high 60s percent rate in 2007 to 2010.[119] In the next decade it climbed back up to the high 70s. Incidentally, in 2019 to 2020 the New York City graduation rate increased by 1 percent despite (or possibly because of) the Covid-19 pandemic.[120] Today high-school attendance is nearly universal; when Snyder was given the mandate to build four high schools, attendance was dramatically lower.

Despite the few and exclusive students attending high school at the turn of the twentieth century, Snyder nevertheless threw himself with gusto into designing buildings to house them. For one thing, he was committed to bringing New York's public schools up to date, making them the equal of, or better than, any school system in the country. Also, he had worked well with the Board of Education, and this was the job assigned him. Finally, he had firsthand faith in high schools: his own in Saratoga Springs had prepared him for Cooper Union, training that enabled him, despite having grown up in a financially strapped family, to hold a highly paid and highly respected job. Moreover, three years after his 1878 graduation, a new state-of-the-art high school had been erected in Saratoga Springs. His small hometown had thus for twenty years outclassed New York City, the place where his own name was now synonymous with public schools.

The first generation of New York City public high schools was located in or close to elite neighborhoods. Wadleigh High School for Girls (1902) was in upper-middle-class Harlem. For boys, DeWitt-Clinton High School (1906) and the High School of Commerce (1903, demolished) were both near the Fifty-Seventh-Street upper-class residential enclave. The mixed Morris High School (1904) was located in the Morrisania section of the Bronx, which had substantial one-family townhouses; the stylistically similar mixed Curtis High School (1904) sat on a hill in the prestigious St. George community above where the Staten-Island ferry docked (fig. 86). The original Stuyvesant High School (1908) was a few blocks south and east of the exclusive Gramercy Park and half a block from Stuyvesant Square with its 1860 Quaker school and 1850s St. George Episcopal Church complex.

For the design of these high schools, Snyder reverted to his previous experience with the design and construction of elementary schools, the H-Plan and Collegiate Gothic in particular. Historian G. W. Wharton put it this way:

> Now, Mr. Snyder up to this time had never built a high school, and the problem, which was to construct . . . four secondary buildings—the finest in the United States—was not one permitting of experiment. The product must be a perfect thing of its kind—not an attempt.[121]

Figure 86. Curtis High School, Staten Island, 1904, with Leap of Faith Ornamentation. LaValle photo.

After a thorough investigation of existing high schools, Snyder chose two styles that he had successfully employed earlier—the H-Plan and Collegiate Gothic. Wharton continued,

> In fact, in the first school erected he departed from all known plans for such structures, and made what might be called a glorified, enlarged edition of an H-type elementary building.[122]

Whereas most school architects designed impressive high-school buildings and then made elementary schools smaller, simpler versions of their high schools, Snyder moved in the opposite direction. Of the twelve first-generation high schools, seven had the H-Plan footprint, but were designed in different styles, including the French Renaissance Wadleigh (1902), Brooklyn's Italian palazzo-style Commercial High School (1906) and Teacher Training School

Figure 87. Erasmus Hall High School, Brooklyn, 1906, West Side. *NYC BOE AFSR 1906–8.*

(1907), the Flemish Renaissance DeWitt Clinton (1906), the French Renaissance/Baroque Stuyvesant (1908), and the Jacobean Eastern District High School (1907).* Grander versions of Snyder's five Collegiate Gothic elementary schools that had all opened in 1900 included Morris (1904), Curtis (1904), and Erasmus Hall (1906) High Schools, Erasmus being the one school with a quadrangle (fig. 87). Snyder's strategy worked. Judging by the fact that five of the first twelve have been landmarked, he did make each "a perfect thing of its kind."

About the four high schools for which in 1897 New York City had earmarked $2.5 million, the newspapers were full of superlatives. The *New York Times* called Wadleigh (1902), "the finest high school building in the world . . . its equipment and . . . the opportunities of learning . . . without an equal anywhere," its ninety-five teachers "the best that money could procure."[123] Wadleigh also had the first two elevators in a city school. More importantly, these impressive features were in the service of a school designed exclusively for girls. Morris High School (1904)†—considered by many

---

*The High School of Commerce, Brooklyn Teacher Training School, and Stuyvesant have interior courtyards.

†Snyder had originally named it Cooper High School after his alma mater, but the neighborhood prevailed in honoring the area's most prominent family, including George

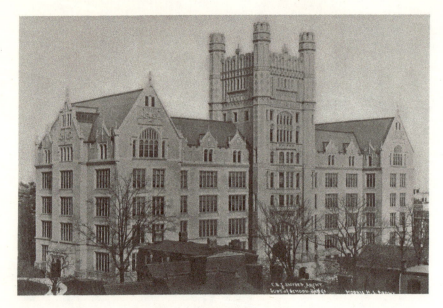

Figure 88. Snyder's Masterpiece: Morris High School, Bronx, 1904. Landmarked Outside and Inside. *1908 American Architect and Building News* (AABN).

Snyder's masterpiece and landmarked outside and inside—would not, according to Snyder himself, "have its equal in the United States" (fig. 88).[124] A later article said, "It is a landmark for the neighborhood and can be seen towering above the surrounding buildings for miles in any direction."[125] The former DeWitt Clinton (1906), now serving CUNY, was hailed at its groundbreaking as "the largest high school building in the United States and one of the most perfect in its appointments."[126] And about the former Stuyvesant High School (1908), now a consortium of small schools, the *New York Times* had this to say:

> With the same care and circumspection that a chemist exercises in studying a new element, the educators have planned this institution. Before it was finally projected an investigation was made of all the leading technical institutions west of the Mississippi with a view to profiting by their experience. The best points of all are incorporated in the equipment and course of study of the new institution. In consequence, New York has provided a school which excels anything of a similar nature in the country.[127]

Morris, signer of the Declaration of Independence; Gouveneur Morris, penman of the Constitution; and Roger Morris, governor of New York State.

Snyder's willingness to heed the advice of educators and to benefit from research contributed to the preeminence of his buildings.

With the high schools Maxwell and Snyder confirmed the transformation of New York City from an educational pariah to a "model of excellence." The giant beauties, designed to align New York's public schools with the city's post-Consolidation position as second-largest city in the world, were sources of pride then and are still today. Stuyvesant is a household name even outside of New York City. DeWitt Clinton and Erasmus, both of which opened in 1906, vie for the title of the greatest number of famous alumni. Mayor Bloomberg chose the Bronx's ornate Morris High School auditorium from which to give his 2012 State of the City address.

Snyder's description of Morris encapsulates his defining principles for high schools and shows the richness of what they had to offer:

> The upper floors of the tower have been designed to provide laboratories for the special work of the professors, a provision which, while badly needed, has often been overlooked in many high school buildings. . . .
>
> Above the basement are five stories of rooms for school work, seventy-one rooms in all. . . .
>
> Forty-six section rooms of the usual size [are] placed, with the long side of about 28 feet, to the light so that the shorter dimension of 21 feet is the depth of the room, bringing the farthest seats sufficiently near the light. Each room is amply lighted by a large window or rather a group of windows in a single opening. . . .
>
> In addition to the section rooms there are twelve laboratories for chemical, physiological, biological, physiographical, and other purposes and three lecture rooms. . . . There will be provided four large study halls, once on each of the floors.
>
> A large library has been provided for the second floor and five other rooms to be assigned for special purposes. Separate gymnasiums have been provided for boys and girls, each with its running track, shower baths, locker rooms, doctor's examination room. . . .
>
> The ventilating system will be that which is known as the "Plenum"—so called because a full supply of fresh air is forced by powerful fans into all the rooms, driving out, by pressure, the air that has become contaminated by use.
>
> The lighting will be by electricity throughout, developed by a complete plant of dynamos and high speed engines or obtained from one of the lighting companies.[128]

There was also an interior telephone system and, in the basement, lunchrooms and bicycle rooms. Morris is the one Snyder school about which a book has been written—Gary Hermalyn's *Morris High School and the Creation of the New York City Public High School System* (Bronx County Historical Society, 1995).

High schools differed from elementary schools on all fronts. Visually they were more magnificent; Wadleigh and Morris, for instance, have dramatic towers, 125 and 180 feet respectively. Generally, they were more than twice the size of the typical elementary school, with elevators. They had large, elaborate, well-equipped auditoriums; some had impressive foyers. Snyder describes the entrance to DeWitt Clinton as

> A loggia, thirty-five feet in length and ten feet deep. The ceiling of the loggia is of stone and formed with intersecting vaults. The marble foyer is connected with the loggia by eight doors and from the foyer corridors to the right and left lead to the main stairways of the school.[129]

The loggia featured a ceiling of Guastivino tiles like those at the Municipal Building's self-contained subway entrance in Lower Manhattan.*

High schools were also more complex functionally. Something as conventional today as a bell system had to be devised—this one, for instance, in the principal's office at Wadleigh High School:

> It is an electric clock, consisting of a large steel cylinder that revolves once every hour. All the way around the cylinder are lines of little holes, sixty in each line. By inserting pegs in these holes the Principal can make bells ring in every classroom in the building at any minute of the day that he sees fit.[130]

Most important, the curriculum required numerous differentiated spaces such as study halls, lunchrooms, science laboratories, gymnasiums, faculty offices, libraries, and music rooms. Study halls were described by the *New York Times* in this way:

> The study room is for those whose overcrowded homes make the preparation of day school tasks almost an impossibility, and is taken advantage of also by serious-minded young people who wish to prepare for civil service or Regents' examinations. In this room, with its atmosphere of study-conducing quiet, there are not only books of reference, but also sympathetic and helpful teachers who are competent to give assistance on difficulties of almost every variety, from the multiplication table to algebra or Greek.[131]

---

*Guastavino vaulting, which composes the ceiling of the loggia, is also found at PS 188 in Manhattan and PS 5 in Brooklyn.

The original Stuyvesant had at least one study hall on each floor. Although going home for lunch from one's neighborhood elementary school remained common through the 1960s, high-school students who often traveled long distances to school needed lunchrooms—in the basement at Wadleigh and Morris, on the fifth floor at New Utrecht High School and Manual Training School in Brooklyn. The fifth floor of Wadleigh was devoted chiefly to five laboratories "with all the necessary instruments and material"[132]—for biology, botany, and chemistry, taught by nine teachers. Gymnasiums were often floor-through with a banked running track encircling the second floor; such an arrangement can still be seen at Manual Training High School and the former Stuyvesant. Finally, in the towers of Wadleigh and Morris, Snyder located science laboratories for the professors.[133]

For the new high schools, Snyder also looked to the theories and requirements for contemporary skyscrapers. He explained that

> From the very first there has been borne in upon [me] in unwavering pressure, by the highly intelligent public-spirited men of which the various Boards [of Education] have been composed, the fact they expected that the improvement in planning and construction of school buildings should keep pace with the rapid development of improved methods in buildings constructed through commercial enterprise.[134]

Snyder's ten years of commercial work before his appointment with the Board of Education served him well in keeping pace with new construction techniques, for his high schools possessed all the up-to-date developments and conveniences of modern office buildings. About Wadleigh High School, historian Wharton wrote that the visitor "will be struck by the fact that in construction, fittings, means of communication, and convenience the building is more like one of the new Broadway office structures than a school house,"[135] and about Morris High School, he said that everything noticed in Wadleigh

> applies equally to this structure, and for that matter to all schools now being constructed in New York City. All are schools with the appliances and accessories of great office buildings. In all of them the latest devices for heating and ventilating, the most approved plumbing and sanitary arrangements, the latest type of engines, the most approved system of fireproofing and construction, the latest discoveries in furnishing are employed.[136]

The uniqueness of Snyder's high schools thus consisted partly in their reflection of contemporary design features beyond those traditionally associated with educational buildings.

Even though high schools, in keeping with their status, tended to be highly ornamented, Snyder made the front elevations impressive without undue expense. When it was suggested that Wadleigh, New York's first high school, had excessive ornamentation, Snyder

> readily demonstrated that much of the so-called ornamentation was due almost wholly to the choice of color and of materials, thus, the quoins on the salient angle of the building ... which aid in giving color and dignity to the building would, if eliminated, have to be replaced, since a void is impossible, with some other material with little or no difference in cost; also that, for instance, a terra-cotta window sill, which through its form and contrasting color looks ornamental, costs less than a good bluestone sill, which is used in factories [and] on the rear of houses.[137]

He continued that the school was built as designed because "no one desired that this City should erect a high school building which would be the subject of the scorn and ridicule of the entire country."[138] He also used the occasion to provide the *New York Times* with a schedule showing that the construction cost per pupil of New York high schools was considerably lower than that in Boston, Philadelphia, or Springfield—$233 per student in New York, for example, versus $496 in Boston. At that rate, to accommodate the 2,500 students at Wadleigh would, Snyder said, "cost the City of Boston $1,228,000 while this board proposes to spend only $600,000 for the same number."[139] New York had the advantage of practicing economy of scale and of having a cleverly frugal and pro-active superintendent of school buildings. A city commissioner who had complained about the superfluous ornamentation on Wadleigh had his own architect do a cost analysis. The finding was that, at most, $20,000 could be saved out of the overall $600,000 cost of the school.

In addition to academic high schools, Snyder also designed New York's first vocational, commercial, and teacher-training high schools. Manual-training rooms for general activity classes such as cooking and carpentry, intended to increase students' manual dexterity, were included in almost all of his elementary schools. High schools offered vocational training classes in particular trades such as millinery and plumbing, with the intent of making students more marketable. The first two vocational high schools were, the name notwithstanding, Manual Training High School in Park Slope (1905), which was unusual in being co-ed, and the all-male Stuyvesant in Manhattan (1908), before it became a competitive math-science school. As suggested by the French Renaissance style of both buildings, a strong academic component complemented a solid grounding in technical subjects.

The experience of two students in the second graduating class at Stuyvesant illuminates aspects of high schools, particularly vocational ones, in the early twentieth century. They were demanding and rigorous. First, according to his biographer Phyllis Ross, the training that future furniture and industrial designer Gilbert Rohde received "in materials, mechanical processes, fabrication methods, wood joinery, cabinetmaking and blueprint drawing, to say nothing of his familiarity with electrical wiring and metalworking—would have made him a strong candidate for architecture school."[140] Second, the reaction to Stuyvesant of Lewis Mumford, future historian, literary critic, and author, a true Renaissance man, shows that the student base of high schools was already radically diversifying. Mumford, who came from an Upper West Side middle-class family, felt "jarred" and "unsettled" when he discovered that many of his classmates experienced "poverty on a grand scale, massive, extensive, blighting vast neighborhoods, altering the whole character of life."[141] Phyllis Ross imagines that students, especially those commuting from "congested immigrant neighborhoods to this palace of learning," were dazzled by "the grand scale of the $1.5-million building, with its opulent marble-clad foyer and stairway."[142] The student body at Stuyvesant, with all its trappings of elitist institutions, was a microcosm of society as a whole. Snyder was no longer building high schools attended primarily by the elite.

To take advantage of New York's position as the financial capital of the world, the Board of Education also opened two commercial high schools. Superintendent of Schools Maxwell had reasoned that "New York is . . . the commercial metropolis of America. It would seem obvious, therefore, that great attention should be paid in her public schools to commercial education."[143]

In 1901 Snyder traveled to Philadelphia to look at high schools and "to ascertain more particularly what had been done in commercial high school work."[144] His own Greek Revival High School of Commerce in Manhattan, "designed with a view of securing for this school a business-like appearance which at the same time suggests its scholastic purposes,"[145] was the first high school in America devoted exclusively to commercial education.[146] It was followed by Brooklyn's Commercial High School in Crown Heights, in the garb of an elegant Italian palazzo-style counting house (fig. 89).*

Then there were the teacher-training high schools. In fact, one of the early rationales for having high schools in the first place was to provide teachers for elementary schools. Two such high schools were the New York

---

*Commercial High School later became Alexander Hamilton High School. It's now Paul Robeson High School.

Figure 89. Commercial High School, Brooklyn, 1906. *NYC BOE AFSR 1906–8.*

Free Academy for men (established in 1847, progenitor of City College) and Normal College for women (established in 1870, now Hunter College). Both of these schools, administered by the Board of Education until the 1920s, had been accepting eighth-grade students since the nineteenth century and had as their mission the education of teachers. However, around the turn of the twentieth century, as the line between high school and college became more blurred, teacher-training high schools came into being. In 1907 Snyder completed a purpose-built teacher-training high school in the Crown Heights section of Brooklyn, yoked by means of the auditorium and gymnasium to an elementary school, PS 138, which functioned as the lab school for student teachers. New York's teacher-training high school had opened in 1899 in the new and grand H-Plan PS 159, the high school on the upper floor and a model primary and grammar school on the lower floors, where training-department pupils took their "observation lessons."[147] It was later moved to another Harlem H-Plan, PS 81M. Not until 1925 did Manhattan get its own purpose-built teacher-training high school on the southeast corner of the City College campus (attributed to Snyder's successor, William Gompert), but because university schools of education had by this time taken over teacher training, it lasted only a decade before being reconfigured as the High School of Music and Art. It is now A. Philip Randolph High School.

Snyder wanted all of his buildings, but especially high schools, to make students feel their own worthiness as well as the value of their education. Historian Michael Henry Adams, describing Wadleigh High School for Girls, wrote in *Harlem Lost and Found* (Monacelli Press, 2002),

As much as salutes to the flag or demanding curriculums, architecture was enlisted in the effort to provide a free education that would create an assimilated, self-sufficient, and productive citizenry. . . . [Wadleigh is] decorated with star-spangled, stripe-emblazoned shields. . . . A beautiful and regal building, the Wadleigh school was a profound reminder to students of individual and collective dignity. . . . All over Harlem Snyder reinforced the notion of the specialness of young citizens with splendid new buildings.[148]

Promoting "individual and collective dignity" was Snyder's core value. He made this revolutionary statement about the grand entrance to the Flemish Renaissance DeWitt Clinton:

It is the intention that the entire school shall enter through this logia [*sic*], thus . . . giving [the students] a sense of dignity and part-ownership in the building.[149]

Up to this point only faculty and visitors ascended the main grand staircase of a school, while students entered on the sides and used the workaday double staircases. Even though New York's first high schools were attended primarily by the children of families with means, Snyder's faith in the students themselves as well as the increasing democratization of high schools throughout the twentieth century led Maryann Dickar in *Corridor Culture* (1998) to write that "every Snyder high school was designed to physically embody the vision of the high school as the 'everyman's college.'"[150]

In this first decade of the twentieth century, Snyder had put at least one striking and imposing high-school building in each borough. These early high schools were just the beginning. By the time he retired, New York City had twenty-six public high schools, two of which were additions. After the twelve second-decade (1900–10) high schools, twelve new buildings plus two additions were built during his final decade (1911–22), the final four designed by Snyder but completed by Gompert as late as 1925. Except for the High School of Commerce, which stood where Lincoln Center does today, all are still being used as schools—twenty-three public schools, one a private Jewish high school, and one now part of City University of New York. While more than half were co-ed, five were for boys and seven for girls, a distribution that reflects the progressive agenda for women as well as the fact that by 1917 women constituted the clear majority of high-school students. Two were commercial and five vocational. Nine of them, more than a third, have been landmarked.*

---

*To elaborate—For boys: Manhattan's High School of Commerce, the former DeWitt Clinton, the former Stuyvesant, Brooklyn's Boys' High School for which Snyder did a 1912 addition, and Bushwick High School. For girls: Wadleigh, Brooklyn's Girls' High School for

These buildings contributed to New York's burgeoning new identity as the cultural capital of the country. Snyder's sons both attended brand new high schools their father had built—Howard, the Manual Training High School and Robert, Erasmus.*

And thus closed Snyder's remarkable second decade. In addition to the construction of New York's first high schools, the heyday of the H-Plan schools, and the transformation of grade schools, he realized an annual average of twenty-one new buildings and additions spread throughout all five boroughs. On the march toward further standardization, the more restrained Italian palazzo-style historicism had supplanted the ornate historicism of Snyder's first decade in pre-Consolidation New York. Beyond his collaboration with Superintendent of Schools William Maxwell, Snyder's second-decade accomplishments included the versatility of load-bearing or steel-skeleton structures and striking functional advances—the city's first auditoriums in particular but also science laboratories, music rooms, study halls, and lunchrooms. Further, Snyder was prolific in his new role as a leading authority in school design, about which he lectured and published widely. One would be hard-pressed to find in the history of school design another such period to rival the volume and creativity of this first decade of the new century in New York City.

A coda: I like to think that Erasmus High School, which Phyllis Ross describes as "an elegant building encoded with lofty academic ideals and high expectations,"[151] imbued my own secondary education. During the century when grand high-school edifices came to symbolize a community's cultural aspirations, my hometown of Montgomery, Alabama, built its "Million Dollar School" from which my father and I both graduated. To design and construct Sidney Lanier High School, which opened in 1929, the city not only chose one of its prominent architects and its foremost builder but also brought in consultants from Columbia University. Only the best was

---

which Snyder did a 1912 addition, Bay Ridge, Washington Irving, Manhattan Trade School for Girls, Hunter High School for Girls occupying what was built as Thomas Hunter Hall for Normal College, and Julia Richman. Commercial: Manhattan's High School of Commerce, Brooklyn's Commercial High School. Vocational: Manual Training, the former Stuyvesant, Washington Irving, Bushwick, and Manhattan Trade School for Girls. Landmarked: Wadleigh, Morris, Curtis, Erasmus, Stuyvesant, Girls' High School, Boys' High School, Flushing, Newtown.

*Howard went on to graduate from Cornell and became a successful civil engineer, in practice with Lawrence Ball; their office was on the twentieth floor of 110 West Fortieth Street. The family reports that Howard worked on the Chanin Building and for their acquaintance Robert Moses on several buildings at the 1939 World's Fair. Robert also went to Cornell but spent only one year.

good enough for the statement of enlightenment the city wanted to make. Perhaps the resulting Collegiate Gothic "castle" so reminiscent of Erasmus High School might never have materialized in its moving and impressive form without Charles Snyder's example (figs. 90 and 91).

Figure 90. Erasmus Hall High School, Brooklyn, 1906. *NYC BOE AFSR 1906–8.*

Figure 91. Sidney Lanier High School, Montgomery, Alabama. Photo by Chris Pruitt. CC BY-SA 3.0, https://commons.wikimedia.org/w/index.php?curid=21848799.

Chapter 5

The Standardizing Decade 1911–1922

A Dimming of the Glory

> The usual attitude of a school architect toward a teacher is "mind your own business, this is mine." It seems to me that [Snyder's] policy of interchange of views corrects and broadens both the builder and the occupant.
> —William McAndrew

IN THE FINAL phase of his career, C. B. J. Snyder garnered official, ceremonial recognition and appreciation. To celebrate his twenty-fifth year as superintendent of school buildings, his employees gave him a silver chest containing a flatware set of twenty-four twelve-piece sterling-silver place settings, and the Board of Education presented him with a Tiffany grandfather clock. Six years later, in 1922, Snyder's retirement imminent, Superintendent of Schools William L. Ettinger praised Snyder's "great contribution to the advancement of school architecture in the United States." He originated "many features . . . now considered essentials of school building planning" and reached "the highest mark of artistic and executive efficiency," all the while heading a department "conspicuously free from all political scandal."[1] That same year, Snyder received a medal from the American Institute of Architects "for distinguished work and high professional standing" (fig. 92).

However, these accolades were just the silver lining of a stormy, dark period—personal, professional, and societal. In 1910 the country experienced a recession that dragged on for four years. In 1912 the charismatic former president Theodore Roosevelt, with whom Snyder had worked

Figure 92. Accolades from Employees, the NYC Board of Education, and the American Institute of Architects. LaValle photo.

indirectly, possibly directly, during Roosevelt's mid-1890s tenure as New York City police commissioner, failed in his bid for the U.S. presidency as a Progressive Party candidate. After 1914, World War I loomed. During the war, Snyder's Building Bureau faced shortages because materials and labor were being diverted to the war effort. In 1918, Quentin Roosevelt, Theodore and Edith's youngest son, a popular American hero, was shot down by German warplanes. One year later, in 1919, President Roosevelt died at the age of sixty.

After World War I ended the United States struggled with high inflation. All new construction of New York City schools was curtailed for three full years. Doing repairs to existing buildings was also difficult to complete. Snyder wrote that "maintenance of the nearly 700 buildings so they could be kept in use was the most difficult because of the shrinkage in purchasing power of the appropriations, due to high prices of labor and materials."[2]

On a personal front, Snyder's sister Kitty died of breast cancer in 1912 at age fifty, and his mother died in 1919. Further, his younger son Robert eloped after his sophomore year at Cornell, not continuing to graduate as his older brother Howard had. Snyder's visionary collaborator, Superintendent of Schools William Maxwell, the pedagogical architect of the schools, started having major health problems in 1915 that forced him to take lengthy leaves of absence until his retirement in 1918 as superintendent emeritus. He died two years later.

Maxwell's health problems and Snyder's professional frustrations were exacerbated by the school system's disastrous experiment from 1914 to 1918 with a plan developed for Gary, Indiana, to utilize its school buildings more efficiently. New York City adopted the plan hoping it would alleviate the perennial overcrowding in its own schools. As far back as 1900, four years after the practice of half-day double sessions had commenced in New York, Snyder had written,

> To keep children in school three or four hours per day is, indeed, vastly better than to permit them to roam the streets in idleness, or worse; but it is far from creditable to this great and wealthy City that sufficient schoolhouses are not provided to meet all demands.[3]

"This great and wealthy City" had let the situation persist and worsen for eighteen years. The Gary plan, developed by William Wirt, superintendent of schools for Gary, Indiana (1907–38) was designed to more efficiently utilize facilities by providing double sessions and keeping the students at school all day, effectively doubling the capacity of each school. One set of students attended academic classes in the morning and performed various activities in the auditorium, gymnasium, or vocational-training rooms in the afternoons; another set of students used the freed-up academic classrooms in the afternoons, having completed their other activities in the mornings.

Politicians and bureaucrats, finding the economics of the Gary Plan irresistible, adopted it precipitously. Grueling for teachers and chaotic for students, the scheme used the "new lights" of education Snyder had brought to New York City—auditoriums, gymnasiums, vocational-training rooms—to "warehouse" and "platoon" students rather than embellish their academic experience.[4] The Gary Plan was dispiriting to Snyder not just because it was unsound educationally but because it exploited features he and his staff had designed to advance learning. The Gary Plan turned out to be so disastrous in New York City that a backlash against it contributed to the 1918 defeat of the reform mayor John Mitchell at the hands of the Tammany candidate, John F. Hylan, who in turn would eventually force Snyder out of office.

Snyder faced other discouragements, one with a particularly modern ring to it. He found himself inundated by onerous new record-keeping requirements such that, he wrote, "the viewpoint of the man who must also think and plan ways and means becomes much narrowed, his initiative is sapped, and the man rapidly deteriorates into a machine."[5] With the Building Bureau now numbering 450 employees, an elevenfold increase since the forty employees he had started with in 1891, he also faced a miasma, not encountered by private employers, created by the Building Bureau's vested system: namely, "the demoralizing effect on the younger men" of others "drawing the maximum salary . . . who, for one reason or another, fall very far short of any real standard of efficiency."[6]

Perhaps hardest for Snyder to deal with was a highly publicized investigation into the condition of the schools, not unlike the one by Wehrum in 1895 at the beginning of Snyder's career. This time it was his own buildings that were being criticized rather than those of others, even though most of the violations were minor, and often because of delayed maintenance over which Snyder had little control. He had built or done an addition for fully half of the schools targeted as faulty. Critics wrote of PS 4 in the Bronx, a star of the new order when it opened in 1898 and the seat from 1908 to 1913 of the renowned Progressive principal Angelo Patri, "fire hazard great, play facilities poor, teachers' rest rooms inadequate." Accusations about Snyder's PS 139 (1903) in Brooklyn included, "Not an old school, but in shocking condition." PS 20 in Queens, originally built by architects Boring and Tilton, to which Snyder had added a wing in 1908, was described as "sanitary equipment good, but dirty; small general repairs needed, insufficient lighting in about half of the rooms."[7]

For the very issues about which Snyder had felt most deeply and had provided for in new and better ways—light, fireproofing, play space, well-functioning bathrooms for students and lounges for teachers—he was encountering criticism. Novelist Upton Sinclair in the 1920s wrote that in New York, the wealthiest city in the world, "the children of the poor are herded into dark, unsanitary fire-traps, some of them seventy-five years of age; and even of these there is an insufficiency!"[8] He sounded like Jacob Riis writing in the 1890s. An insufficiency, yes, but Sinclair's alarmist rhetoric made it sound as if Snyder's career and all his "new order" schools had never happened.

Despite these disheartening factors, Snyder continued doing his best. He capitalized upon the virtues of "standardization," a practice that had been widely assumed to be the enemy of creativity and individuality for much of his career. But as noted on so many fronts, Snyder had the courage and vision to buck the status quo and pioneer more modern techniques. Using standardization, Snyder took advantage of economies of scale in several previous instances: in 1900, when he produced five Collegiate Gothic elementary schools; between 1901 and 1903, with the seven almost identical Naughton-tribute schools; and spanning his second decade, during various eras of H-Plan school construction. Harrison & Dobbin's 1931 manual *School Buildings of Today and Tomorrow* asserted,

> In a city like New York, that demanded 252 new school projects, providing 310,000 sittings, over a period of ten years, standardization was not only advisable but necessary. The Architectural Bureau of the Board of Education of the City of New York began to standardize more than 20 years ago and was practicing it on a large scale when leading architects were claiming that it could not be done. By standardizing everything that can and ought to be standardized, it has now practically won its fight for adequate school facilities. In the light of this accomplishment, the former prejudice against the very idea of standardizing architecture has gradually disappeared and other localities have adopted this expedient to a greater or lesser degree.[9]

Now in the final decade of his career, Snyder became an outspoken proponent of standardization. In the 1918 *American Architect*, he wrote or provided the material for a three-part article, "Department of Architectural Engineering: Standardized School House Design." Countering "the usual interpretation of the word" standardization—"that is, something which is fixed, uninteresting and monotonous"[10]—he made the following statement:

> A careful study and thorough understanding of standards will not in any way hamper the efforts of architects, but will rather broaden the scope of the knowledge possessed and insure [sic] the inclusion of those essentials necessary to the satisfactory use of the building.[11]

Standardization would enhance architects' efforts, not hamper them, Snyder argued. Part I of the article gave standards for size, capacity, equipment, and storage, accompanied by drawings, for various spaces in a school: classrooms, commercial rooms, domestic science departments, drawing rooms, electric wiring shops, gymnasiums, libraries, and kindergartens. Part II progressed to more specialized types of spaces such as machine shops, millinery rooms, music rooms, plumbing shops, printing shops, science rooms, sewing rooms, sheet metal shops, woodworking shops, and auditoriums. Part III specifically addressed school floor plans. The skepticism and hostility surrounding standardization all changed when the desire for efficiency arose during and after World War I and rendered standardization the byword, the desired goal, the golden axiom.

Snyder's repeatedly working out new plans showed he enjoyed the challenge of designing the optimally standardized layout, efforts that did not go unnoticed. *New York 1930* asserted that Snyder "struggled heroically both to evolve a rationalized ground plan on, typically, tight urban midblock sites and to suggest in [the schools'] architectural expression a stepping-stone toward public life." In 1918 George G. Gerwig commended Snyder's skill and ingenuity in standardizing city schools despite the vast volume of the undertaking. Gerwig wrote,

> Mr. Snyder has been in charge of the almost impossible task of providing school quarters to meet the phenomenal growth of New York City. . . . Many of the schoolhouses built under Mr. Snyder's supervision are models of their kind.[12]

During Snyder's final decade in office, he built one-third of his career total, or 134 schools. However, that number represented a significant drop from his second-decade high of 210 schools. Brooklyn was again the borough that dominated the building efforts, with fifty new schools. Manhattan by this time, with subways extending further and further into the outer boroughs, was losing population such that it, like the smaller Bronx and Queens, received only twenty-four schools. The Bronx saw twenty-seven new schools added, while Queens increased its count by twenty-eight. Staten Island netted five.

Simplified Collegiate Gothic had become the uniform of almost all the public schools (PSs). It was the twelve high schools—the same number as during his second-decade heyday—into which Snyder poured much of his creative energy. They were clad in Collegiate Gothic, Dutch Renaissance, Georgian, or Colonial garb* and provided more and better offerings—art

---

*Collegiate Gothic: Bushwick High School (1913), Normal College building, later Hunter High School for Girls (1913), Flushing High School (1915), the original Evander Childs High

studios with northern exposures, chapel-like music rooms, and shops for ever-more specialized subjects such as electric wiring, printing, dressmaking, and embroidery-machine-operating. Once again Snyder's third-decade overall efforts fall into the categories of appearance, construction, and functionality.

Modernizations in Appearance

Snyder's third decade saw an across-the-board change in the appearance of schools. From the Renaissance-Revival and Collegiate Gothic people's palaces of his first decade, he had moved to the plainer, more institutional, primarily Italian palazzo-style buildings of his second decade. The transition from Italian palazzo-style to Simplified Collegiate Gothic had begun toward the end of his second decade when, on a few of his Italian palazzo-style schools, he began placing over the top-floor windows flat Tudor arches connected and defined by a pronounced terra-cotta stringcourse (fig. 93). Then in 1909 in Brooklyn, instead of the overhanging cornice, Snyder used a crenellated, medieval castle-like roofline between the bays and a shallow, finial-topped pediment over each bay, the end pediments larger and having more terra-cotta ornamentation than the inner ones. In addition to eliminating the cornice, he had done away with other Italian palazzo-style features such as quoins, cartouches, and rusticated bottom floors. Simplified Collegiate Gothic was born.

Then the recession of 1910 prompted, or at least witnessed, a complete break to Simplified Collegiate Gothic, not a single additional Italian palazzo-style building. Instead, in this final decade, the Simplified Collegiate Gothic style dominated. His progression toward greater streamlining paralleled the transition in society as a whole from Beaux Arts to the clean austerity of the twentieth-century International Modernism of Corbusier and Gropius. Simplified Collegiate Gothic flourished for the rest of Snyder's career, the medieval castle motifs emblematically fighting off ignorance.

While about half of Snyder's second-decade schools had been Italian palazzo-style, well over 80 percent of his third-decade schools were Simplified Collegiate Gothic: three- to five-story buildings with three, five, or seven bays. The projecting outside bays on five-bay buildings and the

---

School (1916), and Manhattan Trade School for Girls (1917). Dutch Renaissance: Bay Ridge High School (1915) and Newtown High School (1922). Georgian: Julia Richman High School (1923), Thomas Jefferson High School (1924), and New Utrecht High School (1924). Colonial: George Washington High School (1925). Washington Irving High School defies the categories.

Figure 93 PS 29K, 1921: Sylvie's Elementary School. Ron LaValle photo.

projecting middle-bay on seven-bay buildings were further ornamented with terra-cotta designs. Characteristically, the top-floor windows had Tudor arches—usually one long, low arch over the sixteen-foot window expanses. Toward the end of the decade, instead of the single Tudor arch, some buildings had quadruplet Tudor-arched window units.

Almost all had a two-story projecting medieval-looking entranceway— with hexagonal turrets on each side or with a large pointed arch over the doorway (fig. 94). Tall, narrow, pointed-arched windows were located above the doorways, sometimes topped by crenellations. Often the horizontal spaces between and underneath the set of windows at each floor level—the spandrels—had designs in the brick, with each bay subtly outlined by a double row of ender bricks.

The rooflines varied. Sometimes a fence-like balustrade connected the pediments of the outside bays as in the five-bay PS 171K and in the seven-bay

Figure 94. PS 97Q, 1917: Simplified Collegiate Gothic Entranceway. LaValle photo.

PS 47X, both from 1912 and the seven-bay PS 93Q from 1917 (fig. 95). Sometimes the window surrounds were full and keyed—all heavily outlined in terra-cotta. More commonly, the buildings had a crenellated roofline, the medieval feel amplified by lancet windows or shield ornaments. Some small three-bay schools, with only a suggestion of crenellation along the roofline, had highly defined Gothic drip moldings over the windows. Each of the aforementioned patterns was repeated in two to seven sister schools.

After the three-year hiatus in school construction during and after World War I, in the rush to make up for lost time in the early 1920s, Snyder increased exponentially the phenomenon of standardization, or sister schools.

Figure 95. PS 93Q, 1917: Simplified Collegiate Gothic, 7 Bays, Quadruplet Tudor-Arched Windows. Municipal Archives.

In an early move toward a more suburban type of school, he designed three-story, five-bay buildings with a heavy stringcourse over the first floor to emphasize the building's horizontality. But the plan he most favored, for a total of twenty-four sister schools, was the five-story, seven-bay elementary school that could hold almost 2,000 students. It had all the Simplified Collegiate Gothic components: a slightly crenellated roofline, top-floor Tudor arches, and pediments often emphasized with finials, to name a few. Snyder's office designed as many Simplified Collegiate Gothic schools in the two years after the war as it had in the seven years before the war,* most of them for Brooklyn and the Bronx. Clearly, standardizing was providing the kind of efficiency the Building Bureau needed.

While primary schools in his third decade became stylistically simpler, Snyder poured his creative energies into high schools, both academic and

---

*Some weren't completed and opened until as late as 1925.

vocational. Although the number of schools overall fell off by a third from his second-decade high, the number of high schools remained the same—half of his career total; plus, he made two significant additions to Naughton's two Brooklyn high schools.

The ambivalence Snyder had felt during his second decade about providing high schools that served primarily the well-to-do was dispelled in his third decade when high schools started being geared more toward the immigrant population than the privileged. By this decade high-school attendance was becoming more universal—an estimated 30 percent of eighth-graders continued on to high school by 1920—double the number of the previous decade. New Utrecht and Thomas Jefferson High Schools were both in Brooklyn working-class neighborhoods. Bay Ridge, Bushwick, and George Washington High Schools also opened in immigrant neighborhoods—Bay Ridge, the only high school with classes taught in Norwegian; Bushwick, a vocational school for boys; and George Washington, serving Italians and Jews whom public transportation had allowed to leave or bypass the Lower East Side. Washington Irving High School and Manhattan Trade School for Girls—both located in the central, easily accessible Union Square area that had become commercial and institutional, no longer primarily residential—provided vocational training for girls. Now Snyder's mandate and his values were aligned.

The academic high schools he designed for this new clientele were as grand as the earlier exclusive ones. For Normal College, founded to train teachers and still administered by the Board of Education, he designed an imposing, ornate Collegiate Gothic building (1913), which still lords over narrow Lexington Avenue at Sixty-Eighth Street (fig. 96). Subsequently it became the Hunter College High School for Girls, and currently it is the Hunter College student-activities building. The dance studios in the old gymnasiums at each end of the top floor are elegant spaces with spectacular views. Flushing High School (1915), with its asymmetrical auditorium wing, is Collegiate Gothic complete with a campus. The original Evander Childs High School (1916), an H-Plan building with Gothic trappings and an old-fashioned pitched roof, looms unusually large. It's not just the narrow street that creates that impression; the ceiling heights require thirty-two stair risers between floors instead of the customary twenty-eight. And Newtown High School (1922), featuring "stepped gables and a dramatic 169-foot, centrally placed tower topped by a cupola and turrets,"[13] combines Dutch Renaissance elements with Collegiate Gothic to create a dramatic one-of-a-kind building worthy of the Boring & Tilton

Figure 96. Normal College, 1913, Now Part of Hunter College. LaValle photo.

original building (now demolished) to which Snyder's was built as an addition. George Washington High School, Snyder's only Colonial building, was so impressive it was said early graduates referred to it, without irony, as the country club.

The vocational high schools were impressive in their own right. An H-Plan school, Bushwick High School, has three receding levels of crenellated rooflines. Bay Ridge High School, a Flemish Renaissance Revival building, visually dominates the area. Washington Irving High School (1913) drew the *New York Times* headline, "Most Remarkable Girls' School in the World" (fig. 97). It and the Manhattan Trade School for Girls (1917) were revolutionary not only in having been created exclusively for girls but also in their height, the tall building having "heretofore been almost entirely confined to business structures or the towering apartment houses."[14] Manhattan Trade at ten stories and Washington Irving at eight (with a later sixteen-story addition) were both taller than any previous public schools. Writing about Manhattan Trade in the *Real Estate Record and*

Guide, Snyder said, "The structure will be the tallest building of its kind in the city and will be a model of school architecture and planning."[15] Unique in its curriculum and the way it functioned, the school had a unique appearance—a loft-like Collegiate Gothic building clad in white terra-cotta, the figures on the cornice holding tools as well as books (fig. 98).

But, by the end of his third decade, even high schools were standardized—large, handsome, dignified Georgian buildings, lacking the spark of his earlier unique high schools. The quintuplets—Julia Richman, Thomas Jefferson, New Utrecht, Prospect Heights, and Monroe High Schools—all opened in 1923 and 1924. The first three were designed by Snyder and completed by his successor, William Gompert; Prospect Heights and Monroe were attributed to Gompert alone. All involve a simple, dignified red-brick exterior with only the faintest suggestion of Gothic. All have a U-shaped footprint, a large lobby leading into the two-story auditorium, hallways wide enough to be used now as lounges with sofas, a fifth-floor student cafeteria and a sixth-floor teacher cafeteria, two gyms, and one or two swimming pools. When Julia Richman opened, it even had a bank and store on the second floor.[16]

George Washington High School, completed by Gompert, was the last Snyder-designed school to open in 1925. When the northern Manhattan neighborhood association had lobbied for a high school on the site of the abandoned Fort George Amusement Park, for some unknown reason rather than working with the Department of Education and Snyder, the association retained George and Edward Blum to prepare plans and specifications for the proposed school.[17] Snyder, the designated school architect, created his one and only colonial-style school, totally different from the Blums' proposal. It gave the neighborhood a structure with a cupola visible from Fort Tryon Park to the west and from the Bronx to the east. A long balustrade stretches along the roof, broken by a central tower with eagles looking out in all four directions (fig. 99). About the Colonial façade, a recent student said, "The complex angles make me want to come to school. I can imagine I'm entering a palace." A teacher observed, "I love the building. It's an example of what schools used to be. It has a sense of permanence that's important for these kids whose lives are often so transient." The Colonial George Washington inspired several other schools such as Jamaica High School in Queens and Franklin Lane in Brooklyn. With the exception of the Hunter College Student Activities building, all of Snyder's final-decade high schools remain public schools.

Figure 97. Washington Irving High School, 1913, 8 Stories. *Modern School Houses*, Part II, 1915.

Figure 98. Manhattan Trade School for Girls, 1917, 10 Stories. Drawing in American Architect, 1917.

Figure 99. George Washington High School, Completed by Gompert, 1925: Eagle Ornamentation Surrounds Cupola. Arrington photo.

Construction Innovations and Refinements

Snyder honed fireproofing techniques, defining parameters for new buildings and continuing to make old buildings more fire-resistant. In 1912, he announced that all the school buildings in the five boroughs were now equipped with mechanical or electrical fire alarms. In his 1913 annual report, Snyder discussed the fire protection work being carried out in older buildings, including "the replacing of wood stairways with those of fireproof construction, the placing of fire stops in attics, installation of proper signaling apparatus, protection of all boiler rooms, etc., etc."[18] Writing in 1914 about Bushwick High School, he laid out the multiple considerations that went into containing fire and evacuating the building without injury.[19] In 1916, while adequate fireproofing of a school building added to its cost of construction, Snyder felt that the comparative increase in cost between the fireproof and non-fireproof type is continually being lowered, due to improvements in methods and materials, so that under normal market conditions the authorities in every community, whether large or small, should refuse to authorize the construction of non-fireproof buildings.[20]

In 1918, improving upon one of his first innovations, the interlocking staircases for emptying a school quickly in case of fire, he found a way to reduce ceiling heights for classrooms by shaving off fifteen inches from the fifteen feet, six inches that previously he had felt necessary between floors in order to have enough headroom.* Finally, responding in 1921 to the published investigation of the schools, he asserted that no fire perils existed in any school, that no "public school building in the city today ... is unsafe for occupancy." He said that the fire violations found by the investigating committee were for the most part unimportant and that in some instances they represented a difference of opinion as to what is most desirable. He made a distinction between fire hazard and fire peril.[21]

---

*Snyder and Dobbin, "Standardized School House Design," *American Architect*, 1918, 627. Snyder wrote, "A careful checking over of the minimum space to be assigned to each item led to the discovery that the lines of vertical vent flues, which have heretofore been provided between nearly all the classrooms in school buildings, could be eliminated, and the vents from the various rooms could be carried above the corridor ceilings and taken up to the roof through trunk lines located in out-of-the-way corners. This expedient, which has never before been adopted so far as is known, has resulted in reducing the length of the building 5 ft. 6 in. and the length of the two wings 2 ft. over previous buildings of this type, thus saving a very large amount of floor space and cubature. The omission of the ducts between classrooms also made it possible to eliminate an attic space of 4 ft. 6 in. in height, which was required for the collection of the vents. It was also found that by providing recesses for steam risers at the side of windows, instead of placing the risers on the face of the wall, the width of the classrooms and of the building was reduced without decreasing the seating or aisle space in the rooms. ... A further reduction in the height of the building was obtained by changes in stair construction. For many years the floor-to-floor story height of New York schools was fixed at 15 ft. 7½ in., which seemed to be the minimum height that could be used in connection with the type of double-run stairways which had been found so economical of space. On study it was found that by a change in the construction of the stairs enough headroom could be saved to permit of reducing the story height to 15 ft. In a five-story building this makes a savings of more than 3 ft. in the height of the building and permits of a reduction of 4 in. in the thickness of the outside walls as required by the New York Building Code. As a result of these changes in the flues and stairways, this building contains 203–450 cubic feet less than a similar building without these changes and with the same service for pupils."

In this third decade Snyder had to rethink the lighting in the schools. With electricity now standard, the term "well-lit" meant significantly more light than it had two decades earlier. He wrote, "In artificial lighting there has been, as we all know, a most complete revolution. Up to a few years ago the need was almost entirely confined to illumination for evening school work." To meet people's expectations for more and better artificial lighting, Snyder took several steps: In corridors and stairwells, he installed artificial lighting instead of relying solely on borrowed light from classrooms. In the classrooms themselves, he reduced the mullions to a minimum,[22] and nine years later called for the removal altogether "of all transom bars and sash in exterior windows."[23]

He did extensive experiments with shades for the windows, working with considerations of cost, durability, color, translucence, stability, ability to adjust for fresh air, and projected repair frequency. And he assigned the chief of the electrical division to undertake a thorough study of various incandescent lighting fixtures, both those used in other school systems and those available on the market.[24] In his article "The Lighting of School Rooms,"[25] he reported that artificial lighting was positioned so that "whatever shadow was created was delivered in a direction such as to be received under the pupil's hand in writing, there being an absence of shadow forward of the pencil which would tend to confuse." Snyder considered all aspects of lighting as being of "fundamental importance,"[26] and none was too small for his close scrutiny.

During this decade, there were also various other construction refinements. He succumbed to designing additional "portable [temporary] classrooms"—a practice he had opposed earlier in his career. He replaced "the present toilet ranges and urinals which are objectionable, although they represented the best of practice at the time of installation."[27] He instituted changes in floor construction to that used in mercantile buildings, effecting a savings of $3,000 per fifty classrooms.[28] And finally, in a major change that alleviated the Building Bureau's dependence on steel, he started using reinforced concrete, "a form of construction which should be continued as an alternate with steel, leaving market conditions to decide which shall be actually used."[29]

Regarding heating and ventilation, what Snyder had done at the beginning of his career to make mechanically ventilating the schools feasible—that is, developing his own machines and putting them out for bids rather than purchasing the prohibitively expensive market versions—was now impeding repairs. He therefore moved away from the specialized machinery of his earlier years and toward appliances and equipment that were more aligned with what was available commercially. He also changed the location of ventilation flues so that school interiors could be more easily reconfigured. Despite having had to confront the limitations of his original machines, Snyder continued to be guided by the conviction that a school must be built with the future in mind as well as the present.

With his usual concern about quality of life in the schools, Snyder addressed the issue of students' most-asked question, "Can I get a drink of water?" Early on students had waited in a long line at a single spigot with a communal cup. By 1898 Snyder had designed a system unprecedented for its high volume and effective delivery. He wrote,

> Drinking facilities are furnished so that from fifty to sixty children can obtain water at the same time, the troughs to receive the waste being so designed that the clothing of the children, either large or small, is not wet from the spattering of the water.[30]

But he hadn't addressed the health risks of the system. In 1911, the *New York Times* ran the following:

> C. B. J. Snyder, Superintendent of Buildings of the Department of Education, declares that the common drinking cup used in the schools helps spread disease among the children, and he is looking about for a practicable substitute.
>
> He turned his attention first to the various kinds of sanitary fountains, but so far has been unable to find any that is entirely satisfactory. It would require a great number of fountains to supply the needs of the schools, and the additional cost had to be taken into account. He is now endeavoring to invent one which he hopes will meet every requirement.[31]

Two companies at the time manufactured water fountains. However, the cost was prohibitive, especially considering the number that would be needed for the entire school system. So once again Snyder designed his own, the manufacturing of which could be put out for bids. His handling of the water fountain issue sums up his priorities and ways of proceeding—awareness of needs, focus on the solution rather than the problem, practicality and cost consciousness, and confidence in his own resourcefulness. In some schools today, the original fountains still work, while additional ones installed fifty or seventy years later collect dust.

Advances in Functionality

Further broadening of the high-school experience occurred nationwide during the second decade of the new century, Snyder's third decade on the job, nowhere more so than in New York City. A 1919 study of American high schools analyzed the floor plans of 156 high schools built during the years 1908 to 1917; researchers found "multiplication of facilities for specialization, differentiation, and enrichment of the work of the high-school student"[32]— specifically, 109 differentiated spaces (fig. 100). While some categories seem to overlap, for example, "forge or blacksmithing room or shop," "foundry or molding room or shop," "forge and foundry room or shop," nevertheless, the study laid out the spectrum of possibilities: shops and allied work, domestic science suites, science laboratories, commercial art studios, music rooms, libraries, gymnasiums, recreation rooms for clubs and extracurricular activities, auditoriums, study rooms, lunchrooms. By this time almost 100 percent of schools nationwide had gymnasiums and auditoriums. But only 10 to 20 percent of the schools nationwide even approached having the numerous types of facilities New York City schools possessed. One surviving artifact

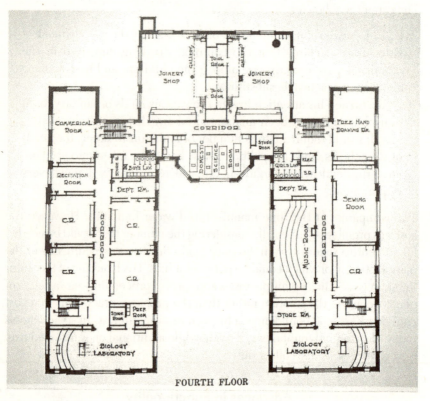

Figure 100. Bushwick High School, Brooklyn, 1913: Fourth-Floor Specialty Areas. *Modern School Houses*, Part II, 1915.

from Snyder's office is a wall chart of a dozen Brooklyn schools under construction during 1916, with a column for each potential specialized space and a checkmark showing which ones each school had.

Snyder was successful at broadening the functionality of schools, in part at least because he relied on the advice and input of teachers and principals. In the evolution of school design in the United States, he was an early example of an architect surveying users about the architectural program. His great-granddaughter, Cynthia LaValle, in her career as a project manager, has commented, "If there's anything I inherited from him, it might be the ability to listen. There is little chance of success when managing a project unless you listen to [communicate with] the stakeholders." About the new building Snyder designed for Washington Irving High School, he wrote, "Its interior planning is the result of the most painstaking and careful study on the part of the architect who has been able to receive the embodied ideas of the faculty of teachers and reduce them to a practical and architectural possibility."[33]

Subsequently the principal, William McAndrew, in a letter expressed

> sincere appreciation for your policy of using the judgment of those whom you expect to occupy a projected building. That every room and piece of equipment involved in the educational work of the school was freely submitted to all the teachers by every member of your staff who had the plans is instance of an intelligence and a courtesy to be found in very few school systems. The usual attitude of a school architect toward a teacher is "mind your own business, this is mine." It seems to me that your policy of interchange of views corrects and broadens both the builder and the occupant.[34]

Snyder, this paean suggests, possessed courtesy, intelligence, openness, and respect for others—all of which resulted in satisfied occupants of the school and a highly functional building, one "that may be safely said to provide a model for similar classes of buildings throughout the country."[35] Washington Irving High School (1913), a model school visited by educators of the nation and worldwide, epitomized Snyder's "intelligent and convenient disposition of space with conveniences for other than the mere traditional restricted use of school-houses."[36]

William McAndrew praised the placement of the science labs, sewing rooms, storage spaces, and gymnasiums, as exemplified here:

> The arrangement and equipment of [the Natural Science rooms] is the admiration and the envy of many science teachers who visit the

school. The transportation of illustrative material from one room to the other without going into the corridors is a great convenience. The arrangement of common preparation rooms between pairs of these science rooms is another economy often noted.[37]

Further, two lecture rooms on the fifth and sixth floors with stereopticon equipment (a slide projector able to create dissolving views) in each could be scheduled for use by various classes as well as by outside groups. Corridors were wide enough for girls to walk seven abreast, making it easy for teachers to check their posture; there were ten enclosed fire- and smoke-proof stairways and four elevators, each large enough to carry a whole class. In keeping with his philosophy to provide facilities for use by multiple organizational entities at the same time,[38] the layout of the school was such that

> It has been possible for the Authors' Club of New York, the Allied Artists of America, and other organizations to hold receptions while the school was in session, and to suffer no interference between periods as the classes passed from room to room.[39]

For all the amenities and conveniences it offered, Washington Irving High School cost, the *Real Estate Record and Guide* reported in 1912, only $.19 per cubic foot, in contrast to the Bronx County Court House and the Municipal Building, which cost $.70 and $.65 per cubic foot, respectively.[40] Snyder still made frugality a high priority—and highlighted it.

Despite the fact that Washington Irving provided a lesson in remarkable aids to education, the school was not without problems. Food had to be carried through the corridor because the demonstration kitchen did not connect directly with the dining room. There were too few men's bathrooms. The roof playground lacked a sunshade. Retracting the screen in the auditorium to pull up the world map for geography classes was slow, causing teachers to complain. Movable instead of fixed chairs in certain rooms answered the desires of many educators and made cleaning easier, but they tipped over too readily.

As the progressive curriculum continued broadening to include additional primarily vocational but also academic and athletic options, these new areas of study requiring new specialized spaces marked, according to the *American Architect*, "the advent of a new epoch in the history of public education in America" and demanded of the architect "an amount of ingenuity and originality not required in following well-beaten paths."[41] Rising to the occasion during his third decade on the job, as he did at Washington Irving High School, Snyder expanded and refined earlier functional innovations he'd made—to accompany science labs, for example, he provided lecture halls and apparatus, preparation, and specimen rooms; in the Bushwick High School (1913) auditorium, a lab table could be rolled to the middle of the stage where through a trapdoor gas, electric, water, steam, and drainage connections were available. Additionally, he designed other improvements such as athletic fields, art studios, motion-picture booths in auditoriums, and ever more sophisticated vocational-training facilities.

Snyder was working at a time when mechanical/vocational training was so thoroughly in its heyday as a panacea for the ills of society that Woodrow Wilson could say with impunity,

> We want one class of persons to have a liberal education, and we want another class of persons, a very much larger class of necessity in every society, to forgo the privilege of a liberal education and fit themselves to perform specific difficult manual labor.[42]

Wilson's brand of elitism is one of the key reasons that vocational training has all but been eliminated from public schools today. But in 1909, his words were a rousing call for more and better vocational training. Thus, in addition to the mechanical-training rooms for carpentry, cooking, sewing, and drawing, Snyder introduced increasingly sophisticated spaces such as model "flats" and printing shops. Manhattan Trade School for Girls (1917) took vocational training a step further. Having a rolling admission so students could start each month, the school offered one-year training programs in a variety of trades such as dressmaking, embroidery-machine-operating, and novelty work. Snyder designed the ten-story building such that each floor housed a different type of factory shop. Its permanent record cards show that the school had an in-house employment bureau and kept track of its students' employment history for years after they had graduated.[43]

Washington Irving High School itself illustrates the spectrum of attitudes toward a vocational school. Its vocational program was described in elevated terms by the *American Architect* as offering "a course of study that promotes the highest ideals and inculcates domestic virtues," and the principal said, "It fits for college, for business, and for matrimony."[44] In down-to-earth contrast, the *New York Times* quoted the Board of Education president Charles Burlington as saying that the school functioned to "teach the girls to get away from chewing gum and send them downtown to work with an ambition to make more than $6 a week."[45] At the same time the school functioned like a conservatory for the fine arts with a competitive admission policy. Artist Lee Krasner, who would marry Jackson Pollock, was turned down the first time she applied but was accepted to her delight after a year at Erasmus High School.[46]

One of Snyder's earlier functional advances in New York Schools—auditoriums to replace partitioned assembly rooms—had by this decade become problematic. Ironically, the grand step forward in 1902 to auditoriums proper ended up undermining the communal, unifying function that assembly rooms had managed so well. In those, the principal had started each school day by leading the students in songs and the pledge of allegiance and giving an informal inspirational reading or talk. Auditoriums proper had seemed highly desirable in the effort to eliminate the partitioned, poorly sound-proofed classrooms after the morning meeting and to make the school more available for community use. But a large auditorium did not lend itself to informal morning assemblies, and its size made discipline difficult. As a consequence, the tradition dropped away. Snyder's radical improvement ended up compromising the very reason for having a large gathering space to begin with. Not until the 1920s were the costs of having upgraded from assembly room to auditorium overcome by the homeroom concept,[47] which once again brought students together first thing every morning and created a sense of belonging.

Despite this, however, Snyder continued designing spectacular high-school auditoriums. The Palladian windows and handsome chandeliers in the George Washington High School auditorium echo those same features in the elegant, adjacent entrance lobby. At Bushwick High School, the foyer between the main entrance and the auditorium was lit by skylights and handsome light fixtures, and the doors into the auditorium had stained-glass panels. The Washington Irving High School auditorium, commented a Municipal Art Society officer, "is in itself a lesson in beauty and refinement. In this structure the city speaks. Its message is symmetry, order, and unostentatious richness. It is simple, it is dignified, it is an inspiring work of art."[48] The auditorium lobby, with its dark mahogany trim, Barry Faulkner murals depicting New York City's history, and huge stone fireplace surmounted by a marble sculpture of girls reading Washington Irving aloud, resembled a room in a private clubhouse. Large enough for receptions up to 400, it functioned for a time as the Municipal Gallery of the City of New York. Sculptor Daniel French called its second-floor gallery "a beauty. Its color and design are in the best of taste."[49] Mark Twain himself, living nearby at the time, petitioned that the auditorium be equipped with simple scenery and a drop curtain to make it more usable by the people in the neighborhood.[50] It became the first high-school auditorium so equipped (figs. 101, 102). Addressing Snyder, the principal commended, "The machine devised by a member of your bureau whereby all the windows of the auditorium are

Figure 101. Washington Irving High School, 1913: Auditorium. *1913 American Architect and Building News* (AABN).

Figure 102. Washington Irving High School Auditorium after 2014 Renovation. Arrington photo.

from one station darkened at once" as "a feat of cleverness and convenience."[51] Once again, Snyder succeeded at designing ever-more complicated specialized devices and spaces.

He worked in other ways as well to increase the functionality of the large spaces. All over town school auditoriums had separate formal entrances for people attending the evening lectures. Starting in 1913, Snyder introduced projection booths in elementary as well as high-school auditoriums. He worked out designs even for the shutter construction of the projectors, explaining,

> The shutters for the machine and for the operator are controlled by fusible plugs, the arrangement, however, being such that they will close in the event of fire and thus prevent fire and smoke from being communicated to the audience.[52]

A screen descended from above in some schools and in others came up out of the floor. In the 1920s high schools, the girls' gymnasium was located directly behind the auditorium in order to make possible large-scale events such as, Snyder explained,

> graduation exercises, plays, pageants and many other uses which now seem essential for the school and for the community.... In order to meet these demands without devoting a thousand or more square feet of floor space to only occasional use... a movable partition operated by electric power will [open up] a clear, unobstructed opening of about sixty feet [and] afford accommodations for a mass meeting or other gatherings of about two thousand, five hundred people.[53]

Lunchrooms became prevalent during this period for students traveling long distances to high school and more and more in elementary schools for low-income students. Even though at least four of Snyder's second-decade high schools had had lunchrooms, about the Washington Irving High School lunchrooms on the fourth and fifth floors with a seating capacity of 882, he wrote,

> An original departure in planning is the introduction of student dining rooms in space usually allotted to classroom purposes.... Every minute of the pupil's life is conserved for educational purposes and during the time passed in the dining room, she is under the scrutiny of competent teachers who correct any lapse of table manners and by this means instill knowledge of the refinements of daily life.[54]

Snyder seems to have felt the need to overcome the view that a lunchroom was a frill by justifying it on pedagogical grounds. However, by the following year, lunchrooms seem to have become standard, as he could simply write, "Lunchrooms for boys and girls are placed above the shops, on what is practically the sixth floor alongside a 12,000-square-foot recreation space."[55] In 1917, the Manhattan Trade School for Girls included plans, never materialized, for a restaurant on the first floor, with the idea that students could take the skills learned in ninth-floor lunchroom and practice them there. The high schools built in the 1920s—Thomas Jefferson High School, New Utrecht High School, Julia Richman High School—had lunchrooms for students on the fifth floor and for teachers on the partial sixth floor. More and more elementary schools also began providing lunches for undernourished children, who, it was estimated in the early 1920s, constituted one-third of the school population of nearly one million. Lunchrooms functioned during off hours as study halls or playrooms.

Even though public schools were often located close to a public library—there was, for instance, a public library either adjacent to or across the street from Wadleigh High School, Eastern District High School, Julia Richman High School, PS 186M, PS 147K, and PS 67K, to name a few—libraries in the school itself became another widespread specialized space, especially in high schools. Snyder worked out the floor plans and furnished them with dark wood shelving, tables and chairs, and a built-in check-out area in the front. In his 1912 addition to Brooklyn's Girls' High School, one floor was devoted to the library that had Tiffany stained-glass windows, since lost. At New Utrecht High School and its sister schools, Snyder placed the library along one wing of the first floor and made the corridor wall above the bookshelves out of plate glass, "thus affording, from the corridor, an uninterrupted view of the interior of the library, which will be made most attractive."[56] At New Utrecht High School brass railings that line the stairs going to an office and storage room under the main library show Snyder's concern about every individual in the school, since only the librarians would see and appreciate such quality trappings.

In accordance with the progressive belief that a child should experience the arts as well as learn the three R's, Snyder designed music and art rooms (fig. 103). The 1919 addition to Curtis High School included a top-floor hallway of art studios with northern exposures, believed to offer the best of light. Music rooms were charming, small, homey like a chapel, with a stage and grand piano, stadium-style seating for 100, dark wood finishes and fancy moldings, and a storage room for musical instruments. Most have now been modernized, though a few such as the one at New Utrecht High School remain intact. This type of specialized space was located in the tower in Flushing High School (1915) and on the fifth floor of the former Evander Childs High School (1916). But by the time he introduced high schools of the 1920s, Snyder had moved the music room to the first floor behind the auditorium and library, "having in mind the vast opportunities which [it] present[s] for community use [without] interfering with their use for school purposes."[57]

Figure 103. Flushing High School, Queens, 1915: Music Room. *Modern School Houses*, Part II, 1915.

Additional design problems were posed by new progressive offerings Superintendent Maxwell initiated for crippled, anemic, deaf, blind, and mentally challenged children.[58] Some classrooms had wheelchair-type desks. In response to parental appeal in 1908, an old, unused building on East Twenty-Third Street had been renovated as one of the first public day schools for deaf children in the country: PS 47M, so numbered because of its opening enrollment of forty-seven students. Snyder designed a new building for the site, the School for the Deaf, which opened in 1925 and still serves this function. The school's façade, a window expanse nearly that of a modern glass tower, seemed to compensate for the students' lack of one sense by playing to another (fig. 104).

Open-air classrooms, designed to improve the health of anemic and tubercular children, had proved so successful, the *New York Times* reported in 1911, that the Board of Education now regarded them as beyond the experimental stage and planned to open twenty more in addition to the existing nine.[59] Snyder did not let the fact that the urban setting lacked peaceful outdoor instruction areas stand in his way. The open-air class at PS 102M (1914), on the Upper East Side, met on a wood platform in Jefferson Park, and a class from PS 95M (1912) convened on the open top floor of a

THE STANDARDIZING DECADE 1911–1922 · 193

Figure 104. PS 47M, 1925: School for the Deaf. Municipal Archives.

Parks Department building across from the school on West Clarkson Street. In many schools Snyder retrofitted a classroom for this special purpose.*

---

*Snyder, "Annual Report of the Superintendent of School Buildings" (1913), 131–33. He explained all the considerations involved:

In the effort to extend the fresh-air classroom movement in our schools it was found that in many localities there was no available space other than classrooms.

This necessitated study as to the possibility of admitting into such a room large quantities of fresh air and sunlight, while at the same time protecting its occupants from storms. . . .

[The room was placed] at about the third floor level, which brought it above the ordinary street dust line and not too high for the children to reach quite easily. . . .

[The total area of windows is] equivalent to about 60 percent of the floor area of the room. . . .

Provisions for heating are such that the temperature even in the coldest weather can be held at about 45 degrees with the windows wide open. . . .

[Each pupil needs] a sleeping bag in a special form, a sweater, cap or hood, mittens and overshoes, and costs about $14. This outfit receives severe usage and will last perhaps, on the average, two years. . . .

It is considered to be most desirable that the children should be in the sunlight as much as possible even when studying.

In his third decade Snyder also made swimming pools a more common amenity in schools. He had been experimenting with them since as early as 1903 at the High School of Commerce and in 1906 at both DeWitt Clinton High School and, in an unusual decision to put a pool in an elementary school, at PS 66; George Washington High School has two. At Julia Richman High School, located adjacent to the Second Avenue El, Snyder placed as a buffer "a separate building along the entire Second avenue frontage of some six stories in height, the first floor being devoted to a swimming pool, dressing rooms, showers, medical examiner, corrective training, offices and laundry."[60] Some elementary schools, such as PS 11M (1924) in Chelsea, were built with pools. The 1917 additions brought pools to others, such as PS 4 and PS 32 in the Bronx. Short of a pool, reported the *New York Times,* the Board of Education was installing "shower baths in all of the new school buildings and was placing them in several of the older ones."[61] For some children at PS 70X (1924, attributed to Gompert), those showers were "the only water they saw from one week to the next," wrote E. L. Doctorow in *World's Fair.*[62]

Responsive as always to what educators were asking for, Snyder undertook another new foray, designing New York's first two public-school athletic fields. One in Astoria, Queens, now gone, sat on a spit of land that sticks out into Hell's Gate in the East River. The other, the field for Edward R. Murrow High School in Midwood, Brooklyn, had several innovative features. The Brooklyn Athletic Field, Snyder wrote, "is entirely of reinforced concrete, and in it are presented some novel features"—namely, as a result of "careful investigation," two innovations to improve the audience's view.[63] Instead of having the usual long straight side of stadiums in this country, Snyder reproduced the curve of the long side of the Athens stadium where the 1906 Olympics had been held, and he adjusted heights and distances so people in the first row didn't have to stand to see over the people standing along the fence between the track and the stand.[64] Again, it is clear that Snyder loved defining and solving problems.

Both primary and secondary schools of this period continued the idea that the school should be a neighborhood nucleus, open to young and old alike, an idea fundamental to Snyder's thought. He said,

> The development of the public school building is due largely to the need for a structure that will render much community service. . . .

The reflection of light from the white paper which is so trying on the eyes can be met by the use of a light screen, just large enough to contain the book, the support for which may be adjusted to any desired angle.

Buildings so planned . . . can be used by the people of the neighborhood. The whole top part of the school where the classrooms are can be shut off from the lower part of the building. If there is night school in the building, the classes can go on, while there may be a dance in the gymnasium, a concert in the music room or a lecture in the auditorium. A schoolhouse of this kind can fill a great social need in the community.[65]

In 1912, the Board of Education gave the Greenwich Settlement House permission to establish intergenerational social centers in two public schools, and in 1914, it planned large-scale summer activities so children wouldn't be idle.[66] "By 1914 the Board of Education was running the most varied and extensive program of socialized activities of any public school system in the country,"[67] educational historian Sol Cohen wrote. Snyder was participating in a school system that saw itself in the business of transforming society, a system that strove to be a model of excellence in the Americanization of immigrants. Sociologist Clarence Perry idealistically saw the school as the setting for a "self-supporting, democratically organized and administered neighborhood institute whereby people could become progressively better and happier through leisure-time occupations."[68] In New York during the academic year 1929–30, more than 5.5 million people used school facilities after hours.

Snyder forged a path that we are still following. During his thirty-one-year career, schools had changed dramatically. From buildings of only classrooms when he had started the job in 1891 to buildings about which, at the time of his retirement in 1922, he could say,

> The changes that have been made are many. When I went to school we did not have any extra activities. Now we have gymnasiums, swimming pools, open-air class rooms, rooms for cardiac children, roof playgrounds, shower baths, model kitchens for teaching domestic science, and a great many other things we never dreamed of thirty years ago.[69]

Numerous up-to-date facilities made a school sound desirable then, as they do today. About a school that opened in 2013 (replacing, sadly, the unique PS 133, one of Snyder's earliest in Brooklyn), we get this description: "The new PS 133 boasts . . . 39 standard and six special education classrooms, high-tech science labs, a gleaming stainless steel kitchen, an inviting library, and a state-of-the-art medical suite."[70] A century earlier, Snyder had publicized Bay Ridge High School (1915) similarly as having special rooms for typewriting, drawing, sewing, cooking, music, and commercial studies; a library; laboratories for zoological, chemical, and physical science; two student lunchrooms and one for teachers; a 1,500-seat auditorium with a roof playground on top; a gymnasium and running track.[71] Snyder's early twentieth-century approach of enumerating amenities is still used today.

Although the advances of Snyder's final decade were accompanied by hard times and criticisms, disappointment and frustration, they continued to demonstrate his far-reaching progressivism. He designed facilities for the voiceless—for truant, crippled, anemic, and deaf children. During his third decade high schools were located in immigrant neighborhoods and vocational schools were provided for girls and boys alike. Far from dismissing girls, Snyder designed for them the two tallest public schools in the system. One of them, Washington Irving, is the single school whose interior has garnered the most admiration even to this day. The dimming of his glory from the two decades of remarkable creativity and productivity seems to have allowed him to shift his attention from major milestones. He and his staff had changed the metaphor for New York public schools from factories to palaces and moved New York City from public-school laggard to leader. In the third and final decade of his career, he was free to express his progressive essence more thoroughly.

Epilogue

Retirement and Successors

CHARLES B. J. Snyder had assumed the position of superintendent of school buildings when he was thirty-one years old. He held that position for the next thirty-one years. Toward the end of his public-school career, the hard times, criticisms, and disappointments he faced ended with the biggest blow of all. In 1922 he was "virtually forced out of the post under pressure by former Mayor Hylan."[1] John Francis Hylan, who had been elected to a second term in 1922 on the campaign slogan of "A Seat for Every Child," pressured Snyder to speed up the school construction process. But Snyder was unwilling to sacrifice quality for speed. Ever gracious and concerned about having a smooth transition, Snyder issued this bittersweet statement,

> Since 1904, that is a long time, I have had no vacation. . . . I am tired and completely worn out. I think it is time for me to go fishing. I have been asked to take the position of consulting architect. . . . I have the best of feelings toward all the members of the Board of Education, and my asking to be retired has nothing to do with any friction between me and any of them. . . . I am asking for retirement on July 1 in order that my successor may have two months in Summer to become acquainted with the duties of the office.[2]

Clearly Snyder was giving a generous account of events. He was prevailed upon to remain but take a vacation of three or four months, "beginning today."[3] Snyder's resignation became official on January 1, 1923 (fig. 105).

Figure 105. Snyder in His Later Years. Snyder Family Archives.

Having started at a salary of $6,000, Snyder was earning $14,000, an amount in keeping with other superintendents' salaries, but about which the president of the board, Ettinger, said, "I know of no one who will accept the job at the salary we pay." Hylan, after some contention with the Board of Education, increased the superintendent of school buildings' salary to $25,000. That amount was sufficient to attract Pratt-Institute-trained William Gompert, but after four years he left the job under uncontested allegations of leaky buildings and shoddy construction.

For fourteen years after Snyder's retirement, school design generally followed Charles B. J. Snyder's patterns. The typical Gompert elementary school was basically a Snyder school, stripped of most ornamentation and the medieval entrance replaced by a Greek Revival entrance of four or six two-story columns. Walter Martin, who followed Gompert as superintendent of school buildings from 1928 until 1938, for the most part eliminated distinctive entranceways altogether and experimented with various locations for the auditorium and gymnasium(s), but he preserved the five-floor, symmetrically massed Snyder building. Some of Martin's schools are plain and utilitarian and some are in the Art Deco tradition. High schools for two decades after Snyder's retirement used versions of the H-Plan: Jamaica, Far Rockaway, Lincoln, Fort Hamilton, Lafayette, and Tilden, to name a few. Many private and parochial schools throughout the city were designed in

Figure 106. Harriet and Charles. Snyder Family Archives.

the wake of Snyder's lead. As late as the 1960s, architect Richard Dattner cites as design precedents for his PS 234 on Chambers Street, in addition to Mackintosh's 1903 Scotland Street School, "the prototypical 'H' Plan School designed for New York City in 1898 by C. B. J. Snyder."[4] Both were important to Dattner for having restricted urban sites and courtyards enclosed by strong, protective walls and gates.

Meanwhile, Snyder himself had been serious about the fishing. Almost immediately after retiring, he and his wife, Harriet, took their two six-year-old granddaughters out of school, loaded their automobile onto a coastal steamer, and went to Florida for four months (fig. 106). A few years later, Harriet died on May 25, 1927, having succumbed to injuries received when struck by a taxicab in NYC. After Harriet's death,[5] Babu, as the family called Snyder, left his house on Bedford Avenue in Brooklyn and lived with his son Howard's family on Wellington Street in Garden City, Long Island, New York.

Snyder kept his hand in architecture. From 1924 to 1925, he is listed as consulting architect for the New York City Board of Education with an office at 505 Fifth Avenue (at Forty-Second Street), and he is mentioned in several newspaper articles as a consulting architect on schools in the New Rochelle area.* From 1931 to 1936, Architects in Practice in New York City, 1900–1940,[6] lists him at 183 Madison Avenue (and Thirty-Fourth Street). For many years he shared his son Howard's office at 110 West Fortieth Street. Both father and son worked into their eighties.† However, it appears that only one building, a 1939 three-story brick convent on Audubon Avenue between West 172nd and 173rd Streets, is attributed solely to Snyder during this period. The convent has the distinction of having been alluded to by J. D. Salinger, who had attended Snyder's PS 166 on West Eighty-Ninth Street. Holden Caulfield, main character in Salinger's famous novel *Catcher in the Rye*, having breakfast in a little sandwich bar near Grand Central Station, talks with two nuns who "were school teachers and . . . going to start teaching at some convent on 168th Street or 186th Street or one of those streets way the hell uptown."[7]

Snyder chose Babylon, Long Island, New York, a community with cool summer breezes, for his vacation home. Ironically this unassuming man had effected an almost Robert Moses–type transformation in New York City public schools. His modest summer home was located in the same village that Robert Moses had chosen for his retirement home.

Almost everything else that is known about the last twenty-two years of Charles B. J. Snyder's life is personal, from the reminiscences of his granddaughters, Howard's children, Libby and Shirley (fig. 107). His son Robert's only daughter, Gail, perished in 2001. "Babu (their name for their grandfather) took Gail and me on day trips to New York to see some of the schools," Libby said, and remembered being impressed. In addition to fishing, Charles B. J. Snyder enjoyed his huge vegetable garden.

During the warm months Snyder took people for rides, swimming, and clam digging on the Great South Bay on the *Emily*, his boat, which he kept moored behind the house in Babylon, New York. His granddaughters remember Babu as a quiet, gentle, modest, sociable person, who never boasted about his numerous achievements and was not one to argue. In retirement Snyder became involved with the Catholic Diocese of Westchester, hosting an annual luncheon for the monsignors. Often on the way home from the Babylon, Long Island, train station, he would stop to socialize at

---

*Plans for a school were submitted by Howard Loeb in conjunction with C. B. J. Snyder, Consulting Architect to Loeb, for the Columbus School (*Standard Star*, 1923). Edward Hahn was chosen for Larchmont High School, with C. B. J. Snyder as consulting architect.

†This building notice appeared in the *New York Times*, June 15, 1934, within the Manhattan Alterations column: Church of St. Bernard, 330 W. 14th St., retained "C. B. J. Snyder, architect" for alterations at a cost of $10,000.

Figure 107. Granddaughters Elizabeth Orr and Shirley Skeffington. LaValle photo.

St. Joseph's Roman Catholic Church. He was also involved in Christ Episcopal Church in Babylon. Charles remained active with the Masons. He was involved in the New York chapter of the American Institute of Architects as a member of the Committee on Uneconomic Practices (AIA).

On November 11, 1945, a week after his eighty-fifth birthday and a month after he had been honored as a fifty-year member at the Masons' Annual Dinner, he, along with his son Robert, died in a tragic accident (fig. 108). Robert had been staying with his father at his summerhouse, which had no central heating. One of them would get up in the morning, light the oven, and use a cookie cutter to hold the oven door open to warm up the house. The iceman, making a delivery that morning, wondered why the dog didn't bark. All three residents, Babu, Robert, and their dog, had been asphyxiated by the gas from the open gas jet. Perhaps one of them thought he had lit the flame but hadn't. In any case, gas, not heat, had spread from the kitchen through to the rest of the house.[8]

The shock of two healthy family members dying unexpectedly occurred right at the end of World War II. Libby's second child was six months old, and Shirley had just had her first child. The family did not manage to arrange for a headstone, and the Department of Education, in chaos at the time, did not manage to notify the *New York Times*. Charles B. J. Snyder was

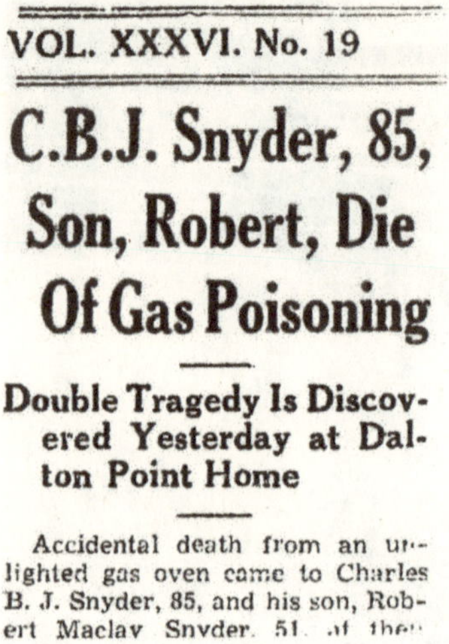

VOL. XXXVI. No. 19

C.B.J. Snyder, 85, Son, Robert, Die Of Gas Poisoning

Double Tragedy Is Discovered Yesterday at Dalton Point Home

Accidental death from an unlighted gas oven came to Charles B. J. Snyder, 85, and his son, Robert Maclav Snyder, 51, at the

Figure 108. *The Babylon Leader*, November 12, 1945. Belle Baxter and the Babylon Library.

buried in an unmarked grave in the Bronx in the Woodlawn Cemetery plot where he had provided flat headstones for the women in his life—his wife, sister, and mother. Finally, in 2008 his great-granddaughter, Cynthia LaValle, provided for installation of a flat headstone in remembrance of C. B. J. Snyder, Public School Architect, 1860–1945, BABU, in the family plot (fig. 109).

Figure 109. Snyder's Grave at Woodlawn Cemetery. Skeffington photo.

Figure 110. Snyder Family Members and Author at Gravesite. LaValle photo.

To celebrate the occasion, Cindy arranged a bus tour to visit some of Charles B. J. Snyder's schools for his descendants and family friends. Granddaughter, Libby Snyder Orr, at 91, once again got to experience and learn more about her grandfather's impressive schools, this time with her own and her sister's children instead of with her grandfather Charles B. J. Snyder (fig. 110).

LISTS OF SNYDER PUBLIC SCHOOLS

Snyder Schools by Borough and Name/PS Number

LEGEND
a—Built as an addition
a→ Built as an addition, building became stand-alone school
A—Addition to a current public school
AO—Addn now used for another purpose
DA—Demolished addition
es—East Side, ws—West Side, ns—North Side, ss—South Side

S—Current public school
O—Building now used for another purpose
O—Built for a purpose other than a school
DB—Demolished building
Boldfaced—Landmarked
<u>Underlined</u>—NRHP designation

BOROUGH	ORIGINAL DESIGNATION	YEAR	DECADE	STATUS	LOCATION
Bronx	Evander Childs High School (original)	1916	III	S	E 184 St/Field Pl x Morris/Creston Ave
Bronx	**Morris High School**	**1904**	**II**	**S**	**E 166 St/Home St x Boston Rd/Jackson Ave**
Bronx	PS 1 a	1895	I	DA	E 145th/E 146th St x College Ave
Bronx	PS 2 a	1902	II	DA	E 169th/E 170th St x Third Ave
Bronx	PS 3 a	1908	II	DA	E 157th St x Courtlandt/Melrose Ave
Bronx	PS 4	1898	I	S	E 173rd/174th x Fulton/Third Ave
Bronx	PS 6	1904	II	S	E Tremont Ave x Bryant/Vyse Ave

LEGEND

a—Built as an addition
a→ Built as an addition, building became stand-alone school
A—Addition to a current public school
AO—Addn now used for another purpose
DA—Demolished addition
es—East Side, ws—West Side, ns—North Side, ss—South Side

S—Current public school
O—Building now used for another purpose
O—Built for a purpose other than a school
DB—Demolished building
Boldfaced—Landmarked
<u>Underlined</u>—NRHP designation

BOROUGH	ORIGINAL DESIGNATION	YEAR	DECADE	STATUS	LOCATION
Bronx	PS 7	1895	I	DB	W 232 St x Kingsbridge/Corlear Ave
Bronx	PS 8	1898	I	DB	E 201st St /Mosholu Pkwy x Bainbridge/Briggs Ave
Bronx	PS 10 a	1906	II	DA	E 163rd St x Eagle Ave
Bronx	<u>**PS 11 a**</u> **(former PS 91)**	**1905**	**II**	**A**	**Ogden/Merriam Ave x W 169th St**
Bronx	PS 12	1915	III	S	Overing St x Frisby/Tratman Ave
Bronx	PS 13 a	1900	I	DA	E 216th St x Willett Ave
Bronx	PS 16 a→b	1909	II	S	E 239th St/E 240th St x Carpenter/Matilda Ave
Bronx	<u>**PS 17**</u> **(former PS 102)**	**1898**	**I**	**SO**	**Fordham St x King Ave**
Bronx	PS 19	1893	I	DB	E 234th/E 235th St x Kepler/Katonah Ave
Bronx	PS 20	1895	I	DB	E 167th St x Simpson/Fox St
Bronx	PS 21 a→b	1900	I	DB	E 225th St/E 226th St x White Plains Rd
Bronx	PS 23	1904	II	DB	E 165th St x Tinton/Union Ave
Bronx	PS 25	1898	I	S	E 149th St x Tinton/Prospect Ave
Bronx	PS 26	1899 & 1923	I	S	West Burnside Ave & Andrews Ave S
Bronx	PS 27	1898	I	S	E 147th St/E 148th St x St. Ann's Ave
Bronx	PS 28	1898	I	S	Anthony Ave x Mount Hope Pl/E Tremont Ave
Bronx	PS 29	1898	I	DB	E 135th St/E 136th St x Cypress Ave

LISTS OF SNYDER PUBLIC SCHOOLS

LEGEND
a—Built as an addition
a→ Built as an addition, building became stand-alone school
A—Addition to a current public school
AO—Addn now used for another purpose
DA—Demolished addition
es—East Side, ws—West Side, ns—North Side, ss—South Side

S—Current public school
O—Building now used for another purpose
O—Built for a purpose other than a school
DB—Demolished building
Boldfaced—Landmarked
Underlined—NRHP designation

BOROUGH	ORIGINAL DESIGNATION	YEAR	DECADE	STATUS	LOCATION
Bronx	PS 30	1900	I	S	E 141st St x Brook Ave
Bronx	**PS 31**	**1900**	**I**	**DB**	**E 144th St/E 146th St x Walton Ave**
Bronx	PS 32	1900	I	S	E 183rd St/Grote St x Cambreleng/Beaumont Ave
Bronx	PS 33	1901	II	S	E 184th St/Fordham Rd x Walton Ave/Jerome Ave
Bronx	PS 34	1904	II	DB	Victor/Amethyst St x Morris Park Ave
Bronx	PS 35	1902	II	S	E 163rd St x Morris/Grant Ave
Bronx	PS 36	1902	II	S	Castle Hill Ave x Blackrock/Watson Ave
Bronx	PS 37	1905	II	SO	E 145th/E 146th St x Willis/Brook Ave
Bronx	PS 38	1921	III	DB	E 157th/158th St x Third/Brook Ave
Bronx	PS 39	1905	II	S	Beck/Kelly St x Longwood Ave
Bronx	PS 40	1906	II	DB	Ritter Pl/Jennings St x Union/Prospect Ave
Bronx	PS 41	1906	II	S	Olinville Ave x Magenta St
Bronx	PS 42	1907	II	S	Washington Ave x Claremont Pkwy
Bronx	PS 43	1908	II	S	E 135th/136th St x Brown Place ws
Bronx	PS 43 Annex	1921	III	S	E 135th/136th St x Brown Place es
Bronx	PS 44	1911	III	S	Prospect Ave x E 176th St
Bronx	PS 45	1913	III	S	E 189th St x Lorillard Pl/Hoffman St

LEGEND

a—Built as an addition
a→ Built as an addition, building became stand-alone school
A—Addition to a current public school
AO—Addn now used for another purpose
DA—Demolished addition
es—East Side, ws—West Side, ns—North Side, ss—South Side

S—Current public school
O—Building now used for another purpose
O—Built for a purpose other than a school
DB—Demolished building
Boldfaced—Landmarked
Underlined—NRHP designation

BOROUGH	ORIGINAL DESIGNATION	YEAR	DECADE	STATUS	LOCATION
Bronx	PS 46	1912	III	S	E 196th St x Briggs/Bainbridge Ave
Bronx	PS 47	1912	III	S	E 172nd St x St Lawrence/Beach Ave
Bronx	PS 48	1917	III	S	Spoffard Ave x Coster/Faile St
Bronx	PS 50	1914	III	S	E 172nd /E 173rd St x Vyse Ave
Bronx	PS 51	1915	III	DB	E 158th St x Trinity/Jackson Ave
Bronx	PS 52	1914	III	S	Kelly St x Leggett Ave/Ave St. John
Bronx	PS 53	1914	III	S	E 168th St x Findlay/Teller Ave
Bronx	PS 54	1917	III	DB	Intervale Ave x Freeman/Chisholm St
Bronx	PS 55	1917	III	S	St Paul's Pl x Washington/Park Ave
Bronx	PS 56	1915	III	S	E 207th St x Hull/Decatur Ave
Bronx	PS 57	1921	III	S	E 180th St/E 181st St x Crotona/Belmont Ave
Bronx	PS 58	1922	III	S	E 176th St x Washington/Park Ave
Bronx	PS 59	1922	III	S	E 182nd St x Bathgate Ave
Bronx	PS 60	1922	III	S	E 163rd St x Rev J. A. Polite Ave
Bronx	PS 61	1922	III	S	Crotona Pk E/Boston Rd x Charlotte St
Bronx	PS 62	1922	III	S	Fox St x Leggett Ave

LEGEND

a—Built as an addition
a→ Built as an addition, building became stand-alone school
A—Addition to a current public school
AO—Addn now used for another purpose
DA—Demolished addition
es—East Side, ws—West Side, ns—North Side, ss—South Side

S—Current public school
O—Building now used for another purpose
O—Built for a purpose other than a school
DB—Demolished building
Boldfaced—Landmarked
Underlined—NRHP designation

BOROUGH	ORIGINAL DESIGNATION	YEAR	DECADE	STATUS	LOCATION
Bronx	PS 63	1924	III	S	E 168th/E 169th St x Franklin Ave
Bronx	PS 64	1923	III	S	E 171st/E 172nd St x Townsend/Walton Ave
Bronx	PS 65	1924	III	S	E 141st St x Cypress/Powers Ave
Bronx	PS 66	1924	III	S	Jennings/E 172nd St x Longfellow/Boone Ave
Bronx	PS 67	1924	III	S	E 178th/E 179th St x Mohegan Ave
Bronx	PS 69	1924	III	S	Randall Ave x Theriot/Leland Ave
Brooklyn	Bay Ridge High School	1915	III	S	4th Ave x 67th/Senator St
Brooklyn	**Boys' High School a**	**1912**	**III**	**A**	**Marcy Ave x Putnam Ave/Madison St**
Brooklyn	Bk HQ BoE	1907	II	O	Livingston St x Red Hook Lane/Smith St
Brooklyn	Bushwick High School	1913	III	S	Irving Ave x Woodbine/Putnam St
Brooklyn	Commercial High School	1906	II	S	Albany Ave x Bergen/Dean St
Brooklyn	Eastern District High School	1907	II	SO	Marcy Ave x Rodney/Keap St
Brooklyn	**Erasmus Hall High School**	**1906**	**II**	**S**	**Flatbush/Bedford Ave x Church/Snyder Ave**
Brooklyn	**Girls' High School a**	**1912**	**III**	**A**	**Nostrand/Marcy Ave x Halsey/Macon St**
Brooklyn	Thomas Jefferson High School	1924	III	S	Pennsylvania Ave x Dumont Ave

LEGEND

a—Built as an addition
a→ Built as an addition, building became stand-alone school
A—Addition to a current public school
AO—Addn now used for another purpose
DA—Demolished addition
es—East Side, ws—West Side, ns—North Side, ss—South Side

S—Current public school
O—Building now used for another purpose
O—Built for a purpose other than a school
DB—Demolished building
Boldfaced—Landmarked
Underlined—NRHP designation

BOROUGH	ORIGINAL DESIGNATION	YEAR	DECADE	STATUS	LOCATION
Brooklyn	Manual Training High School	1905	II	S	7th/8th Ave x 4th/5th St
Brooklyn	New Utrecht High School	1924	III	S	16th/17th Ave x 79th/80th St
Brooklyn	Teachers' Training School (PS 138)	1903	II	S	Prospect/Park Pl x Nostrand/Rogers Ave
Brooklyn	PS 16 a→b	1924	III	S	Wilson/Taylor St x Bedford/Lee Ave
Brooklyn	PS 17	1921	III	S	N 4th/5th St x Driggs ws
Brooklyn	PS 18 a→b	1916	III	S	Maujer St x Leonard/Manhattan Ave
Brooklyn	PS 19 a→b	1911	III	S	S 3rd St x Keap St
Brooklyn	PS 24 a	1908	II	DA	Beaver St x Belvidere St/Arion Pl
Brooklyn	PS 27 a	1906	II	A	Huntington St x Hicks St
Brooklyn	PS 28 a→b	1914	III	S	Herkimer/Fulton St x Ralph/Howard Ave
Brooklyn	PS 29	1921	III	S	Henry St x Harrison/Baltic St
Brooklyn	PS 30 a→b	1907	II	SO	Conover St x Sullivan/Walcott St
Brooklyn	PS 36 a	1915	III	DA	Stagg/TenEyck St x Bushwick/Waterbury Ave
Brooklyn	PS 42	1907	II	DB	St Marks Ave x Classon Ave
Brooklyn	PS 47	1904	II	DB	Pacific/Dean St x 3rd Ave/Nivens St
Brooklyn	PS 48	1915	III	S	18th Ave x 60th/61st St
Brooklyn	PS 50	1915	III	S	Roebling St/Driggs Ave x S 2nd/3rd St
Brooklyn	PS 53 a→b	1901	II	DA	Starr/Troutman St x Central/Hamburg Ave

LEGEND

a—Built as an addition
a→ Built as an addition, building became stand-alone school
A—Addition to a current public school
AO—Addn now used for another purpose
DA—Demolished addition
es—East Side, ws—West Side, ns—North Side, ss—South Side

S—Current public school
O—Building now used for another purpose
O—Built for a purpose other than a school
DB—Demolished building
Boldfaced—Landmarked
Underlined—NRHP designation

BOROUGH	ORIGINAL DESIGNATION	YEAR	DECADE	STATUS	LOCATION
Brooklyn	PS 54	1923	III	S	Sanford St x Willoughby/Dekalb Ave
Brooklyn	PS 56 a	1901	II	DA	Bushwick Ave x Madison St
Brooklyn	PS 63 a	1900	I	DA	Hinsdale/Williams St x Glenmore/Liberty Ave
Brooklyn	PS 64	1901	II	DB	Berriman St/Atkins Ave x Belmont/Pitkin Ave
Brooklyn	PS 66	1906	II	S	Osborn St/Watkins St (now Mother Gaston Blvd) x Sutter/Blake Ave
Brooklyn	PS 67	1923	III	S	St. Edwards St x Auburn Pl
Brooklyn	PS 70 a	1901	II	AO	Patchen/Ralph Ave x Macon St
Brooklyn	PS 72 a	1902	II	DA	New Lots Ave x Schenck Ave
Brooklyn	PS 73 a	1921	III	A	Rockaway Ave x Sumpter/McDougal St
Brooklyn	PS 75 a→b	1909	II	S	Evergreen/Central Ave x Grove St
Brooklyn	PS 80	1905	II	DB	W 17th St/W 19th St x Neptune/Mermaid Ave
Brooklyn	PS 83 a→b	1907	II	SO	Schenectady Ave x Dean/Bergen St
Brooklyn	PS 84 a	1904	II	DA	Stone/Watkins St x Glenmore Ave ss
Brooklyn	PS 85 a→b	1906	II	DB	Evergreen Ave x Eldert/Covert St
Brooklyn	PS 89 a	1906	II	DA	Newkirk Ave ns x 31st/32nd St
Brooklyn	PS 91	1904	II	S	Albany Ave x East New York Ave/Maple St

LEGEND

a—Built as an addition
a→ Built as an addition, building became stand-alone school
A—Addition to a current public school
AO—Addn now used for another purpose
DA—Demolished addition
es—East Side, ws—West Side, ns—North Side, ss—South Side

S—Current public school
O—Building now used for another purpose
O—Built for a purpose other than a school
DB—Demolished building
Boldfaced—Landmarked
Underlined—NRHP designation

BOROUGH	ORIGINAL DESIGNATION	YEAR	DECADE	STATUS	LOCATION
Brooklyn	PS 92 a→b	1906	II	S	Rogers/Bedford Ave x Parkside Ave/Winthrop St
Brooklyn	PS 93	1909	II	S	New York Ave x Herkimer St
Brooklyn	PS 94	1908	II	S	6th Ave x 50th/52nd St
Brooklyn	PS 95	1915	III	S	Van Sicklen St x Gravesend Neck Rd
Brooklyn	PS 97 a→b	1921	III	S	Ave S/Highlawn Ave x Stillwell Ave/W 13th St
Brooklyn	PS 99	1914	III	S	Ave K/L x E 9th/E 10th St
Brooklyn	PS 100	1921	III	S	W 3rd/2nd St x W Brighton Ave/W 2nd Pl
Brooklyn	PS 102	1901	II	S	Ridge Blvd/3rd Ave x 71st/72nd St
Brooklyn	PS 103 a→b	1906	II	SO	14th/15th Ave x 53rd/54th St
Brooklyn	PS 104 a→b	1907	II	DB	92nd St x Gelston/5th Ave
Brooklyn	PS 109 a	1907	II	DA	Dumont/Lavonia Ave x Junius/Powell St
Brooklyn	PS 110 a	1906	II	A	Monitor St/Kingsland Ave x Driggs Ave
Brooklyn	PS 112	1905	II	S	15th Ave x 73rd/74th St
Brooklyn	PS 114	1907	II	S	Glenwood Rd/Bay View Pl x Remsen Ave/E 92nd St
Brooklyn	PS 115	1922	III	S	E 92nd St x Ave M/Ave L
Brooklyn	PS 119	1904	II	S	Ave K x E 38th/39th St
Brooklyn	PS 120	1901	II	DB	Barren Island
Brooklyn	PS 122	1902	II	SO	Harrison Ave/Broadway x Rutledge/Heyward St
Brooklyn	PS 123	1903	II	S	Irving/Wykoff Ave x Willoughby Ave/Suydam St

LEGEND

a—Built as an addition
a→ Built as an addition, building became stand-alone school
A—Addition to a current public school
AO—Addn now used for another purpose
DA—Demolished addition
es—East Side, ws—West Side, ns—North Side, ss—South Side

S—Current public school
O—Building now used for another purpose
O—Built for a purpose other than a school
DB—Demolished building
Boldfaced—Landmarked
Underlined—NRHP designation

BOROUGH	ORIGINAL DESIGNATION	YEAR	DECADE	STATUS	LOCATION
Brooklyn	PS 124	1901	II	S	4th Ave x 13th/14th St
Brooklyn	PS 125	1901	II	SO	Blake Ave x Rockaway Ave
Brooklyn	PS 126	1902	II	S	Meserole Ave/Calyer St x Lorimer St/Guernsey St
Brooklyn	PS 127	1902	II	S	Fort Hamilton Pkwy x 78th/79th St
Brooklyn	PS 128	1902	II	S	21st Ave x 83rd/84th St
Brooklyn	PS 129	1903	II	DB	Quincy St/Gates Ave x Stuyvesant/Lewis Ave
Brooklyn	PS 130	1903	II	S	Ocean Pkwy/E 5th St x Fort Hamilton Ave
Brooklyn	PS 131	1902	II	S	Fort Hamilton Pkwy x 43rd/44th St
Brooklyn	PS 132	1902	II	S	Manhattan Ave x Metropolitan Ave/Conselyea St
Brooklyn	PS 133	1901	II	DB	Butler/Baltic St x 4th/5th Ave
Brooklyn	PS 134	1902	II	S	18th/Webster Ave x E 4th/E 5th St
Brooklyn	PS 135	1923	III	S	Linden Blvd x Schenectady Ave/E 48th St
Brooklyn	PS 135	1909	II	DB	Linden Blvd x Schenectady Ave/E 48th St
Brooklyn	PS 136	1902	II	S	4th Ave ws x 40th/41st St
Brooklyn	PS 137	1902	II	S	Saratoga Ave x Chauncey/Bainbridge St
Brooklyn	PS 138 (Teachers' Training School)	1907	II	S	Prospect Pl/Park Pl x Nostrand/Rogers Ave
Brooklyn	PS 139	1903	II	S	Cortelyou Rd x Rugby Rd/Argyle Rd

LEGEND

a—Built as an addition
a→ Built as an addition, building became stand-alone school
A—Addition to a current public school
AO—Addn now used for another purpose
DA—Demolished addition
es—East Side, ws—West Side, ns—North Side, ss—South Side

S—Current public school
O—Building now used for another purpose
O—Built for a purpose other than a school
DB—Demolished building
Boldfaced—Landmarked
Underlined—NRHP designation

BOROUGH	ORIGINAL DESIGNATION	YEAR	DECADE	STATUS	LOCATION
Brooklyn	PS 140	1902	II	DB	60th St x 3rd/4th Ave
Brooklyn	PS 141	1903	II	DB	Leonard St x Boerum St/McKibbin St
Brooklyn	PS 142	1904	II	S	Henry St x Rapelye St/4th Pl
Brooklyn	PS 143	1904	II	S	Havemeyer St x N 6th/7th St
Brooklyn	PS 144	1904	II	DB	Howard Ave x St Marks/Prospect Pl
Brooklyn	PS 145	1904	II	S	Noll St x Central Ave
Brooklyn	PS 146	1905	II	S	18th/19th St x 6th/7th Ave
Brooklyn	PS 147	1906	II	S	Bushwick Ave x McKibbin St/Seigel St
Brooklyn	PS 148	1907	II	S	Ellery/Hopkins St x Delmonico Pl/Throop Ave
Brooklyn	PS 149	1906	II	S	Sutter Ave x Wyona/Vermont St
Brooklyn	PS 150	1908	II	S	Sackman St/Christopher Ave x Belmont/Sutter Ave
Brooklyn	PS 151	1906	II	S	Knickerbocker Ave x Halsey/Weirfield St
Brooklyn	PS 152	1908	II	S	Glenwood Road x E 23rd/24th St
Brooklyn	PS 153	1909	II	S	E 12th St/Homecrest Ave x Ave T
Brooklyn	PS 154	1908	II	S	11thAve x Windsor Pl/Sherman St
Brooklyn	PS 155	1908	II	S	Herkimer/Fulton St x Eastern Pkwy
Brooklyn	PS 156	1909	II	DB	Sutter Ave x Grafton St
Brooklyn	PS 157	1909	II	S	Taaffe Pl/Kent Ave x Park/Myrtle Ave

LEGEND

a—Built as an addition
a→ Built as an addition, building became stand-alone school
A—Addition to a current public school
AO—Addn now used for another purpose
DA—Demolished addition
es—East Side, ws—West Side, ns—North Side, ss—South Side

S—Current public school
O—Building now used for another purpose
O—Built for a purpose other than a school
DB—Demolished building
Boldfaced—Landmarked
Underlined—NRHP designation

BOROUGH	ORIGINAL DESIGNATION	YEAR	DECADE	STATUS	LOCATION
Brooklyn	PS 158	1909	II	S	Belmont Ave x Warwick/Ashford St
Brooklyn	PS 159	1908	II	S	Pitkin Ave x Hemlock/Crescent St
Brooklyn	PS 160	1909	II	S	Fort Hamilton Ave x 51st/52nd St
Brooklyn	PS 161	1923	III	S	Crown St x New York Ave/Nostrand Ave
Brooklyn	PS 162	1909	II	S	St Nicholas Ave x Willoughby Ave/Suydam St
Brooklyn	PS 163	1909	II	S	Benson Ave x 17th Ave/Bay 14th St
Brooklyn	PS 164	1910	II	S	14th Ave x 42nd/43rd St
Brooklyn	PS 165	1912	III	S	Lott Ave x Amboy St/Thomas S Boyland St
Brooklyn	PS 167	1911	III	S	Schenectady Ave x Eastern Pkwy/Lincoln Pl
Brooklyn	PS 168	1912	III	SO	Throop Ave x Whipple/Bartlett St
Brooklyn	PS 169	1915	III	S	7th Ave x 43rd/44th St
Brooklyn	PS 170	1915	III	S	71st/72nd St x 6th/Stewart Ave
Brooklyn	PS 171	1912	III	S	Ridgewood Ave x Lincoln/Nichols Ave
Brooklyn	PS 172	1914	III	S	4th Ave x 29th/30th St
Brooklyn	PS 173	1913	III	S	Pennsylvania Ave x Liberty/Glenmore Ave
Brooklyn	PS 174	1913	III	S	Dumont Ave x Williams/Alabama Ave
Brooklyn	PS 175	1914	III	S	Blake Ave x Thomas S Boyland/Bristol St

LEGEND

a—Built as an addition
a→ Built as an addition, building became stand-alone school
A—Addition to a current public school
AO—Addn now used for another purpose
DA—Demolished addition
es—East Side, ws—West Side, ns—North Side, ss—South Side

S—Current public school
O—Building now used for another purpose
O—Built for a purpose other than a school
DB—Demolished building
Boldfaced—Landmarked
Underlined—NRHP designation

BOROUGH	ORIGINAL DESIGNATION	YEAR	DECADE	STATUS	LOCATION
Brooklyn	PS 176	1914	III	S	68th St/Bay Ridge Ave x 12th Ave
Brooklyn	PS 178	1915	III	S	Dean/Pacific St x Thomas S Boyland St/Saratoga Ave
Brooklyn	PS 179	1915	III	S	E 2nd/3rd St x Ave C
Brooklyn	PS 181	1922	III	S	New York Ave/E 34th St x Snyder/Tilden Ave
Brooklyn	PS 182	1921	III	SO	Wyona/Vermont St x Dumont Ave
Brooklyn	PS 183	1923	III	S	Riverdale Ave x Strauss/Herzl St
Brooklyn	PS 184	1923	III	S	Newport St x Watkins St/Mother Gaston Blvd
Brooklyn	PS 185	1921	III	S	86th/87th St x Ridge Blvd
Brooklyn	PS 186	1923	III	S	19th Ave x 76th/77th St
Brooklyn	PS 187	1923	III	S	64th/65thSt x 11/12 Ave
Brooklyn	PS 188	1924	III	S	Neptune Ave x W 33rd/W 35th St
Brooklyn	PS 189	1923	III	S	East New York Ave x E 96th St/Rockaway Pkwy
Brooklyn	PS 190	1924	III	S	Sheffield Ave x New Lots/Riverdale Ave
Brooklyn	PS 192	1924	III	S	18th Ave x Bergen Ln/48th St
Brooklyn	PS 193	1924	III	S	Ave L x Bedford Ave / E 26th St
Manhattan	The original DeWitt Clinton High School (Formerly Boys' High School)	1906	II	SO	W 58th/59th St x 10th Ave

LEGEND

a—Built as an addition
a→ Built as an addition, building became stand-alone school
A—Addition to a current public school
AO—Addn now used for another purpose
DA—Demolished addition
es—East Side, ws—West Side, ns—North Side, ss—South Side

S—Current public school
O—Building now used for another purpose
O—Built for a purpose other than a school
DB—Demolished building
Boldfaced—Landmarked
Underlined—NRHP designation

BOROUGH	ORIGINAL DESIGNATION	YEAR	DECADE	STATUS	LOCATION
Manhattan	George Washington High School	1925	III	S	W 191st/W 192nd St x Audubon Ave
Manhattan	GS 1	1899	I	S	Henry St x Catherine/Oliver St
Manhattan	GS 24 a	1895	I	DA	E 128th St x Madison/Fifth Ave
Manhattan	High School of Commerce	1903	II	DB	W 65th/W 66th St x Amsterdam/Broadway
Manhattan	Julia Richman High School	1923	III	S	E 67th/E 68th St x First/Second Ave
Manhattan	Manhattan Trade School for Girls	1917	III	S	E 22nd St x Lexington Ave
Manhattan	Normal College	1913	III	SO	E 68th/E 69th St x Lexington Ave
Manhattan	PS 2	1899	I	DB	Henry St/Madison x Pike/Rutgers St
Manhattan	PS 3	1907	II	S	Grove St x Bedford/Hudson St
Manhattan	PS 4	1908	II	SO	Rivington Ave x Ridge/Pitt St
Manhattan	PS 4 a	1895	I	DA	Rivington ss x Ridge/Pitt St
Manhattan	PS 5	1895	I	DB	W 140th/W 141st St x Edgecombe/Frederick Douglass Ave
Manhattan	PS 6	1894	I	DB	E 85th/E 86th St x Madison Ave es
Manhattan	PS 7	1893	I	DB	Hester x Christie St
Manhattan	**PS 9 (former GS 9)**	**1896**	**I**	**S**	**W 82nd St x West End Ave**
Manhattan	PS 10	1895	I	DB	W 117th St x St Nicholas

LEGEND

a—Built as an addition
a→ Built as an addition, building became stand-alone school
A—Addition to a current public school
AO—Addn now used for another purpose
DA—Demolished addition
es—East Side, ws—West Side, ns—North Side, ss—South Side

S—Current public school
O—Building now used for another purpose
O—Built for a purpose other than a school
DB—Demolished building
Boldfaced—Landmarked
<u>Underlined</u>—NRHP designation

BOROUGH	ORIGINAL DESIGNATION	YEAR	DECADE	STATUS	LOCATION
Manhattan	PS 11	1925	III	S	W 20th/W 21st St x Eighth/Ninth Ave
Manhattan	PS 12	1908	II	SO	Madison St x Jackson St
Manhattan	PS 13 a→b	1898	I	DB	East Houston St x Essex/Norfolk St
Manhattan	PS 15	1906	II	S	E 4th St x Ave C/Ave D
Manhattan	PS 16a	1899	I	AO	W 13th St x Seventh/Eighth Ave
Manhattan	PS 17	1909	II	S	W 47th/W 48th St x Eighth/Ninth Ave
Manhattan	PS 18 a→b	1903	II	DB	E 51st/E 52nd St x Lexington/Park Ave
Manhattan	PS 19 a→b	1894	I	DB	E 13th/14th St x First/Second Ave
Manhattan	PS 20	1899	I	SO	Rivington St x Forsyth/Eldridge St
Manhattan	PS 21/106	1904	II	DB	Spring/Prince St x Elizabeth/Mott St
Manhattan	PS 22 a→b	1902	II	DB	Stanton St x Sheriff St
Manhattan	PS 23	1893	I	SO	Mott St x Bayard St
Manhattan	PS 24	1905	II	S	E 128th St x Madison/Fifth Ave
Manhattan	PS 25 a→b	1894	I	S	E 4th/E 5th St x First/Second Ave
Manhattan	PS 27	1908	II	DB	E 41st/E 42nd St x Second/Third Ave
Manhattan	PS 29	1894	I	DB	Washington St x Albany/Carlisle St
Manhattan	PS 30	1896	I	DB	E 88th St x Second/Third Ave
Manhattan	PS 31	1904	II	S	Monroe St x Gouverneur St

LEGEND

a—Built as an addition
a→ Built as an addition, building became stand-alone school
A—Addition to a current public school
AO—Addn now used for another purpose
DA—Demolished addition
es—East Side, ws—West Side, ns—North Side, ss—South Side

S—Current public school
O—Building now used for another purpose
O—Built for a purpose other than a school
DB—Demolished building
Boldfaced—Landmarked
Underlined—NRHP designation

BOROUGH	ORIGINAL DESIGNATION	YEAR	DECADE	STATUS	LOCATION
Manhattan	PS 37a→b	1898	I	DB	E 17th/E 18th St x Lexington/Park Ave
Manhattan	PS 38	1906	II	S	Watts/Broome St x Sixth Ave
Manhattan	PS 39 a→b	1904	II	DB	E 125th/E 126th St x Second/Third Ave
Manhattan	PS 40	1900	I	S	E 19th/E 20th St x First/Second Ave
Manhattan	PS 41 a	1908	II	DA	W 10th/W 11th St x Greenwich Ave
Manhattan	PS 42	1898	I	S	Hester St x Orchard/Ludlow St
Manhattan	PS 43 a	1895	I	DA	W 129th St x Amsterdam Ave
Manhattan	PS 44	1902	II	DB	Hubert St x Collister St
Manhattan	PS 46 a	1901	II	DA	W 156th St x St Nicholas Ave
Manhattan	PS 47	1925	III	S	E 23rd St x Second/Third Ave
Manhattan	PS 49 a	1903	II	DA	E 37th/E 38th St x Second/Third Ave
Manhattan	PS 50 a	1908	II	DA	E 20th/E 21st St x Second/Third Ave
Manhattan	PS 51 a→b	1908	II	SO	W 44th/W 45th St x Tenth/Eleventh Ave
Manhattan	PS 52	1915	III	S	Academy St x Broadway/Vermilyea Ave
Manhattan	PS 53 a→b	1894	I	DB	E 79th/E 80th St x Second/Third Ave
Manhattan	PS 54 a	1894	I	DA	W 104th St x Amsterdam Ave

LEGEND

a—Built as an addition
a→ Built as an addition, building became stand-alone school
A—Addition to a current public school
AO—Addn now used for another purpose
DA—Demolished addition
es—East Side, ws—West Side, ns—North Side, ss—South Side

S—Current public school
O—Building now used for another purpose
O—Built for a purpose other than a school
DB—Demolished building
Boldfaced—Landmarked
<u>Underlined</u>—NRHP designation

BOROUGH	ORIGINAL DESIGNATION	YEAR	DECADE	STATUS	LOCATION
Manhattan	PS 56 a	1923	III	DA	W 18th St x Eighth/Ninth Ave
Manhattan	PS 57 a→b	1895	I	DB	E 114th/E 115th St x Lexington/Third Ave
Manhattan	PS 58 a	1895	I	DA	W 52nd St x Eighth/Ninth Ave
Manhattan	PS 59 a→b	1909	II	DB	E 56th/E 57th St x Second/Third Ave
Manhattan	PS 60	1925	III	S	E 11th/E 12th St x First Ave/Ave A
Manhattan	PS 61	1913	III	S	E 12th St x Ave B/Ave C
Manhattan	PS 62	1905	II	DB	Hester St x Essex/Norfolk St
Manhattan	PS 63	1906	II	S	E 3rd/E 4th St x First Ave/Ave A
Manhattan	**PS 64**	**1906**	**II**	**SO**	**E 9th/E 10th St x Ave B/Ave C**
Manhattan	PS 65	1908	II	DB	Hester/Canal St x Eldridge/Forsyth St
Manhattan	PS 66	1908	II	S	E 88th St x First/York Ave
Manhattan	**PS 67**	**1894**	**I**	**S**	**W 46th St x Sixth/Seventh Ave**
Manhattan	PS 68 a	1907	II	AO	W 127th/128th St x Lenox/Seventh Ave
Manhattan	PS 69 a→b	1893	I	DB	W 54th /W 55th St x Sixth/Seventh Ave
Manhattan	PS 71 a	1906	II	DA	E 6th/E 7th St x Ave B
Manhattan	PS 72 Annex	1924	III	S	E 104th/E 105th x Lexington Ave
Manhattan	**PS 72 a→b**	**1914**	**III**	**SO**	**E 104th/E 105th x Lexington Ave ws**

LEGEND

a—Built as an addition
a→ Built as an addition, building became stand-alone school
A—Addition to a current public school
AO—Addn now used for another purpose
DA—Demolished addition
es—East Side, ws—West Side, ns—North Side, ss—South Side

S—Current public school
O—Building now used for another purpose
O—Built for a purpose other than a school
DB—Demolished building
Boldfaced—Landmarked
Underlined—NRHP designation

BOROUGH	ORIGINAL DESIGNATION	YEAR	DECADE	STATUS	LOCATION
Manhattan	PS 74 a	1922	III	DA	E 63rd St x Second/Third Ave
Manhattan	PS 75 a→b	1896	I	DA	Hester St x Essex/Norfolk St
Manhattan	PS 78 a	1912	III	DA	E 119th St x Pleasant Ave
Manhattan	PS 80	1924	III	S	E 120th /E 121st St x First Ave
Manhattan	PS 81	1908	II	S	W 119th /W 120th St x Seventh/Eight Ave
Manhattan	PS 83 a→b	1905	II	DB	E 109th /E 110th St x Second/Third Ave
Manhattan	PS 85	1906	II	SO	E 117th St x First Ave
Manhattan	PS 87 a	1895	I	DA	W 77th St x Amsterdam Ave
Manhattan	PS 88 a	1895	I	DA	Rivington St x Lewis St
Manhattan	PS 89 a	1903	II	DA	W 134th St x Lenox Ave
Manhattan	PS 90	1907	II	SO	W 147th /W 148th St x Seventh/Eighth Ave
Manhattan	PS 91	1908	II	S	Forsyth St x Stanton St
Manhattan	PS 92 a	1898	I	DA	Broome St x Ridge St
Manhattan	PS 93 a	1898	I	DA	W 93rd St x Amsterdam Ave
Manhattan	PS 94 a	1898	I	DA	W 68th St x Amsterdam Ave
Manhattan	PS 95	1912	III	S	Clarkson/Houston St x Hudson/Varick St
Manhattan	PS 96	1895	I	DB	E 81st/E 82nd St x York Ave
Manhattan	PS 97	1915	III	S	Mangin x Stanton St/E Houston St

LEGEND

a—Built as an addition
a→ Built as an addition, building became stand-alone school
A—Addition to a current public school
AO—Addn now used for another purpose
DA—Demolished addition
es—East Side, ws—West Side, ns—North Side, ss—South Side

S—Current public school
O—Building now used for another purpose
O—Built for a purpose other than a school
DB—Demolished building
Boldfaced—Landmarked
Underlined—NRHP designation

BOROUGH	ORIGINAL DESIGNATION	YEAR	DECADE	STATUS	LOCATION
Manhattan	PS 100	1909	II	DB	W 138th/W 139th St x Lenox/Fifth Ave
Manhattan	PS 101	1910	II	S	E 111th/E 112th St x Park/Lexington Ave
Manhattan	PS 102	1914	III	S	E 113th St x First/Second Ave
Manhattan	PS 103	1896	I	DB	E 119th St x Madison Ave
Manhattan	PS 104 a→b	1905	II	DB	E 16th/E 17th St x Ave A/First Ave
Manhattan	PS 105	1897	I	SO	E 4th St x Ave B/Ave C
Manhattan	PS 107 a	1905	II	AO	W 10th St x Greenwich St
Manhattan	**PS 109**	**1901**	**II**	**SO**	**E 99th/E 100th St x Second/Third Ave**
Manhattan	PS 110	1904	II	S	Broome/Delancey St x Cannon/Lewis St
Manhattan	PS 114	1909	II	SO	Oak St x Oliver St/St James Pl
Manhattan	PS 115	1914	III	S	W 176th/W 177th St x St Nicholas/Audubon Ave
Manhattan	PS 119	1901	II	DB	W 133rd/W 134th St x Seventh/Eighth Ave
Manhattan	PS 121/38	1924	III	S	E 102nd/E 103rd St x Second/Third Ave
Manhattan	PS 121 a→b	1908	II	DB	E 102nd/E 103rd St x Second/Third Ave
Manhattan	PS 122	1895	I	SO	E 9th St x First Ave
Manhattan	PS 130	1921	III	S	Hester x Baxter St
Manhattan	PS 132	1905	II	S	W 182nd St x Wadsworth Ave
Manhattan	PS 135 a	1895	I	AO	E 51st St x First Ave

LEGEND

a—Built as an addition
a→ Built as an addition, building became stand-alone school
A—Addition to a current public school
AO—Addn now used for another purpose
DA—Demolished addition
es—East Side, ws—West Side, ns—North Side, ss—South Side

S—Current public school
O—Building now used for another purpose
O—Built for a purpose other than a school
DB—Demolished building
Boldfaced—Landmarked
Underlined—NRHP designation

BOROUGH	ORIGINAL DESIGNATION	YEAR	DECADE	STATUS	LOCATION
Manhattan	PS 137 a	1899	I	DA	Grand St x Ludlow/Essex St
Manhattan	PS 139	1924	III	SO	W 139th /W 140th St x Seventh/Lenox Ave
Manhattan	PS 147	1899	I	DB	Henry St/East Broadway x Gouverneur/Scammel St
Manhattan	PS 150	1905	II	S	E 95th /E 96th St x First/Second Ave
Manhattan	PS 151	1897	I	DB	E 91st St x First Ave
Manhattan	<u>PS 157</u>	1900	I	SO	W 126th/W 127th St x St Nicholas
Manhattan	PS 158	1899	I	S	E 77th/E 78th St x York Ave
Manhattan	PS 159	1900	I	DB	E 119th/E 120th St x Second/Third Ave
Manhattan	PS 160	1899	I	SO	Rivington St x Suffolk St
Manhattan	PS 165	1900	I	S	W 108th/W 109th St x Amsterdam/Broadway Ave
Manhattan	**PS 166**	**1900**	**I**	**S**	**W 89th St x Columbus/ Amsterdam Ave**
Manhattan	PS 168	1901	II	SO	E 104th /E 105th St x First/Second Ave
Manhattan	PS 169	1900	I	DB	W 168th St/W 169th St x St Nicholas Ave
Manhattan	PS 170	1901	II	DB	W 111th/W 112th St x Fifth/Lenox Ave
Manhattan	PS 171	1902	II	S	E 103rd/E 104th St x Fifth/Madison Ave
Manhattan	PS 172	1901	II	SO	E 108th/E 109th St x First/Second Ave
Manhattan	PS 174	1901	II	DB	Attorney St x Rivington St

LEGEND

a—Built as an addition
a→ Built as an addition, building became stand-alone school
A—Addition to a current public school
AO—Addn now used for another purpose
DA—Demolished addition
es—East Side, ws—West Side, ns—North Side, ss—South Side

S—Current public school
O—Building now used for another purpose
O—Built for a purpose other than a school
DB—Demolished building
Boldfaced—Landmarked
Underlined—NRHP designation

BOROUGH	ORIGINAL DESIGNATION	YEAR	DECADE	STATUS	LOCATION
Manhattan	PS 177	1901	II	DB	Market St x Monroe St
Manhattan	PS 179	1901	II	DB	W 101st/W 102nd St x Amsterdam/Columbus Ave
Manhattan	PS 183	1904	II	S	E 66th/E 67th St x First/York Ave
Manhattan	PS 184	1902	II	DB	W 116th/117th St x Fifth/Lenox Ave
Manhattan	PS 186	1903	II	SO	W 145th/W 146th St x Amsterdam/Broadway
Manhattan	PS 188	1903	II	S	East Houston St x Lewis St (Baruch and Lillian Wald Dr)
Manhattan	PS 189	1923	III	S	W 188th/W 189th St x Amsterdam Ave ws
Manhattan	PS 190	1904	II	S	E 82nd/E 83rd St x First/Second Ave
Manhattan	**Former Stuyvesant High School**	1908	II	S	E 15th/E16th St x First/Second Ave
Manhattan	Washington Irving High School	1915	III	S	E 16th/E 17th St x Irving Pl
Manhattan	**Wadleigh High School for Girls**	1902	II	S	W 114th/W 115th St x Seventh/Eighth Ave
Queens	**Flushing High School**	1915	III	S	Union St/ Parsons Blvd x 35th Ave/Northern Blvd
Queens	Long Island City High School (former)	1904	II	S	40th/41st Ave x 28th/29th St
Queens	**Newtown High School**	1922	III	S	48/50th Ave x 90th/91st St
Queens	Parental School	1908	II	SO	Kissena Blvd x Melbourne Ave
Queens	PS 1 a	1906	II	AO	46th Rd x 21st St, LIC

LISTS OF SNYDER PUBLIC SCHOOLS · 225

LEGEND
a—Built as an addition
a→ Built as an addition, building became stand-alone school
A—Addition to a current public school
AO—Addn now used for another purpose
DA—Demolished addition
es—East Side, ws—West Side, ns—North Side, ss—South Side

S—Current public school
O—Building now used for another purpose
O—Built for a purpose other than a school
DB—Demolished building
Boldfaced—Landmarked
Underlined—NRHP designation

BOROUGH	ORIGINAL DESIGNATION	YEAR	DECADE	STATUS	LOCATION
Queens	PS 3 (1907)	1921	III	S	68th Dr/69th Ave x 110 St, Forest Hills
Queens	PS 3 (1921)	1907	II	DB	68th Dr/69th Ave x 110 St, Forest Hills
Queens	PS 4 a	1906	II	DA	Crescent Ave/27th x 40th Ave, LIC
Queens	PS 5	1903	II	DB	29th/30th St x 30th Ave, ns
Queens	PS 6 a→b	1905	II	DB	Steinway/38th St x Broadway/31st Ave
Queens	PS 7 a→b	1911	III	DB	80–55 Cornish Ave, Elmhurst
Queens	PS 9	1907	II	S	57th St x 58th Dr.
Queens	PS 14	1915	III	S	Otis Ave x 108th St.
Queens	PS 16	1908	II	S	104th St x 42nd/41st Ave
Queens	PS 17 a	1905	II	DA	28–37 29th St, LIC
Queens	PS 19	1924	III	S	98–02 Roosevelt Ave, Corona
Queens	PS 20 a	1908	II	DA	142–30 Barclay Ave, Flushing
Queens	PS 23 a	1907	II	DA	35th Ave x Union St, Flushing
Queens	PS 28 a	1905	II	DA	109–10 47th Ave, Corona
Queens	PS 30 a	1905	II	DA	11th St, Whitestone
Queens	PS 39 a	1907	II	DA	Nameoke Street & Dinsmore Avenue
Queens	PS 39	1921	III	DB	Nameoke Street & Dinsmore Avenue
Queens	PS 40	1912	III	S	Union Hall St x Brinkerhoff/109th Ave
Queens	PS 41	1917	III	S	35th Ave x 214th Pl/ 214th Ln

LEGEND

a—Built as an addition
a→ Built as an addition, building became stand-alone school
A—Addition to a current public school
AO—Addn now used for another purpose
DA—Demolished addition
es—East Side, ws—West Side, ns—North Side, ss—South Side

S—Current public school
O—Building now used for another purpose
O—Built for a purpose other than a school
DB—Demolished building
Boldfaced—Landmarked
Underlined—NRHP designation

BOROUGH	ORIGINAL DESIGNATION	YEAR	DECADE	STATUS	LOCATION
Queens	PS 42 a→b	1905	II	DA	488 Beach 66th St, Arverne
Queens	PS 44 a→b	1922	III	DA	Beach 94th St, Rockaway Beach
Queens	PS 45 a→b	1915	III	S	149th/150th St x Sutter Ave/Rockaway Blvd
Queens	PS 50	1922	III	S	101st Ave x Allendale St
Queens	PS 51 a→b	1903	II	DB	117th St x Jamaica Ave/89th Ave
Queens	PS 54	1923	III	S	127th St x Hillside/Jamaica Ave
Queens	PS 56	1909	II	S	114th St x 86th Ave
Queens	PS 57	1922	III	DB	124th St, Morris Park
Queens	PS 58 a	1905	II	DA	97th Ave x 92nd/93rd St
Queens	**PS 66 a**	**1907**	**II**	**A**	**102nd St x 85th Rd**
Queens	PS 68	1907	II	S	St. Felix Ave x Seneca Ave
Queens	PS 69	1924	III	S	37th Ave x 77th/78th St
Queens	PS 70	1924	III	S	42nd St x 30th/31st Ave
Queens	PS 71 a→b	1915	III	S	Forest Ave x Bleecker St
Queens	PS 72 a→b	1922	III	DB	Maspeth Ave near Fresh Pond Rd
Queens	PS 76 a	1907	II	DA	10th St x 36th/37th Ave
Queens	PS 77	1911	III	S	Seneca Ave x Centre/George St
Queens	PS 78	1901	II	DB	Maurice Ave x 67th/68th St
Queens	PS 79	1902	II	S	15th Dr x 147th/149th St
Queens	PS 80	1903	II	SO	Greenpoint Ave x Bradley/Gale Ave

LEGEND

a—Built as an addition
a→ Built as an addition, building became stand-alone school
A—Addition to a current public school
AO—Addn now used for another purpose
DA—Demolished addition
es—East Side, ws—West Side, ns—North Side, ss—South Side

S—Current public school
O—Building now used for another purpose
O—Built for a purpose other than a school
DB—Demolished building
Boldfaced—Landmarked
<u>Underlined</u>—NRHP designation

BOROUGH	ORIGINAL DESIGNATION	YEAR	DECADE	STATUS	LOCATION
Queens	PS 81	1905	II	S	Cypress Ave x Menahan/Bleecker St
Queens	PS 82	1906	II	S	144th St x 88th Ave/88th Rd
Queens	PS 83	1904	II	DB	Vernon Ave/9th St x 34th/35thAve, LIC
Queens	PS 84	1905	II	S	41st St x Ditmars Blvd/23rd Ave
Queens	PS 85	1908	II	S	31st St x 23rd Rd/24th Ave
Queens	PS 86	1908	II	DB	Parsons Blvd x Normal Rd/Highland Ave
Queens	PS 87a→b	1909	II	S	80th St x 67th Dr/68th Ave
Queens	PS 88	1907	II	S	Catalpa Ave x 60th Ln/Fresh Pond Rd
Queens	PS 89	1908	II	S	Britton Ave x Gleane St/Hampton St
Queens	PS 90	1909	II	S	109th St x Jamaica Ave/86th Ave
Queens	PS 91	1915	III	S	Central Ave x 68th Pl/69th St
Queens	PS 92	1913	III	DB	34th Ave x 99th St
Queens	PS 93	1917	III	S	Forest Ave x Madison St/Woodbine St
Queens	PS 94	1914	III	S	Little Neck Parkway x 41st Dr/42nd Ave
Queens	PS 95	1915	III	S	90 Ave x 179th St/179th Pl
Queens	PS 96	1915	III	S	Rockaway Blvd x Lincoln St/130th St
Queens	PS 97	1917	III	S	Stillwell Ave x 82nd St
Queens	PS 102	1923	III	S	Van Horn St x 55th Rd

LEGEND

a—Built as an addition
a→ Built as an addition, building became stand-alone school
A—Addition to a current public school
AO—Addn now used for another purpose
DA—Demolished addition
es—East Side, ws—West Side, ns—North Side, ss—South Side

S—Current public school
O—Building now used for another purpose
O—Built for a purpose other than a school
DB—Demolished building
Boldfaced—Landmarked
<u>Underlined</u>—NRHP designation

BOROUGH	ORIGINAL DESIGNATION	YEAR	DECADE	STATUS	LOCATION
Queens	Queens Vocational High School	1920	III	S	47th Ave x 37th St/38th St
Staten Island	**Curtis High School**	1904	II	S	**Hamilton Ave x St. Mark's Pl**
Staten Island	PS 1	1907	II	S	Summit St x Yetman Ave/Brighton St
Staten Island	PS 3a→b	1907	II	DB	Church St near Sharrott Ave
Staten Island	**PS 4a**	1907	II	S	**4210 Arthur Kill Rd x Storer Ave/Clay Pit Rd**
Staten Island	PS 6	1901	II	DB	Rossville Ave/Totten St
Staten Island	PS 8	1917	III	S	School St x Lindenwood Ave
Staten Island	PS 11	1921	III	S	Jefferson St x Garretson/Cromwell Ave
Staten Island	PS 12a	1901	II	A	Rhine/Danube Ave x Steuben St
Staten Island	PS 13a→b	1909	II	DB	Clifton Ave, Rosebank
Staten Island	PS 16a→b	1906	II	DB	Madison/Monroe x 1st/4th, Tompkinsville
Staten Island	PS 18a	1906	II	DA	Clifton x Anderson St
Staten Island	PS 20a→b	1916	III	S	Park Ave x New St/Vreeland St
Staten Island	PS 21	1907	II	S	Hooker Place x Trantor Pl/Walker St
Staten Island	PS 22	1914	III	S	Forest Ave x Sanders St
Staten Island	PS 23a→b	1906	II	DB	30 Natick St, Richmondtown
Staten Island	PS 26	1905	II	S	Victory Blvd x Melvin Ave
Staten Island	**PS 28**	1908	II	SO	**Center St x St. Patricks Pl**

LEGEND

a—Built as an addition
a→ Built as an addition, building became stand-alone school
A—Addition to a current public school
AO—Addn now used for another purpose
DA—Demolished addition
es—East Side, ws—West Side, ns—North Side, ss—South Side

S—Current public school
O—Building now used for another purpose
O—Built for a purpose other than a school
DB—Demolished building
Boldfaced—Landmarked
Underlined—NRHP designation

BOROUGH	ORIGINAL DESIGNATION	YEAR	DECADE	STATUS	LOCATION
Staten Island	PS 29	1922	III	S	Victory Blvd x Slosson Ave/ Trenton Pl
Staten Island	PS 30	1905	II	S	Wardwell x Leonard Ave/ The Blvd
Staten Island	PS 31	1904	II	DB	Pleasant Ave x Lane, Princes Bay
Staten Island	PS 32	1902	II	SO	Osgood Ave x Van Duzer/ Targee St
Staten Island	PS 33	1905	II	DB	Washington/Franklin x Thompson, Grant City
Staten Island	PS 34	1903	II	DB	Fingerboard Rd x Grant/ Sherman, Rosebank

Snyder H-Plan by Borough and Name/PS Number

LEGEND
a—Built as an addition
a→ Built as an addition, the building became a stand-alone school
S—Current public school
A—Addition to a current public school
SO—Building now used for another purpose
AO—Addn now used for another purpose
O—Built for a purpose other than a school
DB—Demolished building
DA—Demolished addition
Boldfaced—Landmarked
<u>Underlined</u>—NRHP designation

BOROUGH	SCHOOL NAME	YEAR	STATUS	LOCATION	STYLE
		FIRST DECADE—3 total			
Manhattan	PS 147	1899	DB	Henry St/East Broadway x Gouverneur/Scammel St	Romanesque Revival
Manhattan	PS 165	1900	S	W 108th/W 109th St x Amsterdam/Broadway	Chateau
Manhattan	PS 159	1900	DB	E 119th/E 120th St x Second/Third Ave	Chateau
		SECOND DECADE—40 total			
Manhattan	<u>PS 109</u>	1901	SO	E 99th/E 100th St x Second/Third Ave	**Chateau**
Manhattan	PS 179	1901	DB	W 101st/W 102nd St x Amsterdam/Columbus Ave	Chateau
Manhattan	PS 168	1901	SO	E 104th/E 105th St x First/Second Ave	Chateau
Manhattan	PS 170	1901	DB	W 111th/W 112th St x Fifth/Lenox Ave	Chateau
Manhattan	PS 119	1901	DB	W 133rd/W 134th St x Seventh/Eighth Ave	Chateau
Manhattan	PS 171	1902	S	E 103rd/E 104th x Fifth/Madison Ave	Chateau
Bronx	PS 33	1901	S	E 184th St/Fordham Rd x Walton Ave/Jerome Ave	Chateau
Manhattan	**Wadleigh High School for Girls**	1902	S	**W 114th/W 115th St x Seventh/Eighth Ave**	Chateau
Manhattan	PS 184	1902	DB	W 116th/117th St x Fifth/Lenox Ave	Italian palazzo-style
Manhattan	PS 188	1903	S	East Houston St x Lewis St (Baruch and Lillian Wald Dr)	Italian palazzo-style

LEGEND

a—Built as an addition
a→ Built as an addition, the building became a stand-alone school
S—Current public school
A—Addition to a current public school
SO—Building now used for another purpose

AO—Addn now used for another purpose
O—Built for a purpose other than a school
DB—Demolished building
DA—Demolished addition
Boldfaced—Landmarked
Underlined—NRHP designation

BOROUGH	SCHOOL NAME	YEAR	STATUS	LOCATION	STYLE
Manhattan	PS 186	1903	SO	W 145th/W 146th St x Amsterdam/Broadway	Italian palazzo-style
Manhattan	High School of Commerce	1903	DB	W 65th/W 66th St x Amsterdam/Broadway	Misc
Manhattan	PS 21 (originally PS 106)	1904	DB	Spring/Prince St x Elizabeth/Mott St	Italian palazzo-style
Manhattan	PS 150	1905	S	E 95th/E 96th St x First/Second Ave	Baroque
Bronx	PS 37	1905	SO	E 145th/E 146th St x Willis/Brook Ave	Baroque
Brooklyn	PS 146	1905	S	18th/19th St x 6th/7th Ave	Baroque, Jacobean
Brooklyn	Manual Training High School	1905	S	7th/8th Ave x 4th/5th St	Baroque
Manhattan	PS 63	1906	S	E 3rd/E 4th St x First Ave/Ave A	Baroque
Manhattan	**PS 64**	**1906**	**SO**	**E 9th/E 10th St x Ave B/Ave C (LPC)**	**misc**
Manhattan	The original DeWitt Clinton High School	1906	SO	W 58th/59th St x 10th Ave	Baroque, Flemish Renaissance
Brooklyn	PS 66	1906	S	Osborn St/Watkins St (now Mother Gaston Blvd) x Sutter/Blake Ave	Baroque
Brooklyn	PS 147	1906	S	Bushwick Ave x McKibbin/Seigel St	Italian palazzo-style
Brooklyn	PS 149	1906	S	Sutter Ave x Wyona/Vermont St	misc
Brooklyn	Commercial High School	1906	S	Albany Ave x Bergen/Dean St	Italian palazzo-style
Manhattan	PS 90	1907	SO	W 147th/W 148th St x Seventh/Eighth Ave	Gothic
Brooklyn	PS 6	1907	S	Baltic/Warren St x Hoyt/Smith St	Baroque

LEGEND

a—Built as an addition
a→ Built as an addition, the building became a stand-alone school
S—Current public school
A—Addition to a current public school
SO—Building now used for another purpose

AO—Addn now used for another purpose
O—Built for a purpose other than a school
DB—Demolished building
DA—Demolished addition
Boldfaced—Landmarked
Underlined—NRHP designation

BOROUGH	SCHOOL NAME	YEAR	STATUS	LOCATION	STYLE
Brooklyn	PS 148	1907	S	Ellery/Hopkins St x Delmonico Pl/ Throop Ave	Baroque
Brooklyn	Eastern District High School	1907	SO	Marcy Ave x Rodney/ Keap St	misc
Brooklyn	Teachers' Training School (PS 138)	1903–1907	S	Prospect Pl/Park Pl x Nostrand/Rogers Ave	Italian palazzo-style
Manhattan	PS 65	1908	DB	Hester/Canal St x Eldridge/Forsyth St	Italian palazzo-style
Manhattan	**Former Stuyvesant High School**	**1908**	**S**	**E 15th /E 16th St x First/Second Ave**	**Baroque**
Manhattan	PS 27	1908	DB	E 41st /E 42nd St x Second/Third Ave	Gothic
Manhattan	PS 81	1908	S	E 119th/E 120th St x Seventh/Eighth Ave	Baroque
Brooklyn	PS 150	1908	S	Sackman St/Christopher Ave x Belmont/ Sutter Ave	Gothic
Manhattan	PS 17	1909	S	W 47th/W 48th St x Eighth/Ninth Ave	Italian palazzo-style
Manhattan	PS 100	1909	DB	W 138th/W 139th x Lenox/Fifth Ave	Italian palazzo-style
Bronx	PS 45	1913	S	E 189 St x Lorillard Pl/ Hoffman St	Italian palazzo-style
Brooklyn	PS 156	1909	DB	Sutter Ave x Grafton St	Italian palazzo-style
Brooklyn	PS 157	1909	S	Taaffe Pl/Kent Ave x Park/Myrtle Ave	Gothic
Brooklyn	PS 158	1909	S	Belmont Ave x Warwick/ Ashford St	Italian palazzo-style
Queens	PS 90	1909	S	109th St x Jamaica Ave/86th Ave	Italian palazzo-style

LEGEND

a—Built as an addition
a→ Built as an addition, the building became a stand-alone school
S—Current public school
A—Addition to a current public school
SO—Building now used for another purpose

AO—Addn now used for another purpose
O—Built for a purpose other than a school
DB—Demolished building
DA—Demolished addition
Boldfaced—Landmarked
Underlined—NRHP designation

BOROUGH	SCHOOL NAME	YEAR	STATUS	LOCATION	STYLE
THIRD DECADE—9 total					
Manhattan	PS 95	1912	S	Clarkson/Houston St x Hudson/Varick St	Simplified Collegiate Gothic
Brooklyn	Bushwick High School	1913	S	Irving Ave x Woodbine/ Putnam St	Gothic
Brooklyn	PS 28	1914	S	Herkimer/Fulton St x Ralph/Howard Ave	Simplified Collegiate Gothic
Manhattan	PS 115	1914	S	W 176th/W 177th St x St Nicholas/Audubon Ave	Gothic
Bronx	The original Evander Childs High School	1916	S	E 184th St/Field Pl x Morris/Creston Ave	Chateau
Manhattan	PS 72 Annex	1924	S	E 104th/E 105th x Lexington Ave	Simplified Collegiate Gothic
Manhattan	PS 60	1925	S	E 11th/E 12th St x First Ave/Ave A	Simplified Collegiate Gothic
Manhattan	PS 11	1925	S	W 20th/W 21st St x Eighth/Ninth Ave	Simplified Collegiate Gothic
Manhattan	PS 47	1925	S	E 23rd St x Second/ Third Ave	Simplified Collegiate Gothic

Snyder High Schools in Chronological Order

LEGEND
a—Built as an addition
a→ Built as an addition, the building became a stand-alone school
S—Current public school
A—Addition to a current public school
SO—Building now used for another purpose
AO—Addn now used for another purpose
O—Built for a purpose other than a school
DB—Demolished building
DA—Demolished addition
Boldfaced—Landmarked
Underlined—NRHP designation

BOROUGH	SCHOOL NAME	YEAR	STATUS	LOCATION
FIRST DECADE: Some high-school classes met in elementary schools.				
SECOND DECADE: 12 schools				
Manhattan	Wadleigh High School for Girls	1902	S	W 114th/W 115th St x Seventh/Eighth Ave
Manhattan	High School of Commerce	1903	DB	W 65th/W 66th St x Amsterdam/Broadway
Bronx	**Morris High School**	1904	S	E 166th St/Home St x Boston Rd/Jackson Ave
Queens	Long Island City High School	1904	S	40th/41st Ave x 28th/29th St
Staten Island	**Curtis High School**	1904	S	**Hamilton Ave x St. Mark's Pl**
Brooklyn	Manual Training High School	1905	S	7th/8th Ave x 4th/5th St
Brooklyn	Commercial High School	1906	S	Albany Ave x Bergen/Dean St
Brooklyn	**Erasmus Hall High School**	1906	S	**Flatbush/Bedford Ave x Church/Snyder Ave**
Manhattan	Former Boys/ DeWitt Clinton/Haaren High Schools	1906	SO	W 58th/59th St x 10th Ave
Brooklyn	Teachers' Training School (PS 138)	1903	S	Prospect Pl/Park Pl x Nostrand/Rogers Ave
Brooklyn	Eastern District High School	1907	SO	Marcy Ave x Rodney/Keap St
Manhattan	**Former Stuyvesant High School**	1908	S	**E 15th /E16th St x First/Second Ave**
THIRD DECADE: 12 schools & 2 additions				
Brooklyn	Boys' High School	1912	A	Marcy Ave x Putnam Ave/Madison St
Brooklyn	Girls' High School	1912	A	Nostrand/Marcy Ave x Halsey/Macon St
Brooklyn	Bushwick High School	1913	S	Irving Ave x Woodbine/Putnam St
Manhattan	Normal College/Hunter High School for Girls	1913	SO	E 68th/E 69th St x Lexington Ave

LEGEND
a—Built as an addition
a→ Built as an addition, the building became a stand-alone school
S—Current public school
A—Addition to a current public school
SO—Building now used for another purpose
AO—Addn now used for another purpose
O—Built for a purpose other than a school
DB—Demolished building
DA—Demolished addition
Boldfaced—Landmarked
<u>Underlined</u>—NRHP designation

BOROUGH	SCHOOL NAME	YEAR	STATUS	LOCATION
Brooklyn	Bay Ridge High School	1915	S	4th Ave x 67th /Senator St
Manhattan	Washington Irving High School	1915	S	E 16th/E 17th St x Irving Pl
Queens	**Flushing High School**	**1915**	**S**	**Union St/ Parsons Blvd x 35th Ave**
Bronx	Former Evander Childs High School	1916	S	E 184th St/Field Pl x Morris/Creston Ave
Manhattan	Manhattan Trade School for Girls	1917	S	E 22nd St x Lexington Ave
Queens	**Newtown High School**	**1922**	**S**	**48th/50th Ave x 90th/91st St**
Manhattan	Julia Richman High School	1923	S	E 67th/E 68th St x First/Second Ave
Brooklyn	Thomas Jefferson High School	1924	S	Pennsylvania Ave x Dumont Ave
Brooklyn	New Utrecht High School	1924	S	16th/17th Ave x 79th/80th St
Manhattan	George Washington High School	1925	S	W 191st/W 192nd St x Audubon Ave

GLOSSARY

Architectural Terminology

Balustrade A railing with a row of vertical supporting elements of wood, metal, or masonry called balusters.

Baroque Often theatrical, a very decorative style following the Mannerist style in Italy in the seventeenth century, featuring designs with curvilinear surfaces and shapes, spirals, and ovals; highly ornamented surfaces, scrolls, and cartouches.

Bay The space created by any division or subdivision of a building between vertical lines or planes, such as columns, piers, wall sections, etc.

Beaux Arts Neo-classical style promulgated by L'École des Beaux Arts in Paris in the late nineteenth–early twentieth centuries incorporating the monumentality of ancient Greek and Roman influences with rich and decorative detail and formal symmetry.

Cartouche (also Cartouch) A slightly convex oval shield usually containing an inscription or date, often edged with decorative scrollwork and used as an ornamental design element.

Chateau French castle, country manor, or palatial country home, with its counterpart *palais* referring to a grand house in a city.

Classical Columns Greek or Roman supporting pillars consisting of two or three parts. Doric columns consist of shaft and capital while Ionic and Corinthian columns consist of base, shaft, and capital.

Clerestory Window Style An upper story of windows on an interior wall used for lighting and ventilation while maintaining privacy.

Collegiate Gothic Style   A sub-genre of Gothic Revival popular in the United States during the late nineteenth and early twentieth centuries influenced by English Tudor and Gothic buildings. U.S. universities were designed using this style to emulate the elite Oxford and Cambridge universities.

Colonial Style   A broad term referring to architectural styles brought from a home country or area to a new settlement or colony.

Corbel   A structural piece of stone, wood, or metal projecting from a wall to support an overhanging structure or element.

Cornice   Horizontal decorative molding topping a building or over doors and windows.

Crenellations   The alternating indentations and raised portions in a battlement or parapet, traditionally designed for defense but later used as a decorative element.

Cupola   A small dome-like ornamental structure topping a roof or larger dome.

Curtain-wall   A non-load-bearing outer wall of a building, generally lighter and less expensive than a load-bearing wall, and hung on a frame of steel or reinforced concrete.

Drip Molding   A projection from a sill or cornice to protect the area below from water runoff.

Façade   An exterior side of a building considered the architectural front.

Finial   A decorative ornament along the top of a peak of an arch or arched structure such as spire, pinnacle, or gable. Common in Gothic architecture.

Fireproofing   A passive fire protection measure rendering something resistant to fire or incombustible or the materials that are used in making something extremely resistant to fire.

Flemish Renaissance Revival Style   Inspired by the seventeenth-century architecture of Belgium and the Netherlands, it was popular during the first half of the nineteenth century. Most structures are large and made of red brick or of a stone like sandstone or limestone, often featuring light-colored bands in façades, stepped gables, and dormers. Many have carved terra-cotta decorations. The most identifiable feature of Flemish Renaissance Revival is probably the stepped gable.

French Renaissance Revival Style   Popular in Europe and the United States in the late nineteenth and early twentieth centuries; it took inspiration from earlier sixteenth- and seventeenth-century French Renaissance architecture. Structures are usually made of stone or brick, look like castles or chateaus, and often have multiple stories with very steep-pitched, slate-covered roofs. Some have mansard roofs or dormer windows, chimneys, cylindrical towers, and turrets.

Gable   Triangular wall section forming the end of a pitched roof.

Georgian Style (also referred to as Colonial Revival)   Identified by its symmetrical composition and formal, classical details, it was the most prevalent style in the English colonies in the eighteenth century: a stone or brick two-story building with a side-gabled roof and a symmetrical arrangement of windows and doors on the front façade. Usually including five bays across with a center door, the style also commonly features a pedimented or crowned entrance with flanking pilasters. Common details include multi-paned sash windows, a dentiled cornice, and decorative quoins at the corners of the building.

Gothic Style   A style developed in northern France and England in the twelfth century that flourished for over 300 years, featuring pointed arches, high rib vaults, slender columns, flying buttresses, and intricate ornamentation.

Gothic Revival Style   An eighteenth- and nineteenth-century style featuring Gothic characteristics: tall spires, pinnacles, finials, gargoyles, lancet windows, tracery, high-pitched roofs, pointed arches, cluster columns or piers, and decorative Gothic patterns in carvings, tilework, and metalwork.

Greek Revival Style   A style prevalent in the early eighteenth century featuring ancient Greek temples, including symmetrical façades, classical columns and/or pilasters, pediments, and other classical ornamentation.

H-Plan Building   A building that, when looked at from above, forms the letter "H."

Historicism   The recreation, imitation, mixing, or application of historic architectural styles to both old and new building types without regard to complete accuracy and usually while using new technological advances and building techniques. Examples include all the Revival styles of architecture.

International Style   A modern style that evolved during the 1920s and 1930s, tending to use mass-produced materials and rejecting all ornamentation and color. The style is characterized by the use of repetitive modular form, flat surface, industrial materials, and glass.

Italian Palazzo-Style   Palazzo style refers to an architectural style of the nineteenth and twentieth centuries based upon the palazzi (palaces) built by wealthy families of the Italian Renaissance.

Italianate Style   This distinct nineteenth-century style was characterized by a prominently bracketed cornice, towers based on Italian campanili and belvederi, and adjoining arched windows. It also featured flat or low-pitched roofs and projecting eaves supported by corbels.

Jacobean Revival Style   Often referred to as Tudor Revival Style. A style often incorporating both flat and gable roofs, open parapets (a low wall or railing to protect the edge of a roof), columns, pilasters, and large round arches, sometimes referred to as arcades.

Loggia   A room, hall, gallery, or porch open to the air on one or more sides.

Mansard Roof   A type of four-sided roof consisting of two slopes on each side. The lower side is steeper than the upper side to allow extra roof space for the attic rooms. Named after seventeenth-century French architect Francois Mansart.

Northern European Renaissance Style   See Flemish Renaissance Revival Style.

Oriel (or Bay) Window A window that protrudes from a wall, does not reach the ground, and is often supported with corbels or brackets.

Pavilion A projecting element of a façade or subdivision of a monumental building used especially at the center or at each end of the building. Often referred to as a volume or block when describing the architectural form of the structure.

Pediment Triangular element or gable between a horizontal entablature and a sloping roof. Often decorated with sculpture.

Piano Nobile Italian for "noble floor." The main floor of an Italian palazzo-style Renaissance building, containing reception rooms; the basement and first floor were used for functions such as food preparation.

Plenum Ventilation A mechanical system designed to force fresh air through a series of intake ducts into a plenum chamber and from there into rooms at a pressure slightly higher than atmospheric pressure, with the resultant mix of stale air then forced out through a series of exhaust ducts by means of fans and adjustable dampers.

Quatrefoil A four-lobed design used in Gothic and Gothic Revival styles in stone and wood. Patterned after floral petals.

Queen Anne Style In the U.S., this late nineteenth-century style featured asymmetrical façades, steeply pitched roofs, front-facing triangular gables, projecting dormer windows, with turrets, towers, and in residential architecture, large wrap around porches, oriel and bay windows, painted balustrades, and wooden or slate roofs.

Quoining Masonry blocks at building corners for support or decoration, generally used in Renaissance-style buildings adding to the image of strength.

Reinforced Concrete Poured concrete used for floors, walls, or columns with embedded support, usually steel bars or mesh.

Renaissance Architecture The fourteenth- to sixteenth-century Italy-based European revival of ancient Greek and Roman styles. Emphasis was on order, symmetry, proportion, geometry, and the regularity of parts. The use of semicircular arches and domes replaced the complex proportional systems and irregular profiles of medieval buildings.

Retrofitting Bringing an older building up to current standards by furnishing new, modified, or improved systems, technology, or equipment.

Romanesque Revival Style Inspired in part by Romanesque architecture, this style placed emphasis on thick rusticated masonry walls, heavy round arches, towers with conical roofs, and asymmetrical façades.

Rustication The lower part of an exterior wall or a door or window frame consisting of large cut stone blocks separated by deep joins and sometimes with a rough exposed surface, used to give a solid look.

Simplified Collegiate Gothic Style Developed after Collegiate Gothic became popular, this style featured buildings, usually with a two-story crenellated or towered entrance, Tudor windows (especially on the top floor), drip moldings, and decorative stonework—enough to convey the idea of Collegiate Gothic but without the complex, rich ornamentation of full Collegiate Gothic.

Stringcourse A horizontal molding or projecting course of masonry or wood across the façade of a building often used to visually divide a building's registers or stories.

Terra-cotta Glazed or unglazed fired clay used to make bricks, flooring, roof tiles, and ornamentation.

Transom Window A toggle or fixed window above another window or door, usually installed for added air circulation and light.

Tripartite The organization of the façade or another aspect of a building into three parts, either horizontally or vertically.

Tudor Arch A low, wide, pointed arch having a greater span than rise (wider than it is tall).

ACKNOWLEDGMENTS

THIS BOOK HAS seen the light of day entirely owing to Cindy LaValle and Covid-19. Let me explain. On January 9, 2017, I was diagnosed with Parkinson's. I soldiered on, completing the book and submitting it to Fordham University Press. In May 2018, it was soundly rejected with a 9½-page letter detailing all its shortcomings. Disheartened, I shelved the book. I didn't regret the ten years I spent every waking moment doing something Snyder-related. When people ask me if I were "in relationship," I would answer, "Yes, with a dead architect." But, after all, in trying to get to know Snyder's more than 200 buildings that still exist, I had traveled the areas of the city I would never have otherwise seen, met many interesting people, and learned a tremendous amount about architecture and about the history of education in New York City. I did regret that I had failed to provide the opportunity for others, besides mainly architectural historians, to get to know this remarkable man's achievements—others such as the person who feels pleasure at sighting a handsome school building, the person who sees a gem of a school building hidden in plain sight, and people who work inside the buildings: custodians, security guards, office staff, principals, teachers, students, and former students. I was resigned to not having produced a product.

Not so, Cindy. A recently retired healthcare information technology project manager and, most significantly, Snyder's great-granddaughter, she shared the manuscript with friends. They loved it but found sections dry and boring. In the fall of 2019 Cindy approached me about a reboot of the book. Cindy recruited her partner, Michael Janoska, a recently retired land and city survey technician by day and custodian in the Sayville School District, New York, by night, and Dorothy "Dee" Laffin, who comes from a family of public-school educators, a recently retired Executive Dean of Suffolk County Community College, Long Island. The year 2020 found us sequestered within our homes throughout much of the Covid crisis; under these difficult circumstances, our team undertook this project with vigor and determination. We convened weekly on Zoom with each of us reporting progress on assigned tasks, identifying issues, and accepting new assignments. Mike became the resident historian. Dee and I set to making the book more friendly by streamlining dry sections weighed down with too much information, lengthy direct quotations, and labyrinthine sentences. Cindy transformed my parenthetical citations into proper endnote style, formatted the bibliography, and gave the proposed book a stylish look. After addressing identified inadequacies and issues, we resubmitted the manuscript to Fordham. When this version was accepted, we were jubilant. As the beneficiary of the team's efforts, I owe profound thanks to Cindy, Dee, and Mike (and Mike's son-in-law, Hector Janoska, for his beautiful artwork).

A bit more project history: Having noticed impressive school buildings around town and wanting to learn more about them, I was tipped off to see David Ment, Public School Archivist at the Municipal Archives. He sat me down with the enchanting *Annual Financial and Statistical Report, 1906–1908*, of the New York City Board of Education, Bureau of Finance. This huge book pictured, for the only time in the Department of Education's history, every current school in existence or under construction, the last sixteen years of which, of course, were exclusively Snyder-inspired buildings. I was uncharacteristically bold and called Christopher Gray, architectural historian, who wrote the "Streetscapes" column for the *New York Times*, six of which had been about Snyder schools. I called with no introduction. He invited me to meet with him at his office, where he opened a filing cabinet, cleared a space on a table, and told me to read the contents of his files on Snyder. Up until his tragic death in 2017, Christopher Gray was unwaveringly supportive in my endeavor. One item within the folder that first day was a letter from Elizabeth Orr and Shirley Skeffington, two of Snyder's granddaughters, both in their late eighties, who had known their grandfather in person through their mid-twenties. The purpose of the letter was to set the record straight correcting Christopher's statement from a 1999 column titled, "Architect Who Taught a Lesson in School Design," which indicated that no current Snyder descendants had been identified. Thanks to them for showing me family heirlooms, telling me real-life stories of their grandfather, and introducing me to Cindy and several other Snyder family members.

Thank you to Terry Peters of the Outdoors Club for her unwavering willingness to go anywhere with me in search of a school; to the Transponders, Risa Ehrlich, Liz York, and Patricia Aiken (a group of women artists near where I lived at the time in northern Manhattan) who first brainstormed with me on how to pursue this project; and to Annice Alt, who introduced me to Tamara Coombs of the Municipal Arts Society, who made me one of its walking-tour leaders. Other organizations that trusted me enough to give a lecture to their members were the Historic Districts Council, the Victorian Society, the Society of Architectural Historians (SAH-NYC), the Greenwich Village Society for Historic Preservation, Landmark West, the Bronx County Historical Society, the UFT Retired Teachers, and various other teacher organizations, men's clubs, and public libraries.

Andrew Dolkart of Columbia University and Marta Gutman and Jerrilyn Dodds of City College allowed me to sit in on classes in architectural history and the history of New York City. Additional information was gathered through continuing education courses given by Francis Morrone and Gail Cornell of NYU and Barry Levin of Cooper Union. To all I am greatly indebted. My first draft of 120 pages was read by Christopher Gray, Gail Cornell, Annice Alt, and Cindy LaValle, reactions of whom led me to reorganize, add material, and do further research, giving me some idea of how to proceed. Over years out-of-town friends Elizabeth Tannenbaum, Tom Bauso, and Valerie Hall visited for one or two weeks, read drafts, and talked about what they would like to see discussed in the text. Joyce Zonana, Anne Bauso, and Brian Papa heroically suggested edits. Stephanie Golden suggested the title.

I also want to thank attendees at my lectures and participants on my walking tours of the schools for their enthusiasm and loyalty: to name a few, Arthur and Madalyn Castle, Bob Halasz, Mike Miller, Craig Nunn, Tamara Mishiyeva, Linda Rossi, Sifor Ng, Mary Durkee, and Fran Litvack. And many thanks go to multiple other people who helped and encouraged me, including out-of-towners—Mohana Rajakumar, Holly Clayson, Margo Collet, Jill Vickers, Kathy Childs Jones, Elaine Stein Cummins, Marjorie Kornhauser, Brent Brolin, and Jean Harrison; around town—Nancy Russo, Joyce Mendelsohn, Jim Dwyer, Rick Moody, Bill Christenson, Subutay Musluoglu, Ted Mineau, Simeon Bankoff, Frampton Tolbert, Bruce Nelligan, Katy Daugharty (an architect who replaced the cornices on the schools she renovated), Jay Shockley, James Edmondson, Rajul Parekh, Abigail Caro, Thomas Casey, James O'Keefe, Andrea Coyle, Leo Hogan, and Ron Rice;

and many tour guides, such as Tony Robins, Francis Morrone, Justin Ferrate, and Joe Svelank. Also thanks to my twenty-four-hour home-health aides, Sherona Kirkpatrick, Ameena Hussein, Emmanuel Paul, Shea Wilson, and Adbul Pah for, among other things, preventing falls. The staff of Fordham University Press made the publishing process easy and enjoyable and the product much improved. Thank you especially to Director Fredric Nachbaur, meticulous copy editor Aldene Fredenburg, Eric Newman, Will Cerbone, Mark Lerner, and Kate O'Brien-Nicholson.

And, finally, to my three daughters, Kate Arrington, Louise Bauso, and Anne Bauso; to my granddaughters, Sylvie and Marion Shannon; to son-in-law, Mike Shannon, and partner-in-law, Brandon Phillips; to extended family, my surrogate son, Brian Papa, his wife, Lauren, and their daughters, Talulah and Josie; friends Annabelle Peevey, her husband, Anthony Carelli, and their son, Auggie; and my children's father, Tom Bauso (a true believer)—thank you for your patience, solicitude, and love. You kept me alive, literally.

NOTES

Introduction: Hidden in Plain Sight

1. Paul Spencer Byard, *New Schools for New York* (New York: Princeton Architectural Press, 1992), 6.
2. Robert A. M. Stern, "Schools Too Grand to Turn into Trash," *New York Times*, January 22, 2000, A15.
3. David McCullough, "John Adams to Matthew Robinson," March 23, 1786, in *John Adams* (New York: Simon & Schuster, 2001), 340.
4. John Adams, *The Works of John Adams, Second President of the United States: With a Life of the Author, Notes and Illustrations* (New York: Little, Brown, 1854), 9:540.
5. Henry Barnard, *School Architecture, Or Contributions to the Improvement of School-Houses in the United States*, ed. Jean and Robert McClintock (1849) (New York: Teachers College Press, 1970), 31–33.
6. Jonathan Zimmerman, *Small Wonder: The Little Red Schoolhouse in History and Memory* (New Haven, Conn.: Yale University Press, 2009), 71–72.
7. Paul Turner, "Boundless Enthusiasm," in *Campus: An American Planning Tradition* (Cambridge, Mass.: MIT Press), 17–18, 89, passim.
8. Herbert Kohl, "Should We Burn Babar?," in *Essays on Children's Literature and the Power of Stories* (New York: New Press, 1995).
9. Kenneth M. Price and Ed Folsom, "Mannhatta," in *The Walt Whitman Archive*, 404–5, https://whitmanarchive.org/published/LG/1891/poems/271. From 1995 until 2007 the *Archive* operated under the aegis of the Institute for Advanced Technology in the Humanities (IATH) at the University of Virginia. In 2007, the *Archive* moved from a server at IATH to the University of Nebraska–Lincoln, where it is one of the projects sponsored by the Center for Digital Research in the Humanities.
10. "School Fund Too Small—Miss Grace H. Dodge Favors Much Larger Appropriations," *New York Times*, January 5, 1895, 9.
11. Jacob Riis, *The Battle with the Slum* (New York: Macmillan, 1902), 353.

12. "Needs of the Schools; Many Evils Reported by Ex-Commissioner Wehrum Corrected; More New Buildings Still Needed; Abuses That Still Exist Due to Lack of Funds, Says Superintendent Snyder—Health Board Inquiry," *New York Times*, January 3, 1895.

13. Charles B. J. Snyder, "School-Building in New York City," *Educational Review*, January–May 1898, 20.

14. Selma Cantor Berrol, *The Empire City: New York and Its People, 1624–1996* (Westport, Conn.: Greenwood, 1997), 81–87.

15. Snyder, "Annual Report of the Superintendent of School Buildings," *Superintendent of Schools Annual Report to the Department of Education* (1904), 316.

16. "Board of Education Minutes," *Journal of the Board of Education of the City of New York*, 1898, 844–47.

17. Gary Hermalyn, *Morris High School and the Creation of the New York City Public High School System* (New York: Bronx County Historical Society, 1995).

18. Michele Cohen, *Public Art for Public Schools* (New York: Monacelli, 2009).

19. Christopher Gray, "Streetscapes/Charles B. J. Snyder: Architect Who Taught a Lesson in School Design," *New York Times*, November 21, 1999, Real Estate Section, 7.

20. Dolores Hayden, *The Power of Place* (Cambridge, Mass.: MIT Press, 1995).

21. Marta Gutman, Review of "*The Chicago Schoolhouse: High School Architecture and Educational Reform, 1856–2006*, by Dale Allen Gyure; *Das Klassenzimmer vom Ende des 19. Jahrhunderts bis Heute*, by Thomas Mülry Andmüller and Romana Schneider; and *Small Memory*, by Jonathan Zimmerman," *Journal of the Society of Architectural Historians* 71, no. 4 (December 6, 2012): 556.

22. Nikolaus Pevsner, *A History of Building Types* (Princeton, N.J.: Princeton University Press, 1976).

23. Marta Gutman, *Designing Modern Childhoods: History, Space, and the Material Culture of Children* (New Brunswick, N.J.: Rutgers University Press, 2008).

24. Dale Allen Gyure, *The Chicago Schoolhouse: High School Architecture and Educational Reform, 1856–2006* (Chicago: Center for American Places, 2011).

25. Jennifer Nadler Wright, *C.B.J. Snyder, New York City Public School Architecture, 1891–1922*, photography by Roy Wright (self-published, 2020).

26. "Renaming the Schools," *New York Times*, March 25, 1916, 12.

1. The Making of an Architect 1860–1945

1. Evelyn Barrett, *Chronicles of Saratoga* (Saratoga County, N.Y.: Published privately by E. B. Britten, 1959), 202.

2. Issac Edwards Clarke, "Art and Industry: (1897) Industrial and Technical Training in Voluntary Associations and Endowed Institution," in *The Executive Documents Printed by Order of the Senate of the United States for the Second Session of the Forty-sixth Congress 1879–'80 in Seven Volumes* (Washington, D.C.: Government Printing Office, 1898), vol. 7, part 3, Chapter V, the Cooper Union for the Advancement of Science and Art, 348–447,380, https://www.google.com/books/edition/Art_and_Industry_1897_Industrial_and_tec/_Vc BAAAAYAAJ?hl=en&gbpv=1&dq=ANNUAL+REPORT+OF+THE+Trustees+of+the+Cooper+Union+FOR+THE+Advancement+of+Science+and+Art&pg=PA376&printsec =frontcover.

3. Clarke, "Art and Industry," 1898, 409.

4. Clarke, "Art and Industry," 1898, 389.

5. *History and Commerce of New York City* (New York: American Publishing and Engraving, 1891), 115.

6. "New Rochelle Awaking: Village on the Sound Assuming Its Summer Aspect; Many Cottages Already Open, and Most of the Others Will Be Occupied by June 1," *New York Times*, May 17, 1896, 16.

7. "Local News," *New Rochelle Pioneer*, November 22, 1890, 3.

8. "Board of Education Minutes," *Journal of the Board of Education of the City of New York* (1898): 844.

2. Auspicious Times for Snyder's Public-School Mandate

1. "Needs of the Schools; Many Evils Reported by Ex-Commissioner Wehrum Corrected; More New Buildings Still Needed; Abuses That Still Exist Due to Lack of Funds, Says Superintendent Snyder—Health Board Inquiry," *New York Times*, January 3, 1895, 5.

2. Charles Wehrum, *The Common Schools of the City of New York* (New York: Board of Education, 1894), 26.

3. Frances Wilson, "A New Type of School Architecture," *Outlook* 65, 1900, 609.

4. Adele Marie Shaw, "The True Character of New York Public Schools," in *World's Work: A History of Our Time* (New York: Doubleday, Page, 1903), 4,209.

5. Jacob Riis, *The Battle with the Slum* (New York: Macmillan, 1902), 354–55.

6. Riis, *Battle*, 344.

7. Charles B. J. Snyder, "How New York City Has Solved Some Trying School Building Problems," *School Journal*, June 28, 1902, 738.

8. Mary Ruth Moore and Constance Sabo-Risley, "Our Proud Heritage: Sowing the Seeds of Hope for Today; Remembering the Life and Work of Susan Blow," Young Children, National Association for the Education of Young Children (NAEYC), November, 2018, /https://www.naeyc.org/resources/pubs/yc/nov2018/remembering-life-work-susan-blow#:~:text=Des%20Peres%20School%2C%20site%20of,publicly%20funded%20kindergarten%20in%20America.

9. A. Emerson Palmer, *The New York Public School: Being a History of Free Education in the City of New York* (New York: Macmillan, 1908), 186.

10. Riis, *Battle*, 374.

11. "To Improve the Schools the Extensive Work Which Is Planned; Buildings in Need of Repairs Will Be Altered and the Comfort and Safety of Pupils Enhanced," *New York Times*, July 8, 1888, 6.

12. "Frauds in New Schools; The City Swindled on the Construction Work; Testimony Which Reflects upon Ex-Superintendent Debevoise—Galvanized Iron in Place of Lead Pipe—Experts to Investigate," *New York Times*, November 19, 1891, 1.

13. Charles B. J. Snyder, "Mr. Snyder's Re-Election: To the Editor of The New York Times," *New York Times*, February 26, 1898, 6.

14. E. L. Doctorow, *Ragtime* (New York: Random House, 1975), 231.

15. Riis, *Battle*, 382, 396.

16. Shaw, "True Character of Public Schools," 4,205.

17. Snyder, "To the Editor of the New York Times."

18. Riis, *Battle*, 368.

19. Angelo Patri, *A Schoolmaster of the Great City: A Progressive Educator's Pioneering Vision for Urban Schools* (New York: Macmillan, 1917), 10.

20. G. W. Wharton, "High School Architecture in the City of New York," *School Review*, June 1, 1903, 459.

21. Jacob Riis, *A Ten Years' War: An Account of the Battle with the Slum in New York* (Boston and New York: Houghton, Mifflin, 1900), 214.

22. C. B. J. Snyder, "Annual Report of the Superintendent of School Buildings," *Superintendent of Schools Annual Report to the Department of Education*, 1904, 273.

23. C. B. J. Snyder, "Annual Report of the Superintendent of School Buildings," *Superintendent of Schools Annual Report to the Board of Education*, 1892, 250.

24. "New-York's 'Imperial Destiny,'" *New York Times*, February 5, 1888, 4.

25. Jonathan Zimmerman, *Small Wonder: The Little Red Schoolhouse in History and Memory* (New Haven, Conn.: Yale University Press, 2009), 71.

26. Eric Thomas Weber, "Education, American Philosophers On," in *American Philosophy: An Encyclopedia*, ed. John Lachs and Robert B. Talisse (New York and London: Routledge, 2008), 208.

27. Riis, *Battle*, 370.

28. Herbert R. Kohl, *Should We Burn Babar?: Essays on Children's Literature and the Power of Stories* (New York: New Press, 1995), 143, 147–48.

29. Patri, *Schoolmaster of the Great City*, 10.

30. Herbert R., Kohl, Foreword, in *A Schoolmaster of the Great City: A Progressive Educator's Pioneering Vision for Urban Schools*, by Angelo Patri (New York: Macmillan, 1917), xi.

31. Marta Gutman, Review of *The Chicago Schoolhouse: High School Architecture and Educational Reform, 1856–2006*, by Dale Allen Gyure; *Das Klassenzimmer vom Ende des 19. Jahrhunderts bis Heute*, by Thomas Mülry Andmüller and Romana Schneider; and *Small Memory*, by Jonathan Zimmerman, *Journal of the Society of Architectural Historians* 71, no. 4 (December 6, 2012): 556.

32. Dale Allen Gyure, *The Chicago Schoolhouse: High School Architecture and Educational Reform, 1856–2006* (Chicago: Center for American Places, 2011), 80–89.

33. William W. Cutler, "Cathedral of Culture: The Schoolhouse in American Educational Thought and Practice since 1820," *History of Education Quarterly* (1989): 1.

34. Naomi Blumberg and Ida Yalzadeh, "City Beautiful Movement," *Encyclopedia Britannica*, accessed January 4, 2019, https://www.britannica.com/topic/City-Beautiful-movement.

35. Henry Adams, *The Education of Henry Adams* (Boston and New York: Houghton, Mifflin, 1918), 340–41.

36. Paul Goldberger, Review of *New York 1900: Metropolitan Architecture and Urbanism 1890–1915*, by Robert A. M. Stern, Gregory Gilmartin, and John M. Massengale, *New York Times*, March 18, 1984.

37. "New York at the Louisiana Purchase Exposition, St. Louis 1904," *Report of the New York State Commission* (Albany, 1907), 205–6.

38. "Rehabilitating New York's Historic Schools," *Center for Architecture*, https://www.centerforarchitecture.org/video/rehabilitating-new-yorks-historic-schools-03-27-2017/.

39. Robert A. M. Stern, Gregory Gilmartin, and John M. Massengale, *New York 1900: Metropolitan Architecture and Urbanism 1890–1915* (New York: Rizzoli, 1995), 79.

40. C. B. J. Snyder, "Annual Report of the Superintendent of School Buildings," *Superintendent of Schools Annual Report to the Department of Education*, 1904, 17.

41. "Letters," *New York Times*, November 10, 1908.

42. Architectural League of New York, *New Schools for New York: Plans and Precedents for Small Schools*, ed. Public Education Association of the City of New York (New York: Princeton Architectural Press, 1992), 188.

43. "Board of Education Minutes," *Journal of the Board of Education of the City of New York*, 1898, 689.

44. G. W. Wharton, "High School Architecture in the City of New York." *School Review*, June 1, 1903, 408.

45. William W. Cutler, "Cathedral of Culture: The Schoolhouse in American Educational Thought and Practice since 1820," *History of Education Quarterly* (1989): 8.

46. Diane Ravitch, *The Great School Wars: A History of the New York City Public Schools* (New York: Basic Books, 1988).

47. C. B. J. Snyder, *Superintendent of Schools Annual Report to the Board of Education*, 1891, 219, 233.

48. Shaw, "True Character of Public Schools," 4,210, 4,206.

49. "The Magnitude of Current School Building Operations in New York—The Excellent Character of Mr. Snyder's Work," *American Architect and Building News*, no. 1544, July 25, 1905, 33.

50. Shaw, "True Character of Public Schools," 4,207.

51. Christopher Gray, "Streetscapes/Charles B. J. Snyder: Architect Who Taught a Lesson in School Design," *New York Times*, November 21, 1999, Real Estate Section, 7.

3. The Creative Decade 1891–1900: Making Revolutionary Change

1. Christopher Gray, "Streetscapes/Charles B. J. Snyder: Architect Who Taught a Lesson in School Design," *New York Times*, November 21, 1999, Real Estate, Section 7.

2. Jacob Riis, *The Battle with the Slum* (New York: Macmillan, 1902), 353.

3. C. B. J. Snyder, "Annual Report of the Superintendent of School Buildings," *Superintendent of Schools Annual Report to the Board of Education*, 1895.

4. Charles B. Snyder, *The Real Estate Record and Guide*, 1884.

5. Francis Wilson, "A New Type of School Architecture," *Outlook* 65, 1900, 810.

6. Riis, *Battle*, 355.

7. Amy S. Weiser, "Review of The Architecture of Literacy: The Carnegie Libraries of New York City," *Journal of the Society of Architectural Historians* (September 1998): 358.

8. Robert A. M. Stern, "Schools Too Grand to Turn into Trash," *New York Times*, January 22, 2000.

9. "New Public School Buildings," *Real Estate Record and Guide* 45, February 22, 1890, 257–58; quoted in Robert A. M Stern, Gregory Gilmartin, and John M. Massengale, *New York 1900 Metropolitan Architecture and Urbanism 1890–1915* (New York: Rizzoli, 1995), 78.

10. Riis, *Battle*, 354.

11. *New York Times*, September 26, 1895.

12. Stern, Gilmartin, and Massengale, *New York 1900*, 79.

13. Robinson Meyer, "How Gothic Architecture Took over the American College Campus," *Atlantic*, https://www.theatlantic.com/education/archive/2013/09/how-gothic-architecture-took-over-the-american-college-campus/279287/, September 11, 2013.

14. Frederick Stymatz Lamb, "Modern Use of the Gothic: The Possibilities of New Architectural Style," *Craftsman*, 1905, 158–59.

15. Riis, *Battle*, 392.

16. Charles B. J. Snyder, "School-Building in New York City," *Educational Review* 15 (January–May 1898): 25.

17. "May Retain Snyder to Rebuild Schools: Education Officials Considering Plan to Make Him a Consulting Architect; Wants Rest after 31 Years; Remarkable Improvement Made in New York Schoolhouses during His Service as Superintendent," *New York Times*, May 7, 1922, 33.

18. *New York Tribune*, April 9, 1892.

19. Deborah E. B Weiner, *Architecture and Social Reform in Late-Victorian London* (Manchester, UK: Manchester University Press, 1994), 54.

20. Lloyd Ultan and Barbara Unger, *Bronx Accent* (New Brunswick, N.J.: Rutgers University Press, 2006), 84.

21. *Fifty-Fifth Annual Report of the Board of Education of the City of New York for the Year Ending December 31, 1896* (New York: Hall of the Board of Education, 1897), 225, 244.

22. John Beverley Robinson, "The School Buildings of New York," *Architectural Record* 7, January–March 1898, 384.

23. Francis Wilson, "New Type of School Architecture," *Outlook* 65, August 1, 1900, 815–17.

24. *Sun*, January 10, 2008.

25. Christopher Gray, "Streetscapes: Public School 157; A Conversion to Serve Another Generation's Needy," *New York Times*, April 16, 1989, Section 10–12.

26. Michele Cohen, *Public Art for Public Schools* (New York: Monacelli, 2009), 39.

27. Charles B. J. Snyder, "The Construction of Public School Buildings in the City of New York," *Proceedings of the Municipal Engineers of the City of New York* (New York: City of New York, 1904), 46.

28. Wallace K. Harrison and C. E. Dobbin, *School Buildings of Today and Tomorrow* (New York: Architectural Book Publishing, 1931), 59.

29. Riis, *Battle*, 353.

30. William W. Cutler, "Cathedral of Culture: The Schoolhouse in American Educational Thought and Practice since 1820," *History of Education Quarterly* 29 (1989): 1–40.

31. Riis, *Battle*, 381.

32. Stephen Crane, *Maggie, A Girl of the Streets* (New York: Norton, 1897), 4–5.

33. Snyder, "Annual Report of the Superintendent of School Buildings" (1895), 226.

34. "Cooper Union," from Wikipedia, the free encyclopedia, https://en.wikipedia.org/wiki/Cooper_Union#The_Foundation_Building.

35. Snyder, "School-Building in New York City," 21.

36. Snyder, "School-Building in New York City," 20.

37. Bel Kaufman, *Up the Down Staircase* (New York: Vintage/ Random House, 1965).

38. "Fireproofing," *American Architect*, January 27, 1916, 187.

39. Charles B. J. Snyder, "How New York City Has Solved Some Trying School Building Problems," *School Journal*, June 28, 1902, 739.

40. C. B. J. Snyder "Annual Report of the Superintendent of School Buildings" (1896), 223.

41. Jean Arrington, *Interview with Donald Friedman*, November 21, 2009.

42. Snyder, "School-Building in New York City," 21.

43. Robinson, "School Buildings of New York," 377.
44. Metro-Goldwyn-Mayer, *Fame*, 1980, https://en.wikipedia.org/wiki/Fame_(1980_film).
45. Stern, Gilmartin, and Massengale, *New York 1900*, 79.
46. Adele Marie Shaw, "The True Character of Public Schools," in *World's Work: A History of Our Time* (New York: Doubleday, Page, 1905), 4,207.
47. Riis, *Battle*, 371, 364.
48. Snyder, "Annual Report of the Superintendent of School Buildings" (1895), 223.
49. Snyder, "Annual Report of the Superintendent of School Buildings" (1894), 231.
50. Snyder, "Annual Report of the Superintendent of School Buildings" (1902), 210.
51. Riis, *Battle*, 344.
52. Wilson, "New Type of School Architecture," *Outlook* 65, 817.
53. Snyder, "School-Building in New York City," 21.
54. Norm Fruchter, "Spanish Flu, COVID-19, and the City's Schools," *Metropolitan Center for Research on Equity and the Transformation of Schools* (August 2020), https://steinhardt.nyu.edu/metrocenter/spanish-flu-covid-19-and-citys-schools.
55. Snyder, "Annual Report of the Superintendent of School Buildings" (1892), 231.
56. Snyder, "Annual Report of the Superintendent of School Buildings" (1895), 226.
57. Snyder, "How New York City Has Solved," 740, 741.
58. Snyder, "School-Building in New York City," 21.
59. Wilson, "New Type of School Architecture," *Outlook* 65, 812.
60. Snyder, "Annual Report of the Superintendent of School Buildings" (1891), 223.
61. Jacob Riis, "The Making of Thieves in New York," *Century Illustrated Monthly Magazine 40*, November 1894, 116.
62. Shaw, "True Character," 4,209.
63. Snyder, "Annual Report of the Superintendent of School Buildings" (1895), 232.
64. Snyder, "School-Building in New York City," 21.
65. Snyder, "Annual Report of the Superintendent of School Buildings" (1894), 218–19.
66. Snyder, "School-Building in New York City," 21.
67. Frank G. McCann, "The Heating and Ventilation of Schools in Congested City Districts," in *Modern School Houses, Part 2* (New York: American Architect, 1915), 16; https://www.google.com/books/edition/American_Architect_and_Architecture/m5kwAQAAIAAJ?hl=en&gbpv=1&dq=snyder+obviates+the+need+of+steam+coils+in+wardrobes&pg=PA200&printsec=frontcover, 200.
68. Shaw, "True Character," 4,210.
69. Snyder, "Annual Report of the Superintendent of School Buildings" (1893), 250.
70. Snyder, "Annual Report of the Superintendent of School Buildings" (1892), 232.
71. Snyder, "School-Building in New York City," 21.
72. Robinson, "School Buildings of New York," 383.
73. David Reed, and David Widger, producers, *The Project Gutenberg e-Book of Democracy and Education, by John Dewey*, July 26, 2008 [e-book #852], https://www.gutenberg.org/files/852/852-h/852-h.htm, Chapters 12 and 13.
74. Robinson, "School Buildings of New York," 382.
75. Diane Ravitch, *The Great School Wars: A History of the New York City Public Schools* (New York: Basic Books, 2000), 113.
76. Snyder, "Annual Report of the Superintendent of School Buildings" (1894), 217.
77. Snyder, "How New York City Has Solved," 739.

78. Shaw, *World's Work*, 4,207.

79. William Henry Maxwell, *A Quarter Century of Public School Development* (New York: American Book, 1912), 43.

80. "Public School Changes: Twenty Inspectors of Manual Training are to Superintend New Courses of Study," *New York Times*, September 8, 1897, 12.

81. Selma C. Berrol, *Julia Richman: A Notable Woman* (Philadelphia: Balch Institute Press, 1993), 64.

82. Charles B. J. Snyder, "Public School Buildings in the City of New York," Part I, *American Architect and Building News AABN*, January 25, 1908, 29.

83. Robinson, "School Buildings of New York," 377.

84. Snyder, "School-Building in New York City," 20.

85. *Board of Education Journal*, July 8,1894, 1,426–29.

86. Snyder, "Annual Report of the Superintendent of School Buildings" (1894), 219.

87. Snyder, "School-Building in New York City," 22.

88. "Schools Open This Week: Only Four of the New Buildings in Manhattan and the Bronx Ready. Lack of Room in Brooklyn Large Increase in Attendance Expected—Supt. Jasper Says that Manhattan Will Take Care of All Applicants—Brooklyn Not in Such Good Condition," *New York Times,* September 12, 1898, 10.

89. Wilson, "New Type of School Architecture," 810.

90. *Real Estate Record and Guide*, 4th quarter, 1899, 6.

91. Archie Emerson Palmer, *The New York City Public School: Being a History of Free Education in the City of New York* (New York: Macmillan, 1905), 290.

92. Snyder, "How New York City Has Solved," 739.

93. Riis, *Battle*, 347.

94. Snyder, "Annual Report of the Superintendent of School Buildings" (1899), 141.

95. "Roof Playgrounds," *Proceedings of the 2nd Annual Playground Congress*, 1908, 92.

96. William Maxwell, *Superintendent of Schools Annual Report to the Department of Education*, 1899, 141.

97. Riis, *Battle*, 361.

98. *Snyder*, "How New York City Has Solved," 739.

99. Wilson, "New Type of School Architecture," *Outlook 65*, 809–10.

100. Evelyn Barrett, *Chronicles of Saratoga* (1947) (Saratoga County, N.Y.: Published privately by E. B. Britten, 1959), 506–22.

4. The Prolific Decade 1901–1910: Building a World-Class Public-School System

1. Jacob, Riis, *The Battle with the Slum* (New York: Macmillan, 1902), 396.

2. Edward Robb Ellis, *The Epic of New York City* (New York: Carroll & Graf, 1966), 457.

3. Adele Marie Shaw, "The True Character of New York Public Schools," in *World's Work: A History of Our Time* (New York: Doubleday, 1903), 4,205.

4. Ellis, *Epic*, 459.

5. "40,000 Added to Part Time in School Year," *New York Tribune*, September 16, 1906, 3.

6. Charles B. J. Snyder, "Annual Report of the Superintendent of School Buildings," *Superintendent of Schools Annual Report to the Department of Education* (1902), 186.

7. Snyder, "Annual Report of the Superintendent of School Buildings" (1904), 289.

8. Snyder, "Annual Report of the Superintendent of School Buildings" (1902), 239, 342.

9. *American Architect*, January 27, 1916, 186.

10. Snyder, "Annual Report of the Superintendent of School Buildings" (1904), 288–89.

11. Snyder, "Annual Report of the Superintendent of School Buildings" (1902), 186.

12. John Vincent Mooney, "William H. Maxwell and the Public Schools of New York City" (Ph.D. diss., Fordham University, 1981), https://research.library.fordham.edu/dissertations/AAI8119781/#:~:text=Abstract,1904%2C%201910%2C%20and%201916.

13. G. W. Wharton, "High School Architecture in the City of New York," *School Review*, June 11, 1903, 459.

14. Snyder, "Annual Report of the Superintendent of School Buildings" (1904), 288.

15. "How New York Takes Care of Its Army of 600,000 School Children," *New York Times*, September 10, 1905, 30.

16. Robert A. M. Stern, Gregory Gilmartin, and John M. Massengale, *New York 1900: Metropolitan Architecture and Urbanism 1890–1915* (New York: Rizzoli, 1995), 79.

17. *School Journal*, 1913, 179.

18. Andrew Dolkart, *Morningside Heights: A History of Its Architecture and Development* (New York: Columbia University Press, 1998), 134, 140.

19. Donald Presa, *Landmarks Preservation Commission Designation Report Public School 116 (The Elizabeth Farrell School)*, Landmarks Preservation Commission Designation Report (New York, 1975), 2.

20. Snyder, "Annual Report of the Superintendent of School Buildings" (1904), 278–79.

21. Stern, Gilmartin, and Massengale, *New York 1900*, 86.

22. "P. S. 39," *Bronx County Historical Society Journal* 51, 2014, 19.

23. Snyder, "Annual Report of the Superintendent of School Buildings" (1902), 201.

24. Snyder, "Annual Report of the Superintendent of School Buildings" (1906), 372.

25. Snyder, "Annual Report of the Superintendent of School Buildings" (1906), 376.

26. "A Magnificent Architectural Scheme in Progress in Greater New York," *School Board Journal*, July 1905, 16.

27. *School*, January 14, 1909, 223–24; see also the *Board of Education Journal*, October 25, 1916, 1,521–22.

28. Snyder, "Annual Report of the Superintendent of School Buildings" (1901).

29. Snyder, "Annual Report of the Superintendent of School Buildings" (1906).

30. "Making Schoolhouses Fireproof: New York's Tendency in That Direction Has Long Been Marked," *New York Tribune*, February 28, 1904, 7.

31. Snyder, "Annual Report of the Superintendent of School Buildings" (1906), 349.

32. George E. Walsh, "New York's Fireproof School Buildings," *Fireproof Magazine* 9, September 9, 1906, 106.

33. Walsh, "Fireproof," 105.

34. Snyder, "Annual Report of the Superintendent of School Buildings" (1904), 316.

35. Snyder, "Annual Report of the Superintendent of School Buildings" (1904), 307–9.

36. *New York Times*, January 14, 1906.

37. "Public School Buildings in the City of New York," *American Architect and Building News (AABN), Part I*, January 25, 1908, 34.

38. *New York Times*, September 10, 1905, 30.

39. Shaw, "True Character," 4,207.

40. A. Emerson Palmer, *The New York Public School: Being a History of Free Education in the City of New York* (New York and London: Macmillan, 1905), 193, 290, 309; Selma C.

Berrol, "William Henry Maxwell and a New Educational New York," *History of Education Quarterly* 8, 1968, 221.

41. The Trustees, *The Twenty-Fifth Annual Report of the Trustees of the Cooper Union for the Advancement of Science and Art* (New York: Trow's, 1881–1900), Chapter 3, 124.

42. Berrol, "Maxwell," 222.

43. John J. Donovan and Others, *School Architecture: Principles and Practices* (New York: Macmillian, 1921), 18.

44. *New York Times*, September 10, 1905, 30.

45. Charles D. Larkins, "The Manual Training High School, Brooklyn, New York," *School Review 13*, 1905, 741–57.

46. Selma C. Berrol, *Julia Richman: A Notable Woman* (Philadelphia: Balch Institute Press, 1993), 62.

47. "Public School Buildings in the City of New York," 28.

48. Charles B. J. Snyder, "The Construction of Public School Buildings in the City of New York," in *Proceedings of the Municipal Engineers of the City of New York* (New York: City of New York, 1904), 59.

49. "Roof Playgrounds," *Proceedings of the 2nd Annual Playground Congress*, 1908, 93.

50. Riis, *Battle*, 386.

51. "Roof Playgrounds," 92.

52. Riis, *Battle*, 374.

53. Palmer, *New York Public School*, 309.

54. Riis, *Battle*, 389–91.

55. Riis, *Battle*, 386.

56. "Public Schools Abroad: Report on Those of England and One in Paris; Made for Purposes of Comparison, with the Schools of this City—English Schools Have Also the Problem of Overcrowding to Solve," *New York Times*, December 13, 1896, 4.

57. Snyder, "Annual Report of the Superintendent of School Buildings" (1902), 204–5.

58. Berrol, "Maxwell," 222–23.

59. Gerald Kurland, *Seth Low: The Reformer in an Urban and Industrial Age* (New York: Twayne, 1971), 166.

60. *Sun*, September 19, 1897.

61. Snyder, "Annual Report of the Superintendent of School Buildings" (1904), 281.

62. Shaw, "True Character," 4,208.

63. Stern, Gilmartin, and Massengale, *New York 1900*, 78.

64. *New York Times*, September 10, 1905, 30.

65. Avery Corman, *My Old Neighborhood Remembered: A Memoir* (Fort Lee, N.J.: Barricade, 2014), 94.

66. William W. Cutler, "Cathedrals of Culture: The Schoolhouse in American Educational Thought and Practice since 1820," *History of Education Quarterly* (1989): 26.

67. *School Journal*, September 21, 1899.

68. Charles B.J. Snyder, "Annual Report of the Superintendent of School Buildings," *Superintendent of Schools Annual Report to the Department of Education* (1913), 154.

69. Snyder, "Annual Report of the Superintendent of School Buildings" (1902), 197–98.

70. Snyder, "Annual Report of the Superintendent of School Buildings" (1902), 201.

71. Snyder, "Construction of Public School Buildings," 53–54.

72. Snyder, "Construction of Public School Buildings," 53–54.

73. Snyder, "Construction of Public School Buildings," 54.
74. Snyder, "Annual Report of the Superintendent of School Buildings" (1906), 373.
75. *New York Times*, September 10, 1905, 30.
76. Michele Cohen, "C. B. J. Snyder, Superintendent of School Buildings, Sets the Stage for Public Art," *Municipal Engineers Journal* 85 (1998): 34.
77. Michele Cohen, *Public Art for Public Schools* (New York: Monacelli, 2009), and Snyder, "Annual Report of the Superintendent of School Buildings" (1906), 343–49.
78. David Ment, "Public Schools," in *The Encyclopedia of New York City*, ed. Kenneth T. Jackson (New Haven, Conn.: Yale University Press, 1995), 956–60.
79. *New York Times*, September 10, 1905, 30.
80. Clarence Arthur Perry, *Public Lectures in School Buildings: Suggestions for Their Organization and Sources of Speakers and Topics* (New York: Department of Child Hygiene of the Russell Sage Foundation, 1910), 19.
81. Riis, *Battle*, 398; Cutler, "Cathedral," 30.
82. Clarence Arthur Perry, *Wider Use of the School Plant* (New York: Russell Sage Foundation, 1910), 4.
83. Harry Golden, *The Right Time: An Autobiography of Harry Golden* (New York: Putnam, 1969), 44.
84. Snyder, "Annual Report of the Superintendent of School Buildings" (1904), 288.
85. Christopher Gray, "Streetscapes: The Immaculate Conception Church on East 14th; A Protestant Complex Converted to Catholicism," *New York Times*, July 26, 1998, Section 11, 5.
86. Sarah Landau and Carl W. Condit, *The Rise of the New York Skyscraper* (New Haven, Conn.: Yale University Press, 1996), 113.
87. Andrew Dolkart and Matthew Postal, *Guide to NYC Landmarks* (Hoboken, N.J.: John Wiley & Sons, 2009), 31.
88. C. B. J. Snyder, "Annual Report of the Superintendent of School Buildings" *Superintendent of Schools Annual Report to the Board of Education* (1891), 220, 233.
89. *New York Times*, January 3, 1895, 22–23.
90. Snyder, "Annual Report of the Superintendent of School Buildings" (1892), 230.
91. Snyder, "Annual Report of the Superintendent of School Buildings" (1892), 244.
92. Charles B. J. Snyder, "School-Building in New York City," *Educational Review* 15, January–May 1998, 22–23.
93. Snyder, "School-Building in New York City," 24.
94. Snyder, "Construction of Public School Buildings," 57.
95. Snyder, "School-Building in New York City," 24–25.
96. Gilbert Morrison, "School Architecture and Hygiene," Monographs on Education in the United States (Albany, N.Y.: J. B. Lyon, 1900), 25, https://openlibrary.org/books/OL6950650M/School_architecture_and_hygiene.
97. Riis, *Battle*, Chapter 13.
98. *New York Times*, May 7, 1922.
99. Charles C. Johnson, "The Model School House," in *World's Work: A History of Our Time* (New York: Doubleday, Page, 1906), 7,664–68.
100. Christopher Gray, "Streetscapes: Public School 165; The 'Palace Design' Proves a Durable One," *New York Times*, May 17, 1992.
101. *New York Times*, September 10, 1905, 30.
102. Snyder, "Annual Report of the Superintendent of School Buildings" (1904), 286.

103. Shaw, "True Character," 4,207.
104. Snyder, "Annual Report of the Superintendent of School Buildings" (1904), 290.
105. Snyder, "Annual Report of the Superintendent of School Buildings" (1904), 289.
106. Snyder, "Annual Report of the Superintendent of School Buildings" (1904), 292.
107. Snyder, "Annual Report of the Superintendent of School Buildings" (1904), 292.
108. Snyder, "Annual Report of the Superintendent of School Buildings" (1904), 293.
109. Charles B. J. Snyder, "How New York City Has Solved Some Trying School Building Problems," *School Journal*, June 28, 1902.
110. "Told about New Yorkers," *Evening World*, May 29, 1903, 8.
111. Johnson, "Model School House," 7,668.
112. William Maxwell, *Superintendent of Schools Annual Report to the Department of Education* (1899), 7.
113. W. T. Harris, "Recent Growth of Public High Schools in the United States as Affecting the Attendance of Colleges," *Journal of Proceedings and Addresses of the 40th Annual Meeting of the National Education Association*, 1901, 175.
114. "A Model High School," *New York Times*, April 7, 1895.
115. Snyder, "Construction of Public School Buildings," 46.
116. Snyder, "Construction of Public School Buildings," 48.
117. George E. Thomas, "From Our House to the 'Big House': Architectural Design as Visible Metaphor in the School Buildings of Philadelphia," *Journal of Planning History* (2006): 218–40.
118. Robert A. M. Stern, "Schools Too Grand to Turn into Trash," *New York Times*, January 22, 2000, A15.
119. "The Nation's Long and Winding Path to Graduation," https://www.edweek.org/media/34gradrate-c1.pdf.
120. Sophia Chang, "NYC High School Graduation Rate Increased in 2020 Despite (or Because of) Pandemic," January 14, 2021, https://gothamist.com/news/nyc-high-school-graduation-rate-increased-2020-despite-or-because-pandemic.
121. Wharton, "High School Architecture," 459.
122. Wharton, "High School Architecture," 459–60.
123. *New York Times*, March 1, 1903.
124. *New York Times*, February 3, 1901.
125. *New York Times*, January 24, 1904.
126. *New York Times*, May 10, 1903.
127. *New York Times*, October 27, 1907.
128. Snyder, "Annual Report of the Superintendent of School Buildings" (1902), 190–91.
129. Snyder, "Annual Report of the Superintendent of School Buildings" (1904), 290.
130. *New York Times*, March 1, 1903.
131. *New York Times*, September 10, 1905.
132. *New York Times*, March 1, 1903.
133. Snyder, "Annual Report of the Superintendent of School Buildings" (1902), 190.
134. Snyder, "Annual Report of the Superintendent of School Buildings" (1904), 303.
135. Wharton, "High School Architecture," 468.
136. Wharton, "High School Architecture," 471.
137. Snyder, "Annual Report of the Superintendent of School Buildings" (1902), 187.
138. Snyder, "Annual Report of the Superintendent of School Buildings" (1902), 188.
139. *New York Times*, March 30, 1901.

140. Phyllis Ross, *Gilbert Rohde: Modern Design for Modern Living* (New Haven, Conn.: Yale University Press, 2009), 12.

141. Lewis Mumford, "A New York Adolescence: Tennis, Quadratic Equations, and Love," in *Sidewalk Critic: Lewis Mumford's Writings on New York*, ed. Robert Wojtowicz (New York: Princeton Architectural Press, 1998), 42.

142. Mumford, "New York Adolescence," 9.

143. Maxwell, *Annual Report* (1899), 108.

144. *School Journal*, May 10, 1901, 296.

145. Wharton, "High School Architecture," 478.

146. William Henry Maxwell, *A Quarter Century of Public School Development* (New York: American Book, 1912), 77.

147. Wharton, "High School Architecture," 457.

148. Michael Henry Adams, *Harlem Lost and Found* (New York: Monacelli, 2002), 232–33.

149. Snyder, "Annual Report of the Superintendent of School Buildings" (1904), 290.

150. Maryann Dickar, *Corridor Culture: Mapping Student Resistance at an Urban School* (1998; repr. New York: New York University Press, 2008), 27.

151. Ross, *Gilbert Rohde*, 26.

5. The Standardizing Decade 1911–1922: A Dimming of the Glory

1. "Editorial Comment: CBJ Snyder to Retire," *American Architect and Architectural Review*, 1922, 388.

2. C. B. J. Snyder, "Annual Report of the Superintendent of School Buildings," *Superintendent of Schools Annual Report to the Department of Education* (1919), 13.

3. Snyder, "Annual Report of the Superintendent of School Buildings" (1900), 22.

4. John Beverley Robinson, "The School Buildings of New York," *Architectural Record* 7, January–March 1898, 382.

5. Snyder, "Annual Report of the Superintendent of School Buildings" (1913), 108.

6. Snyder, "Annual Report of the Superintendent of School Buildings" (1913), 111.

7. "School Conditions Defended by Prall—Puts Report of Snyder's Findings against That of 40 Civic Associations," *New York Times*, July 10, 1921, 20.

8. Upton Sinclair, *The Goslings: A Study of American Schools* (Pasadena, Calif.: Author, 1924), 63–64.

9. Wallace K. Harrison and C. E. Dobbin, *School Buildings of Today and Tomorrow* (New York: Architectural Book, 1931), 53.

10. Charles B. J. Snyder and C. E. Dobbin, "Department of Architectural Engineering: Standardized School House Design," *American Architect*, Three Parts, November 6, 13, and 20, 1918, 629.

11. Snyder and Dobbin, "Standardized School House Design," 559.

12. George G. Gerwig, *Schools with a Perfect Score: Democracy's Hope and Safeguard* (New York: Macmillan, 1918), 63.

13. Donald G. Presa, *Landmarks Preservation Commission Designation Report on Newtown High School*, Landmarks Preservation Commission Designation Report (New York, 2003), 1.

14. Charles B. J. Snyder, "The Washington Irving High School," *American Architect*, 1913, 146.

15. Charles B. J. Snyder, *The Real Estate Record and Guide*, May 12, 1917, 669.

16. "New School to Have Bank. Plans Filed for the Julia Richman High for Girls," *New York Times*, January 11, 1922, 37.

17. "Washington Heights Taxpayers Urge Selection of Fort George for High School Site Famous Old Amusement Resort Has Been Entirely Cleared of Buildings and Is Now Available for Development—Need of Additional School Facilities in Upper Manhattan Enhances Interest in Proposed Plan," *New York Times*, April 11, 1920, R-1.

18. Snyder, "Annual Report of the Superintendent of School Buildings" (1913), 107.

19. Charles B. J. Snyder, "Bushwick High School," *American Architect*, April 1914, 197–201.

20. *American Architect*, January 27, 1916, 187.

21. "Parents Invited to Inspect Schools; Not a Firetrap Among Them, Says Prall—Charges Investigators Distort Picture. Most Violations Minor; False Impression Conveyed to Play Politics, He Alleges—in Snyder Reports to the Board," *New York Times*, September 15, 1921, 3.

22. Snyder, "Annual Report of the Superintendent of School Buildings" (1913), 127.

23. Snyder, "Annual Report of the Superintendent of School Buildings" (1922), 17.

24. Snyder, "Annual Report of the Superintendent of School Buildings" (1913), 126–30.

25. Charles B. J. Snyder, "The Lighting of School Rooms," *American Architect*, 1915, 170–76.

26. Snyder, "Lighting," 170, 176.

27. Snyder, "Annual Report of the Superintendent of School Buildings" (1922), 17.

28. Snyder, "Annual Report of the Superintendent of School Buildings" (1913), 111.

29. Snyder, "Annual Report of the Superintendent of School Buildings" (1922), 18.

30. Charles B. J. Snyder, "School-Building in New York City," *Educational Review* 15 (January–May 1898), 21.

31. "Drinking Fountains in Schools Planned—Building Supt. Snyder Finds the Use of Cups in Common a Menace to Health," *New York Times*, February 18, 1911, 8.

32. Leonard V. Koos, "Space-Provisions in the Floor-Plans of Modern High-School Buildings," *School Review: A Journal of Secondary Education* 27, no. 8, October 1919, 597.

33. Snyder, "Washington Irving High School," 146.

34. Snyder, "Annual Report of the Superintendent of School Buildings" (1913), 144.

35. Snyder, "Washington Irving High School," 149.

36. Snyder, "Annual Report of the Superintendent of School Buildings" (1913), 158.

37. Snyder, "Washington Irving High School," 161.

38. C. B. J. Snyder, "Duplicate Type School Building," *American Architect*, September 27, 1916.

39. Snyder, "Washington Irving High School," 162.

40. Alfonse Weiner, School Commissioner, "Many New Schools Will Have to Be Built," in *Real Estate Record and Guide*, June 1, 1912.

41. Snyder, "Washington Irving High School," 155.

42. Woodrow Wilson, "The Meaning of a Liberal Education," An Address to the New York City High School Teachers Association, January 9, 1909, in *High School Teachers Association of New York*, vol. 3, 1908–1909, 19–31, https://en.wikisource.org/wiki/The_Meaning_of_a_Liberal_Education.

43. Paul Lukas (blog), "Permanent Record: A Trove of 1920s Report Cards and the Stories They Tell," September 18, 2011, http://permanentrecordproject.blogspot.com/

search/label/Manhattan%20Trade%20School%20Movie, https://www.filmpreservation.org/preserved-films/screening-room/manhattan-trade-school-for-girls-1911.

44. Snyder, "Washington Irving High School," 155.

45. "Washington Irving Dines 'twixt Songs—Hoping between Mouthfuls and Song That They Hustle That New School," *New York Times*, November 20, 1910, C10.

46. Gail Levin, *Lee Krasner: A Biography* (New York: William Morrow/Harper Collins, 2011), 55.

47. Clemmont E. Vontress, "The Demise of the Homeroom," *Clearing House* 36 (September 1961): 16–18.

48. Snyder, "Annual Report of the Superintendent of School Buildings" (1913), 167.

49. Snyder, "Annual Report of the Superintendent of School Buildings" (1913), 167.

50. Snyder, "Annual Report of the Superintendent of School Buildings" (1913), 149.

51. Snyder, "Annual Report of the Superintendent of School Buildings" (1913), 163.

52. Snyder, "Annual Report of the Superintendent of School Buildings" (1913), 139.

53. Snyder, "Annual Report of the Superintendent of School Buildings" (1922), 67–68.

54. Snyder, "Washington Irving High School," 149.

55. Charles B. J. Snyder, "Bushwick High School," *American Architect*, April 29, 1914, 199.

56. Snyder, "Annual Report of the Superintendent of School Buildings" (1922), 68.

57. Snyder, "Annual Report of the Superintendent of School Buildings" (1922), 68.

58. Selma C. Berrol, "William Henry Maxwell and a New Educational New York," *History of Education Quarterly* 8 (1968): 223.

59. "Registration Rush in All the Schools—Mothers Busy Presenting Their Young Hopefuls to the Principals and Aide," *New York Times*, September 7, 1911, 9.

60. Charles B. J. Snyder, *Report on Construction and Maintenance* (1922), 73.

61. "School All the Year Round—Idle Hours Have Danger for City Children," *New York Times*, August 9, 1914, 42.

62. E. L. Doctorow, *World's Fair* (New York: Random House, 2007), 150.

63. Snyder, "Annual Report of the Superintendent of School Buildings" (1913), 142–46.

64. Charles B. J. Snyder, "Locker, Dressing and Toilet Building for Brooklyn Athletic Field," *American Architect*, December 20, 1911, 262–65.

65. "May Retain Snyder to Rebuild Schools: Education Officials Considering Plan to Make Him a Consulting Architect," *New York Times*, May 7, 1922, 33.

66. "School All the Year Round," 42.

67. Sol Cohen, "The Public Education Association of New York City, 1895–1959: Progressives and Public School Reform" (Ph.D. diss., Columbia University, 1963), 135.

68. William W. Cutler, "Cathedrals of Culture: The Schoolhouse in American Educational Thought and Practice since 1820," *History of Education Quarterly* (1989): 32.

69. "May Retain Snyder," 33.

70. Marla Smith, "Borough Briefs in the Schools: Community Welcomes New School Building," *CSA News 16*, 2013.

71. Charles B. J. Snyder, *The Real Estate Record and Guide*, July 6, 1913, 1,178.

Epilogue: Retirement and Successors

1. "Big Shake-Up Likely in Gompert Office: Aides of School Architect Are Expected to Follow Him into Retirement. Dobbin Assumes the Post. He Was Assistant to Snyder,

Who Was Virtually Forced out under Hylan's Pressure," *New York Times*, December 4, 1927, 24.

2. "Supt. Snyder Asks to Quit School Job—Chief of Buildings Since 1891, He Finds Health Is Affected by Press of Duties," *New York Times*, May 4, 1922, 14.

3. *New York Times*, July 2, 1922, 23.

4. Richard Dattner, *Civil Architecture: The New Public Infrastructure* (New York: McGraw Hill, 1995), 102.

5. "Obituary Notice—Mrs. Harriet K. Snyder," *New York Times*, May 27, 1927, 23.

6. Dennis Steadman Francis and James Ward, *Architects in Practice in New York City, 1900–1940* (New York: Committee for the Preservation of Architectural Records, 1980 [Francis] and 1989 [Ward].

7. J. D. Salinger, *Catcher in the Rye* (New York: Little, Brown, 1951), Chapter 15.

8. "C. B. J. Snyder, 85, Son, Robert, Die of Gas Poisoning, Double Tragedy Is Discovered Yesterday at Dalton Point Home," *Babylon Leader*, November 12, 1945, 1.

REFERENCES

"40,000 Added to Part Time in School Year." *New York Tribune*, September 16, 1906.

Adams, Henry. *The Education of Henry Adams*. Boston and New York: Houghton, Mifflin, 1918.

Adams, John. *The Works of John Adams, Second President of the United States: With a Life of the Author, Notes and Illustrations*. Vol. 9. New York: Little, Brown, 1854.

Adams, Michael Henry. *Harlem Lost and Found*. New York: Monacelli, 2002.

"Architect Picked to Speed Schools—Board of Education Head Reported to Have Chosen Henry B. Crosby." *New York Times*, January 12, 1923.

Architectural League of New York. *New Schools for New York: Plans and Precedents for Small Schools*. Edited by the Public Education Association of the City of New York. New York: Princeton Architectural Press, 1992.

Armstrong, Charles G., and Francis J. Armstrong. "Reports on New York Public Schools, Delays in Their Location, Design, and Construction." Consulting Engineer, New York: *Report of Committee on School Inquiry, Board of Estimate and Apportionment, City of New York*, 1913.

"Army of 610,000 Children Went to School." *New York World*, Monday Evening, September 11, 1905.

Barnard, Henry. *School Architecture, or Contributions to the Improvement of School-Houses in the United States* (1842). 2nd ed., ed. Jean and Robert McClintock. New York: Teachers College Press, 1970.

Barrett, Evelyn. *Chronicles Of Saratoga. 1947.* Saratoga County, N.Y.: Published Privately by E. B. Britten, 1959.

Berrol, Selma Cantor. *The Empire City: New York and Its People, 1624–1996*. Westport, Conn.: Greenwood, 1997.

———. *Julia Richman: A Notable Woman*. Philadelphia: Balch Institute Press, 1993.

———. "William Henry Maxwell and a New Educational New York." *History of Education Quarterly* 8 (1968).

"Big Shake-Up Likely in Gompert Office; Aides of School Architect Are Expected to Follow Him into Retirement. Dobbin Assumes the Post. He Was Assistant to Snyder, Who Was Virtually Forced out under Hylan's Pressure." *New York Times*, December 4, 1927.

"Board of Education Minutes." *Journal of the Board of Education of the City of New York*, 1898.

Butler, Nicholas Murray. *Across the Busy Years: Recollections and Reflections*. New York: Scribner, 1939.

Byard, Paul Spencer. *New Schools for New York*. New York: Princeton Architectural Press, 1992.

"The Case of C. B. J. Snyder: Investigation of the Charges Made against the Superintendent of School Buildings Is Resumed." *New York Times*, September 13, 1898, 12.

Caudell, William W. *Toward Better School Design*. New York: F. W. Dodge, 1954.

"C. B. J. Snyder, 85, Son, Robert, Die of Gas Poisoning; Double Tragedy Is Discovered Yesterday at Dalton Point Home." *Babylon Leader*, November 12, 1945.

"A Century of Free Education in New York." *New York Times*, June 5, 1904.

Chang, Sophia. "NYC High School Graduation Rate Increased in 2020 Despite (or Because of) Pandemic." January 14, 2021. https://gothamist.com/news/nyc-high-school-graduation-rate-increased-2020-despite-or-because-pandemic.

"City With Millions to Spend Lacks Schools—More Than 61,000 Children Get Only 'Part Time.'" *New York Times*, August 2, 1903, 20.

Cohen, Michele. "Art to Educate: A History of Public Art in the New York City Public Schools 1890–1976." Ph.D. diss., City University of New York, 2002.

———. "C. B. J. Snyder, Superintendent of School Buildings, Sets the Stage for Public Art." *Municipal Engineers Journal* 85 (1998): 34.

———. *Public Art for Public Schools*. New York: Monacelli, 2009.

Cohen, Sol. *Progressives and Urban School Reform: The Public Education Association, of New York City, 1895–1954*. New York: Teachers College, 1964.

———. "The Public Education Association of New York City, 1895–1959: Progressives and Public School Reform." Ph.D. diss., Columbia University. 1963.

Colon, George L. "P. S. 39." *Bronx County Historical Society Journal*, 2014.

Corman, Avery. *My Old Neighborhood Remembered: A Memoir*. Fort Lee, N.J.: Barricade, 2014.

Cremin, Lawrence A. *The Transformation of the School Progressivism in American Education 1876–1957*. New York: Vintage, 1964.

Cunningham, Hugh. *Children and Childhood in Western Society Since 1500*. New York and Harlow, UK: Pearson Longman, 2005.

Cutler, William W. "Cathedral of Culture: The Schoolhouse in American Educational Thought and Practice since 1820." *History of Education Quarterly* 1989.

Dattner, Richard. *Civil Architecture: The New Public Infrastructure*. New York: McGraw Hill, 1995.

Diamonstein, Barbaralee. *The Landmarks of New York: An Illustrated, Comprehensive Record of New York City's Historic Buildings*. Albany: State University of New York Press. 1988.

Dickar, Maryann. *Corridor Culture: Mapping Student Resistance at an Urban School*. New York: New York University Press. 2008.

Dobbs, Stephen Mark. "The Paradox of Art Education in the Public Schools: A Brief History of Influences." Paper presented at AERA (American Educational Research Association) annual meeting. New York, 1971. https://eric.ed.gov/?id=ED049196.

Doctorow, E. L. *Ragtime*. New York: Random House, 1975.
———. *World's Fair*. New York: Random House, 2007.
Dolkart, Andrew. *Morningside Heights: A History of Its Architecture and Development*. New York: Columbia University Press, 1998.
Dolkart, Andrew, and Matthew Postal. *Guide to NYC Landmarks*. Hoboken, N.J.: John Wiley & Sons. 2009.
Donovan, John J., and Others. *School Architecture: Principles and Practices*. New York: Macmillian, 1921.
Dresslar, Fletcher B. "American Schoolhouses." *U.S. Bureau of Education Bulletin No. 5*.
"Drinking Fountains in Schools Planned—Building Supt. Snyder Finds the Use of Cups in Common a Menace to Health." *New York Times*, February 18, 1911.
Dwyer, Jim. "About New York—A Builder of Dreams, in Brick and Mortar." *New York Times*, October 1, 2008.
"Editorial Comment: CBJ Snyder to Retire." *American Architect and Architectural Review*, May 10, 1922.
"Educational Lectures & Exhibits of the Week." *New York Times*, April 1, 1915.
Ellis, Edward Rob. *The Epic of New York City*. New York: Carroll & Graf, 1966.
"Erasmus Hall High School Designation List 348." Landmarks Preservation Commission, June 24, 2003.
Fass, Paula S. *Encyclopedia of Children and Childhood: In History and Society*. New York: Macmillan Reference USA, 2004.
Fifty-Fifth Annual Report of the Board of Education of the City of New York for the Year Ending December 31,1896. New York: Hall of the Board of Education, 1897.
"A Fine Schoolhouse—(PS 169)." *New York Times*, January 1, 1898.
The First Fifty Years, 1898–1948: A Brief Review of Progress. New York: The Superintendent of the New York (N.Y.) Board of Education, January 1949.
Francis, Dennis Steadman, and James Ward. *Architects in Practice in New York City, 1900–1940*. New York: Committee for the Preservation of Architectural Records, 1980 (Francis) and 1989 (Ward).
Friedman, Donald, Project Manager PS 90M, Interview by Jean Arrington. November 19, 2009.
Gerwig, George William. *Schools with a Perfect Score: Democracy's Hope and Safeguard*. New York: Macmillan, 1918.
Gilmartin, Gregory, Robert A. M. Stern, and Thomas Mellins. *New York 1930: Architecture and Urbanism between the Two World Wars*. New York: Rizzoli, 1987.
Goldberger, Paul. Review of *New York 1900: Metropolitan Architecture and Urbanism 1890–1915*, by Robert A. M. Stern, Gregory Gilmartin, and John M. Massengale. *New York Times*, March 18, 1984.
Golden, Harry. *The Right Time: An Autobiography of Harry Golden*. New York: Putnam, 1969.
"Good Government Club 'E' No.7, Public School Buildings in New York City, Their Condition as Shown in Official Reports." 1896.
Gray, Christopher. "Streetscapes: Charles B. J. Snyder; Architect Who Taught a Lesson in School Design." *New York Times*, November 21, 1999, Real Estate Section.
———. "Streetscapes: The Immaculate Conception Church on East 14th; A Protestant Complex Converted to Catholicism." *New York Times*, July 26, 1998, Section 11.
———. "Streetscapes: Public School 35; A Window on the Blackboard World of the 1890s." *New York Times*, August 16, 1987, Section 8, p. 14.

———. "Streetscapes: Public School 157; A Conversion to Serve Another Generation's Needy." *New York Times*, April 16, 1989, Section 10–12.

Gutman, Marta. Review of *The Chicago Schoolhouse: High School Architecture and Educational Reform, 1856–2006*, by Dale Allen Gyure; *Das Klassenzimmer vom Ende des 19. Jahrhunderts bis Heute*, by Thomas Mülry Andmüller and Romana Schneider; and *Small Memory*, by Jonathan Zimmerman. *Journal of the Society of Architectural Historians* 71 (2012): 556–59. https://Online.Ucpress.Edu/Jsah/Article/71/4/556/60257.

———. *Designing Modern Childhoods: History, Space, and the Material Culture of Children*. New Brunswick, N.J.: Rutgers University Press, 2008.

Gyure, Dale Allen. *The Chicago Schoolhouse: High School Architecture and Educational Reform, 1856–2006*. Chicago: Center for American Places, 2011.

Hamlin, A. D. F., C. B. J. Snyder, and Others. *Modern School Houses: Being a Series of Authoritative Articles on Planning, Sanitation, Heating and Ventilation*. New York: Swetland, 1915.

Harris, W. T. "Recent Growth of Public High Schools in the United States as Affecting the Attendance of Colleges." *Journal of Proceedings and Addresses of the 40th Annual Meeting of the National Education Association*, 1901, 175.

Harrison, Wallace K., and C. E. Dobbin. *School Buildings of Today and Tomorrow*. New York: Architectural Book, 1931.

Hayden, Dolores. *The Power of Place*. Cambridge, Mass.: MIT Press, 1995.

Hermalyn, Gary. *Morris High School and the Creation of the New York City Public High School System*. New York: Bronx County Historical Society, 1995.

History and Commerce of New York City. New York: American Publishing and Engraving, 1891.

Hubbell, Chas. Bulkley. "Personal Note from Chas. Bulkley Hubbell, President, on His Retirement," June 13, 1898.

Johnson, Charles C. "The Model School House." In *World's Work: A History of Our Time* 7664–68. New York: Doubleday, Page, 1906.

Kaufman, Bel. *Up the Down Staircase*. New York: Vintage/Random House, 1965.

Kohl, Herbert. *Should We Burn Babar?: Essays on Children's Literature and the Power of Stories*. New York: New Press, 1995.

Koos, Leonard V. "Space-Provisions in the Floor-Plans of Modern High-School Buildings." *School Review: A Journal of Secondary Education* 27, no. 8, October 1919, 573–99.

Kozol, Jonathan. *Savage Inequalities: Children in America's Schools*. New York: Harper Perennial, 1991.

Krinsky, Carol Hersell. *The Chronicles of Erasmus Hall High School 1937–1987*. New York: New York City Board of Education, 1987.

Kurland, Gerald. *Seth Low: The Reformer in an Urban and Industrial Age*. New York: Twayne, 1971.

Kursham, Virginia. *Public School 31, The Bronx, Designation List 185 LP-1435*. New York: Landmarks Preservation Commission, 1986.

Lamb, Frederick Stymatz. "Modern Use of the Gothic: The Possibilities of New Architectural Style." *Craftsman*, 1905.

Landau, Sarah, and Carl W. Condit. *The Rise of the New York Skyscraper 1865–1913*. New Haven, Conn.: Yale University Press, 1996.

Larkins, Charles D. "The Manual Training High School, Brooklyn, New York." *School Review* 13, 1905.

Levin, Gail. *Lee Krasner: A Biography*. New York: William Morrow/Harper Collins, 2011.

Lukas, Paul (blog). "Permanent Record: A Trove of 1920s Report Cards and the Stories They Tell." September 18, 2011. http://permanentrecordproject.blogspot.com/search/label/Manhattan%20Trade%20School%20Movie; Manhattan Trade School for Girls, https://www.filmpreservation.org/preserved-films/screening-room/manhattan-trade-school-for-girls-1911.

"A Magnificent Architectural Scheme in Progress in Greater New York." *School Board Journal*, July 1905.

"Making Schoolhouses Fireproof: New York's Tendency in That Direction Has Long Been Marked." *New York Tribune*, February 28, 1904.

"May Retain Snyder to Rebuild Schools—Education Officials Considering Plan to Make Him a Consulting Architect." *New York Times*, May 7, 1922.

Maxwell, William Henry. *A Quarter Century of Public School Development*. New York: American Book, 1912.

Mcclintock, Robert M., and Jean Mcclintock. "Architecture And Pedagogy." *Journal of Aesthetic Education*, 1968.

McCann, Frank G. "The Heating and Ventilation of Schools in Congested City Districts." In *Modern School Houses, Part 2*. New York: American Architect, 1915.

McCullough, David. *John Adams*. New York: Simon & Schuster, 2001.

Ment, David. "Public Schools." In *The Encyclopedia of New York City*, edited by Kenneth T. Jackson. New Haven, Conn.: Yale University Press, 1995.

Mintz, Steven. *Huck's Raft: A History of American Childhood*. Cambridge, Mass.: Belknap Press of Harvard University Press, 2006.

"A Model High School." *New York Times*, April 7, 1895.

Mooney, John Vincent. "William H. Maxwell and the Public Schools of New York City." Ph.D. diss, edited collection, Fordham University, 1981. https://research.library.fordham.edu/dissertations/AAI8119781.

Moore, Mary Ruth, and Constance Sabo-Risley. "Our Proud Heritage: Sowing the Seeds of Hope for Today; Remembering the Life and Work of Susan Blow." *Young Children*, National Association for the Education of Young Children (NAEYC), November, 2018, https://www.naeyc.org/resources/pubs/yc/nov2018/remembering-life-work-susan-blow.

Morrison, Gilbert. "School Architecture and Hygiene." Monographs on Education in the United States. Albany, N.Y.: J. B. Lyon, 1908. https://openlibrary.org/books/OL6950650M/School_architecture_and_hygiene.

"Most Remarkable Girls' School in the World." *New York Times*, February 2, 1913.

Mumford, Lewis. "A New York Adolescence: Tennis, Quadratic Equations, and Love." In *Sidewalk Critic: Lewis Mumford's Writings on New York*, edited by Robert Wojtowicz. New York: Princeton Architectural Press. 1998.

"A Municipal Artist." *American Art News* 20, no. 31, May 13, 1922.

"Need of More Schools—Good Government Club G Discusses Present Evils." *New York Times*, January 10, 1895.

"Needs of the Schools; Many Evils Reported by Ex-Commissioner Wehrum Corrected; More New Buildings Still Needed; Abuses That Still Exist Due to Lack of Funds, Says Superintendent Snyder Health Board Inquiry." *New York Times*, January 3, 1895.

"New Public School Building, Details of Fine Structure on St. Ann's Avenue." *New York Times*, April 4, 1897.

"New School to Have Bank. Plans Filed for the Julia Richman High for Girls." *New York Times,* January 11, 1922.

"New Schools to Open. Two Buildings Completed and to Be in Use about Dec 1—Room for 3,000 Pupils." *New York Times,* November 15, 1898.

"New York at the Louisiana Purchase Exposition, St. Louis 1904." *Report of the New York State Commission.* Albany, 1907.

New York School Buildings, 1806–1956. New York: New York City Board of Education, 1956.

"New York's Public Schools." *New York Times.* November 1, 1896, Sunday Magazine Supplement, 2.

Palmer, A. Emerson. *The New York Public School: Being a History of Free Education in the City of New York.* New York and London: Macmillan, 1905.

"Parents Invited to Inspect Schools; Not a Firetrap among Them, Says Prall—Charges Investigators Distort Picture. Most Violations Minor; False Impression Conveyed to Play Politics, He Alleges—in Snyder Reports to the Board." *New York Times,* September 15, 1921.

Patri, Angelo. *A Schoolmaster of the Great City: A Progressive Educator's Pioneering Vision for Urban Schools.* New York: Macmillan, 1917.

Perry, Clarence Arthur. *Public Lectures in School Buildings: Suggestions for Their Organization and Sources of Speakers and Topics.* New York: Department of Child Hygiene of the Russell Sage Foundation, 1910.

———. *Wider Use of the School Plant.* New York: Russell Sage Foundation, 1910.

Pevsner, Nikolaus. *A History of Building Types.* Princeton, N.J.: Princeton University Press, 1976.

Pierce, J. H., ed. "The Magnitude of Current School Building Operations in New York—The Excellent Character of Mr. Snyder's Work." *American Architect and Building News,* no. 1,544, July 29, 1905.

"Plans New York's Largest School—Supt. Snyder Designs a Building with 72 Classrooms and Big Play Space." *New York Times,* June 4, 1922.

Presa, Donald G. *Landmarks Preservation Commission Designation List 337 LP-1975 Public School 116 (The Elizabeth Farrell School).* Landmarks Preservation Commission Designation Report. New York, 1975.

———. *Landmarks Preservation Commission Designation Report on Newtown High School.* Landmarks Preservation Commission Designation Report. New York, 2003.

"Public School Changes—Twenty Inspectors of Manual Training Are to Superintend New Courses of Study," *New York Times,* September 8, 1897.

"Public School Matters—The Board of Education Consolidates the Primary and Grammar Departments—Biennial Census Criticized." *New York Times,* September 9, 1897.

"Public Schools Abroad: Report on Those of England and One in Paris; Made for Purposes of Comparison, with the Schools of this City—English Schools Have Also the Problem of Overcrowding to Solve." *New York Times,* December 13, 1896.

Ravitch, Diane. *The Great School Wars: A History of the New York City Public Schools.* New York: Basic Books, 1988.

Reese, William J. *The Origins of the American High School.* New Haven, Conn.: Yale University Press, 1995.

"Registration Rush in All the Schools—Mothers Busy Presenting Their Young Hopefuls to the Principals and Aide." *New York Times,* September 7, 1911.

Riis, Jacob. *The Battle with the Slum.* New York: Macmillan, 1902.
———. *How the Other Half Lives.* Boston: Bedford and St. Martin's, 2011.
———. *A Ten Years' War: An Account of the Battle with the Slum in New York.* Boston and New York: Houghton, Mifflin, 1900.
Robinson, John Beverley. *Architectural Composition: An Attempt to Order and Phrase Ideas Which Hitherto Have Been Only Felt by the Instinctive Taste of Designers* (1907). Pittsburgh: Creative Media Partners, 2018.
———. "The School Buildings Of New York." *Architectural Record* 7, January–March 1898.
"Roof Playgrounds." In *Proceedings of the 2nd Annual Playground Congress,* 1908.
Ross, Phyllis. *Gilbert Rohde: Modern Design for Modern Living.* New Haven, Conn.: Yale University Press, 2009.
Rothfork, John. "Transcendentalism and Henry Barnard's 'School Architecture.'" *Journal of General Education* (1977): 173–87.
Rury, John L. *Education and Social Change Themes in the History of American Schooling.* Mahwah, N.J.: Lawrence Erlbaum, 2002.
Salinger, J. D., *Catcher in the Rye.* New York: Little, Brown, 1951.
"Saloons Too Near Schools." *New York Times,* June 20, 1895.
Schmidt, H. W. "Heating, Ventilation, and Sanitation in School Buildings." *Review of Educational Research* 8, no. 4 (October 1938): 392–98.
"School All the Year Round—Idle Hours Have Danger for City Children." *New York Times,* August 9, 1914.
"School Fund Too Small—Miss Grace H. Dodge Favors Much Larger Appropriations." *New York Times,* January 5, 1895.
"Schools Open This Week—Only Four of the New Buildings in Manhattan and the Bronx Ready." *New York Times,* September 12, 1898.
"Schools Will Open with 750,000 Pupils—Additional Buildings, Ready for Occupancy, Will Increase Sittings 12,727." *New York Times,* September 13, 1914.
Shaw, Adele Marie. "The True Character of Public Schools." In *World's Work: A History of Our Time,* 4,204–21. New York: Doubleday, Page, 1903.
Shockley, Jay. *(Former) Stuyvesant High School Landmarks Designation: Landmark Site: Manhattan Tax Map Block 922, Lot 8.* Landmarks Preservation Commission Research Department. New York: Landmarks Preservation Commission, 1997.
Shorto, Russell. *The Island at the Center of the World: The Epic Story of Dutch Manhattan, and the Founding Colony That Shaped America.* New York: Doubleday, 2004.
Sinclair, Upton. *The Gosling: A Study of American Schools.* Pasadena, Calif.: Self-published, 1924.
Snyder, Charles B. J. "Bushwick High School." *American Architect,* April 29, 1914.
———. "The Construction of Public School Buildings in the City Of New York." In *Proceedings of the Municipal Engineers of the City of New York.* New York: City of New York, 1904.
———. "The Construction of School Buildings." *Architectural Forum,* March 1928.
———. "Duplicate Type School Building." *American Architect,* September 27, 1916.
———. "How New York City Has Solved Some Trying School Building Problems." *School Journal,* June 28, 1902.
———. "The Lighting of School Rooms." *American Architect,* September 15, 1915.
———. "Locker, Dressing and Toilet Building for Brooklyn Athletic Field." *American Architect,* December 20, 1911.

———. "Mr. Snyder's Re-Election: To the Editor of *The New York Times.*" *New York Times*, February 26, 1898.
———. "Public School Buildings in the City of New York." Parts I–III. *American Architect and Building News (AABN).* January–March 1908.
———. *The Real Estate Record and Guide*, 1884.
———. *The Real Estate Record and Guide*, July 6, 1913.
———. *The Real Estate Record and Guide*, May 12, 1917.
———. *Report On Construction and Maintenance*, 1922.
———. "School-Building in New York City," edited by Nicholas Murray Butler. *Educational Review,* January–May 1898.
———. "Superintendent of Schools Annual Report to the Board of Education," 1891–95.
———. "Superintendent of Schools Annual Report to the Department of Education," 1899–1904, 1906, 1909, 1913,1919.
———. "The Washington Irving High School." *American Architect*, March 19, 1913.
Snyder, Charles B. J., and C. E. Dobbin. "Department of Architectural Engineering: Standardized School House Design." Three Parts. *American Architect*, November 6, 13, and 20, 1918.
Snyder, Thomas D. *120 Years of American Education: A Statistical Portrait. Educational Statistics.* Center For Education Statistics, U.S. Department of Education, New York: Chelsea House, 1993. https://Nces.Ed.Gov/Pubs93/93442.Pdf.
"Snyder Will Not Retire. Superintendent to Take a Vacation Instead." *New York Times*, July 2, 1922.
Stern, Robert A. M. "Schools Too Grand to Turn into Trash." *New York Times*, January 22, 2000.
Stern, Robert A. M., Gregory Gilmartin, and John M. Massengale. *New York 1900: Metropolitan Architecture and Urbanism 1890–1915.* New York: Rizzoli, 1995.
"Supt. Snyder Asks to Quit School Job—Chief of Buildings Since 1891, He Finds Health Is Affected by Press of Duties." *New York Times*, May 4, 1922.
"The Surroundings of Schools." *New York Times*, November 24, 1891.
"This Week's Free Lectures." *New York Times*, December 29, 1907.
Thomas, George E. "From Our House to the 'Big House': Architectural Design as Visible Metaphor in the School Buildings of Philadelphia." *Journal of Planning History* (2006): 218–40.
Trustees (The). *The Twenty-Second Annual Report of the Trustees of the Cooper Union for the Advancement of Science and Art.* New York: Trow's, 1881.
Turner, Paul. "Boundless Enthusiasm." In *Campus: An American Planning Tradition.* Cambridge, Mass.: MIT Press, 1987.
Tyack, David B. *The One Best System: A History of American Urban Education.* Cambridge, Mass.: Harvard University Press, 1974.
Ultan, Lloyd, and Barbara Unger. *Bronx Accent.* New Brunswick, N.J.: Rutgers University Press, 2006.
"Unsafe Public Schools: Many Found to Be Dangerous to Health and Life. Gas Necessary in Some Classrooms. Thousands of Children in Danger from Fire—Unsafe Exits—Foul Odors from Sewers—Lack of Desks." *New York Times*, January 4, 1895.
Upton, Dell. "Lancasterian Schools, Republican Citizenship, and the Spatial Imagination in Early Nineteenth-Century America." *Journal of the Society of Architectural Historians* (September 1996): 238–53.

Vontress, Clemmont E. "The Demise of the Homeroom." *Clearing House* 36 (September 1961): 16–18.

Walsh, George E. "New York's Fireproof School Buildings." *Fireproof Magazine* 9, September 9, 1906.

"Washington Irving Dines 'twixt Songs—Hoping between Mouthfuls and Song That They Hustle That New School." *New York Times*, November 20, 1910.

Weber, Eric Thomas. "Education, American Philosophers On." In *American Philosophy: An Encyclopedia,* edited by John Lachs and Robert B. Talisse. New York and London: Routledge, 2008.

Wehrum, Charles. *The Common Schools of the City of New York.* New York: Board of Education, 1894.

Weiner, Alfonse, School Commissioner. "Many New Schools Will Have to Be Built." In *Real Estate Record and Guide,* June 1, 1912.

Weiner, Deborah E. B. *Architecture and Social Reform in Late-Victorian London.* Manchester, UK: Manchester University Press. 1994.

Weiser, Amy S. "Review of The Architecture of Literacy: The Carnegie Libraries of New York City." *Journal of the Society of Architectural Historians* (September 1998): 358.

Wharton, G. W. "High School Architecture in the City of New York." *School Review,* June 11, 1903.

Wheelwright, Edmund M. "The American Schoolhouse, XVI." *Brickbuilder* 8, March 1899.

———. *School Architecture: A General Treatise for the Use of Architects and Others.* Boston: Rogers & Manson, 1901.

White, Norval, and Elliot Willensky. *AIA Guide to New York City.* New York: Crown, 2000.

Wilson, Francis. "A New Type of School Architecture." *Outlook* 65, August 1, 1900.

Wilson, Woodrow. "The Meaning of a Liberal Education." An Address to the New York City High School Teachers Association, January 9, 1909. In *High School Teachers Association of New York*, vol. 3, *1908–1909*, 19–31. https://en.wikisource.org/wiki/The_Meaning_of_a_Liberal_Education.

Woods, Mary N. *From Craft to Profession: The Practice of Architecture in Nineteenth-Century America.* Berkeley: University of California Press, 1999.

"Would Cut Red Tape to Build Schools—Superintendent Ettinger Proposes Changes in Charter to Expedite Contracts." *New York Times,* December 3, 1922.

Wright, Jennifer Nadler. *C. B. J. Snyder, New York City Public School Architecture, 1891–1922.* Photography by Roy Wright. Self-Published, 2020.

Zelizer, Viviana A. *Pricing the Priceless Child: The Changing Social Value of Children.* Princeton, N.J.: Princeton University Press, 1994.

Zimmerman, Jonathan. *Small Wonder: The Little Red Schoolhouse in History and Memory.* New Haven, Conn.: Yale University Press, 2009.

INDEX

Adams, John, 2
Adams, Michael Henry, 162–63
Addams, Jane, 96
administration: assembly rooms for, 92–93; Board of Education and, 24, 26, 88–89; career in, 197–99, *198*; children and, 78; curriculum for, 38–39; history of, 68–69; Maxwell for, 103, 164; Naughton for, 108; politics of, 119; Progressivism for, 89–90; in public education, 9, 26–27, 38–40; Snyder, C. B. J., in, 197–99, *198*; Snyder schools for, 185; teachers and, 185–86
advertising, 24, *24*
advocacy, x–xi
African Americans, 30
The Age of Innocence (Wharton, E.), 19
Alabama, 164–65, *165*
Almirall, Raymond F., 136
amenities, in architecture, 191–96, *192–93*
American Society of Heating and Ventilating Engineers (ASHVE), 80–83, 80*n*
A. Philip Randolph High School, 162
architecture: advertising for, 24, *24*; advocacy for, x–xi; amenities in, 191–96, *192–93*; for auditoriums, 187–90, *189*; Baroque, 143–46, *144–45*; for Board of Education, 47–48, *67*, 67–68; at Chicago World Fair, 6; for City View Inn, 114, *114*; for colleges, 41; Colonial, 105; for Columbia University, *105*, 105–6; consultants in, 199–200; Cooper Union for, 17–18, 20–22, 129–30; for culture, 159–60; designs for, 25, 51–60, *52–55*, *58*, 60–62, 62–69, *64–65*, *67*, 69–70; for door handles, 50–51, *51*; for entranceways, 106, *106–7*, 173, *174*; functionality in, 43–44, 86–98, *88–89*, *91*, *93–94*, *98*; Guastivino tiles, 158, 158*n*; innovations for, 80–86, *81–82*; Leap of Faith Ornamentation, *154*; of Martin, Walter, 198–99; mechanical innovations for, 70–73, *74–77*, *75*, 77–80, *80*; for Minerva statue, *75*, *77*, 143; modernization in, 172–78, *173–75*, *177*, 179–80; in New York City, ix, 19–20, 20*n*, 40–41, 49–50, 63; policy for, 94, *94*; politics of, 9–10, 26–27, 137–38; Progressivism for, 1; public-school mandate and, 42–48, *44–45*; refinements in, 180–83; for Riis, 53, 56, 63, *75*, 138–39; scholarship on, 11; for skyscrapers, 159; for Snyder schools, 163–64, 163*n*; standardization in, 170–71, 181, 181*n*; standards in,

273

274 · INDEX

architecture (continued)
104–5; Tudor arches, 116, 119, 119n, 147, 172, 173, 174, 175; in United States, 40, 166; for windows, 173–75, 174–75, 182, 188; for World Fair, 6, 42–43. See also specific styles
ASHVE. See American Society of Heating and Ventilating Engineers
Assembly Hall, 150–51
assembly rooms, 92–93
athletic facilities, 123–24, 194
attendance, 38, 38–39, 127
auditoriums, 129, 129–34, 132–33, 187–90, 189, 195–96

Balaikrishna, Anjali, 11
Barnard, Henry, 1–2, 32n, 46–47
Baroque architecture, 143–46, 144–45
Barrett, Evelyn, 17
bathrooms, 85, 94
The Battle with the Slum (Riis), 6, 29, 36, 68–69, 99; architecture in, 138–39; Snyder schools in, 125–26
Bay Ridge High School, 177, 195–96
Beaux Arts architecture, 172
Bellamy, Francis, 39
Bishop, William, 21, 26
Blashfield, Edwin, 133
Bloomberg, Michael, 157
Board of Education: administration and, 24, 26, 88–89; architecture for, 47–48, 67, 67–68; auditoriums for, 133–34; budgets for, 161, 198; Building Bureau and, 102–3; consultants for, 199–200; elevators for, 96; Greenwich Settlement House for, 195; health for, 128; high schools for, 149–57, 150, 154–56, 162, 162; history of, 31–32; Little for, 26–27; in New York City, 10, 24, 37, 66, 92; policy for, 137–38; politics of, 187; Progressivism for, 136n; reform for, 100–2; reputation with, 166–67, 167; research for, 136; rooftop playgrounds for, 90–92; Snyder, C. B. J., for, 46; Snyder schools for, 73, 75, 153; for Wharton, G., 159
Board of Estimate and Apportionment, 102
Board of Health, 127

Boston, 149–50, 160
Brooklyn Athletic Field, 194
Brooklyn Boys' High School, 150
Brooklyn Girls' High School, 150, 191
Brooklyn schools, 108, 109
Brooklyn Teacher Training School, 124
budgets: for Board of Education, 161, 198; contracts for, 100–2; ethics and, 46; politics of, 37–39, 38; safety and, 85; for Snyder schools, 155–56
Building Bureau, 102–3, 169, 175, 182
built machinery, 80–86, 81–82
Bunce, J. Oscar, 24
bureaucracy, 43–44, 103
Burlington, Charles, 187
Burnham, Daniel, 103
Bushwick High School, 51, 82, 143, 146–47, 148, 180–81, 187–88
Butler, Nicholas Murray, 6

California, 148
Catcher in the Rye (Salinger), 200
C.B.J. Snyder (Wright, J.), 11
Central America, 22
charity, 31–32
Chateau-Type H-Plan, 141
Chicago, 11; City Beautiful Movement, 40, 41, 56–57; Columbian Exposition in, 40, 41, 57, 103; culture of, 55–56; Great Fire, 72–73; Hull House in, 96; New York City and, 148–49; World Fair, 6, 42–43
The Chicago Schoolhouse (Gyure), 11, 40
children: administration and, 78; attendance by, 38, 38–39; Child Labor Laws, 30; children's gardens, 92; compulsory education for, 152–53; desks for, 83–84; with disabilities, 192, 193, 196; Gompert elementary school, 198; health of, 123–24; immigration for, 66; lighting for, 91–92, 193n; mentally challenged, 192; in New York City, 125–26; open-air classrooms, 134–35, 135; parks for, 192–93; policy for, 35–36; for politics, 197; poverty for, 68; in Progressivism, 191–96, 192–93; public baths for, 127–28, 128; public education for,

INDEX · 275

30–32, 30n, 31, 90, 100–1; rooftop playgrounds for, 96–97, 124, 124–25; for Snyder, C. B. J., 168; social movements for, 56–57
City Beautiful Movement, 40, 41, 56–57, 104
City College, 133, 162
City Island Historical Society, 73
City University of New York, 163
City View Inn, 114, 114
class sizes, 12–13
Clinton, DeWitt, 30
Cohan, George M., 22
Cohen, Michele, 10, 89, 132–33
colleges, 2, 41, 162–63, 176, 177
Collegiate Gothic architecture, 7, 7–8, 43–44, 44, 140; in H-Plan schools, 146–47, 147–48, 170; Italian Palazzo architecture and, 106, 119, 120; Simplified, 9, 9, 171–75, 171n, 174–75; in Snyder schools, 60, 61–62, 62–63, 65, 69, 113
Colon, George L., 116
Colonial architecture, 105, 177–78, 200
Columbian Exposition, 40, 41, 57, 103
Columbia University, 20, 105, 105–6, 120
Commercial High School, 154–55, 161, 162
community, 193–94
compulsory education. *See* public-school mandate
Consolidation of the Boroughs, 43
construction: of creativity, 70–73, 74–77, 75, 77–80, 80; innovations in, 120–22, 180–83
consultants, 199–200
contracts, for budgets, 100–2
Cooper, Peter, 21
Cooper Union, 49, 72; for architecture, 17–18, 20–22, 129–30; auditoriums at, 129, 129; education at, 6, 17–18, 20–22; Great Hall, 129–30; vocational education for, 123
Cormon, Avery, 127–28
cost of living, 160–61
Crane, Stephen, 70–71
creativity: construction of, 70–73, 74–77, 75, 77–80, 80; for high schools, 175–76; innovations from, 51–60, 52–55, 58,

60–62, 62–69, 64–65, 67, 69–70; Progressivism and, 86–98, 88–89, 91, 93–94, 98; of Snyder, C. B. J., 7–8, 49–51, 51, 80–86, 81–82
culture: for African Americans, 30; architecture for, 159–60; charity in, 31–32; of Chicago, 55–56; community and, 193–94; compulsory education for, 152; evening lectures for, 188; immigration for, 99–100; in New York City, 19, 93, 184, 184–85; Progressivism and, 42–43, 71; of public education, 56; reform in, 24–25, 36; slums in, 70–71; Snyder schools for, 66–67, 94–96; Tammany Era for, 19, 32–33; vacation schools for, 96–97; vocational education for, 187
curriculum: for administration, 38–39; development, 36; for learning, 158–59; for Maxwell, 123; for Progressivism, 186–87; for public education, 86–87
Curtis, Ellen Louise, 18–19
Curtis High School, 153, 154, 155, 191
custom-designed fixtures, 80–86, 81–82
Cutler, William W., 40, 46

Dattner, Richard, 199
Davis, Andrew Jackson, 20
death, 201–3, 202–3
Debevoise, George W., 33, 50, 87
Demorest, William Jennings, 18–19, 22, 26
"Department of Architectural Engineering" (Snyder, C. B. J.), 170–71
Department of Education, 103
Designing Modern Childhoods (Gutman), 11
desks, 83–84
Dewey, John, 39, 86–87
DeWitt-Clinton High School, 78, 132–33, 133, 153, 155–58; Flemish Renaissance Revival architecture for, 163; swimming pools at, 194
Dickar, Maryann, 163
disabilities, 192, 193, 196
Dobbin, C. E., 170
Doctorow, E. L., 127–28, 194
Dolkart, Andrew, 105
Donovan, John J., 73, 74, 123

door handles, 50–51, *51*
drinking facilities, 83
Dutch Renaissance architecture, 54, 55, 60

École des Beaux Arts, 55–57
education: curriculum for, 36, 38–39, 86–87, 123, 158–59, 186–87; pedagogy for, 86–98, *88–89*, *91*, *93–94*, *98*, 190–91. *See also* public education
efficiency, 103, 175
elevators, 96
elitism, 149–57, *150*, *154–56*, *162*, 187
Ellis, Edward Robb, 99
Emigrant Industrial Savings Bank, 136
Encyclopedia of New York City (Jackson), 95n
engineering, 80–82, 80n
England, 126–27, 151–52
entranceways, 106, *106–7*, 173, *174*
Erasmus Hall High School, 132–33, *133*, 155, *155*, 157, 164–65, *165*, 187–88
ethics, 33, 46–47
Ettinger, William L., 166, 198
Europe, 126–27, 137, 139
Evander Childs High School, 143, 147, 176–77, 191
Evening High School, 151
evening lectures, 95–96, 95n, 188

faculty, 78
Fame (film), 54, *54*
families, 90
fashion, 18
Faulkner, Barry, 188
fireproofing, 72–73, 120–21, 180–81
fixtures, 80–86, *81–82*
Flemish Renaissance Revival architecture, 57, *61*, 155, 163
Flushing High School, 150, *150*, 191, *192*
Foster, Norman, ix
Free School Society, 30–32
French, Daniel, 188–89
French Renaissance Revival architecture, 64, 154–55, 160
Friedman, Donald, 75
Frobel, Friedrich, 92

functionality: advances in, 183–91, *184*, *189*; in architecture, 43–44, 86–98, *88–89*, *91*, *93–94*, *98*; innovations in, 122–35, *124*, *128–29*, *132–33*, *135*; Simplified Collegiate Gothic architecture for, 171–72, 171n; for Snyder, C. B. J., 122–35, *124*, *128–29*, *132–33*, *135*, 183–91, *184*, *189*

Gallagher, P., 102
gardens, 92
Gary Plan, 168–69
George Washington High School, 176–78, *180*, 188, 194
Georgian architecture, 178
Germany, 134
Gerwig, George, 171
Gilbert, Cass, ix
Gilded Age, 16–17
girls' schools: Brooklyn Girls' High School, 150, 191; Harlem Boys and Girls Club, 75, *76*; Hunter College High School for Girls, 176, *177*; Manhattan Trade School for Girls, 176–78, *179*, 187, 190–91; Wadleigh High School for Girls, 43, 153, 158–60, 162–63
Golden, Harry, 134
Gompert, William, 162
Gompert elementary school, 198
Goodhue, Bertram, ix
Gothic architecture, 60, 78, 146–47, *147–48*
Gould Library, 57
graduation rates, 153
grammar schools (GS), 11–12, 28–29, 29n
Gray, Christopher, 10, 50, 66–67, 136, 142
Great Depression, 127, 143
Great Fire of Chicago, 72–73
Great Hall (Cooper Union), 129–30
Great Migration, 30
The Great School Wars (Ravitch), 39
Greek Revival High School of Commerce, 161, 198
Greenwich Settlement House, 195
GS. *See* grammar schools
Guastivino tiles, 158, 158n
Gutman, Marta, 10–11, 40
Gyure, Dale Allen, 11, 40, 48

Hall, G. Stanley, 86
Harlem Boys and Girls Club, 75, 76
Harlem Court House, 64
Harlem Lost and Found (Adams, M.), 162–63
Harrison, Wallace K., 170
Hayden, Dolores, 10–11
health: for Board of Education, 128; Board of Health, 127; of children, 123–24; open-air classrooms for, 192–93, 193n; public baths for, 127–28, 128; safety and, 70–73, 74–77, 75, 77–80, 80; sanitation for, 183, 194; water for, 183
heating, 84–85, 182–83
Henry Street Settlement House, 35
Hermalyn, Gary, 10, 158
Herman Ridder school, 12
Herman Ritter Junior High School, 63
high schools: A. Philip Randolph High School, 162; Bay Ridge High School, 177, 195–96; for Board of Education, 149–57, 150, 154–56, 162, 162; Brooklyn Boys' High School, 150; Brooklyn Girls' High School, 150, 191; Bushwick High School, 51, 82, 143, 146–47, 148, 180–81, 187–88; Commercial High School, 154–55, 161, 162; creativity for, 175–76; Curtis High School, 153, 154, 155, 191; DeWitt-Clinton High School, 78, 132–33, 133, 153, 155–58, 163, 194; Erasmus Hall High School, 132–33, 133, 155, 155, 157, 164–65, 165, 187–88; Evander Childs High School, 143, 147, 176–77, 191; Evening High School, 151; Flushing High School, 150, 150, 191, 192; George Washington High School, 176–78, 180, 188, 194; Greek Revival High School of Commerce, 161, 198; High School of Commerce, 153, 155n; High School of English and Classical Studies, 149–50; High School of Music and Art, 162; High School of Performing Arts, 53–54, 54; Hunter College High School for Girls, 176, 177; innovations for, 157–65, 162, 165; Julia Richman High School, 172, 191, 194; Larchmont High School, 200n; learning in, 161; Long Island City High School, 114; Manual Training High School, 123–24, 159, 164; Morris High School, 4, 10, 115–16, 118, 132, 153, 155–59, 156; New Utrecht High School, 159, 176, 191; Revival Wadleigh High School, 142, 142–43; St. Regis High School, 68; Sidney Lanier High School, 164–65, 165; Stuyvesant High School, 123, 132, 155–56; Thomas Jefferson High School, 176, 191; Wadleigh High School for Girls, 43, 153, 158–60, 162–63; Washington Irving High School, 176–78, 179, 185–90, 189; West Side Vocational High School, 88–89, 89
history: of administration, 68–69; of Board of Education, 31–32; City Island Historical Society, 73; of New York City, 20, 40–41, 95n, 188; of public education, 38, 38–42, 41, 50–51, 50n; of public-school mandate, 28–33, 31; of Snyder schools, 1–4, 4–5, 6–11, 7–9; of United States, 10
Hotel de Cluny, 136
"How New York City Has Solved Some Trying School Building Problems" (*School Journal*), 71
How the Other Half Lives (Riis), 36
H-Plan schools: auditoriums for, 129, 129–31; Baroque architecture for, 143–46, 144–45; Chateau-Type H-Plan, 141; Collegiate Gothic architecture in, 146–47, 147–48, 170; early designs for, 8–9, 43, 59, 63–64, 64, 90, 104; Evander Childs High School and, 176–77; innovations in, 136–40, 140n, 141–42, 142–49, 144–45, 147–48; Italian Palazzo architecture for, 104, 116, 117, 119, 143; for New York City, 198–99; for Snyder, C. B. J., 136–40, 140n, 141–42, 142–49, 144–45, 147–48; for vocational education, 177–78
Hubbell, C. B., 97–98, 98
Hull House, 96
Hunt, Richard Morris, 136
Hunter College High School for Girls, 176, 177
Hylan, John F., 169, 197

immigration: for children, 66; for culture, 99–100; in New York City, 15–16, 151–52; in United States, 55–56
Indiana, 168–69
innovations: in appearance, 104–6, *105–7*, 108, *109–15*, 110–16, *117–18*, 119–20; for architecture, 80–86, *81–82*; in construction, 120–22, 180–83; from creativity, 51–60, *52–55*, *58*, 60–62, 62–69, *64–65*, *67*, 69–70; in functionality, 122–35, *124*, 128–29, 132–33, *135*; for high schools, 157–65, *162*, *165*; in H-Plan schools, 136–40, 140n, *141–42*, 142–49, *144–45*, *147–48*; mechanical, 74–77, *75*, 77–80, *80*, 85; in spaces, 87–88, *88*
International Modernism, 172
Italian Palazzo architecture: Collegiate Gothic architecture and, *106*, 119, 120; French Renaissance Revival architecture compared to, 154–55; for H-Plan schools, 104, 116, *117*, 119, 143; in New York City, *8*, 8–9, 57–58, *58*, *61*, 68, 105–6, *105–6*; for Snyder schools, 172
Italian Renaissance architecture, 57–60, *105*, 111–12, *112*
Ittner, William, 40, 47–48

Jackson, Kenneth, 95n
Jacqueline Onassis School of International Studies, *54*
Julia Richman High School, 172, 191, 194

Kaufman, Bel, 73, *74*
Kramer Versus Kramer (Cormon), 127–28
Krasner, Lee, 187–88

Lancaster, Joseph, 30, 30n
Landau, Sarah, 136
Landmark Commission, 63
Larchmont High School, 200n
Late Victorian Architecture (Palliser), 24
LaValle, Cynthia, 185, 202
Leap of Faith Ornamentation, *154*
learning, 158–59, 161, 185–86, 191
lectures, 95–96, 95n, 188

Lenox Library, 136
libraries, 191
lighting, 136; for children, 91–92, 193n; skylights, 131–32, *132*, 188; in Snyder schools, 79–80, *80*, 129–32, *132*, 182
"The Lighting of School Rooms" (Snyder, C. B. J.), 182
Lincoln, Abraham, 129
Little, Joseph J., 26–27, 50n
Loeb, Howard, 200n
London Board Schools, 65
Long Island City High School, 114
Low, Seth, 36–38, 127
Lucy G. Moses Preservation Award, 146n

Mackintosh, Charles Rennie, 104
Maclay, Robert, 35
Macvey, Amnon, 33
Madison Square Garden, 20
Maggie (Crane), 70–71
Manhattan Trade School for Girls, 176–78, *179*, 187, 190–91
manual training, 87–89, 96–97, 123, 160
Manual Training High School, 123–24, 159, 164
Martin, Walter, 198–99
Martin, William, 63
Maxwell, William, 9, 35–36, 44–45, 88; for administration, 103, 164; curriculum for, 123; legacy of, 149; as mentor, 168; Naughton and, 108; New York City for, 157; vacation schools for, 96
McAndrew, William, 166, 185–86
McClellan, George, 36–37
McKim, Charles, 105
Ment, David, 95
mentally challenged children, 192
Mills Building, 136
Minerva statue, 75, 77, 143
Mitchel, John, 36, 169
Model Homes for the People (Palliser), 24
"The Model School House" (*World Work*), 148
modernization, 172–78, *173–75*, *177*, *179–80*
Modern School-Houses (Nelligan), 43

INDEX · 279

"Modern Use of the Gothic" (magazine), 62
Morgan, J. P., 22
Morris High School, 4, 10, 115–16, *118*, 132, 153, 155–59, *156*
Morris High School (Hermalyn), 10, 158
Morrone, Francis, 66
Moses, Robert, 44, 200
moving partitions, 93, 93–94, 130
Mumford, Lewis, 161
Mundie, William, 40, 47–48
Municipal Engineers, 138
music rooms, 191, *192*

National Register of Historic Places, 139–40, 140*n*
Naughton, James, 104, 108, *109*, 151
Naughton-tribute schools, 108, *109–11*, 110–11, 170
Nelligan, Bruce, 43
neo-Classical architecture, 113, *113*
New Utrecht High School, 159, 176, 191
New York 1900 (Stern), ix, 78
New York City: architecture in, ix, 19–20, 20*n*, 40–41, 49–50, 63; Assembly Hall in, 150–51; Board of Health in, 127; Brooklyn Teacher Training School in, 124; Chicago and, 148–49; children in, 125–26; City Island Historical Society, 73; City University of New York, 163; Consolidation of the Boroughs in, 43; cost of living in, 160–61; culture in, 19, 93, *184*, 184–85; elitism in, 149–57, *150*, *154–56*, *162*; Evening High School in, 151; evening lectures in, 95–96, 95*n*; families in, 90; fashion in, 18; Fire Department, 102–3; Gary Plan for, 168–69; graduation rates in, 153; Harlem Boys and Girls Club in, 75, 76; historical preservation in, 146*n*; history of, 20, 40–41, 95n, 188; H-Plan schools for, 198–99; immigration in, 15–16, 151–52; Italian Palazzo architecture in, 8, 8–9, 57–58, *58*, *61*, 105–6, *105–6*; for Maxwell, 157; New York Training School for Teachers, 64, 154–55; Parental School in, 114; policy in, 11–12, 86–87; politics in, ix–x, 26, 30–31; poverty in, 35, 66–67, 169–70; Progressivism in, 3, 85–86; public education in, 7, 47–48, 84, 183–84; rooftop playgrounds in, 90–92, 94, 96; St. Mary's Park in, 59–60, 67; for SHPO, 4; slums in, 6, 29, 35–36; for Snyder, C. B. J., 18–23, *23*, 104–6, *105–7*, 108, *109–15*, 110–16, *117–18*, 119–20; Snyder schools for, 170, 188; social class in, 161; Tammany Hall in, 19; for United States, 99–100; after World War II, 2–3. *See also specific topics*
The New York City Public School (Palmer), 50*n*
Normal College, 162, 176, *177*

open-air classrooms, 134–35, *135*, 192–93, 193*n*
Orr, Elizabeth, 200–3, *201*, *203*

Palace of Education, 42
Palliser, George, 24
Palmer, A. E., 50*n*, 86, 86*n*
Panama Canal, 99
Parental School, 114
Paris, France, 55, 136
Parker, Francis, 39
parks, 192–93
Patri, Angelo, 39–40, 169
pedagogy, 86–98, *88–89*, *91*, 93–94, *98*, 190–91
Perkins, Dwight, 40
Perry, C. A., 134, 195
Philadelphia, 160–61
philanthropists, 95–96
physical education, 89–90, *91*
playgrounds, 90–92, 94, 96–97, *124*, 124–25
Pledge of Allegiance, 38
plenum technology, 122
policy: for architecture, 94, *94*; for Board of Education, 137–38; for children, 35–36; Consolidation of the Boroughs, 43; in New York City, 11–12, 86–87; for public education, 30–31, 127; for Snyder schools, 85–86, 171

politics: of administration, 119; of architecture, 9–10, 26–27, 137–38; of Board of Education, 187; of budgets, 37–39, 38; of Building Bureau, 182; of bureaucracy, 43–44; children for, 197; in New York City, ix–x, 26, 30–31; of Progressivism, 34–35, 169; of public education, 2–3, 37; reform in, 151; for Snyder, C. B. J., 10–11, 45–46; Tweed in, 32
Post, George, 19, 136
poverty: for children, 68; in New York City, 35, 66–67, 169–70; for philanthropists, 95–96; public education for, 100; reform for, 125–26; settlement houses and, 195; social movements for, 70–71; in United States, 70–71, 127–28, 128
The Power of Place (Hayden), 10
primary schools (PS), 11–12, 57–60, 58, 60–61
Progressivism: for administration, 89–90; for architecture, 1; for Board of Education, 136n; children in, 191–96, 192–93; creativity and, 86–98, 88–89, 91, 93–94, 98; culture and, 42–43, 71; curriculum for, 186–87; in New York City, 3, 85–86; for physical education, 89–90, 91; politics of, 34–35, 169; public education in, 89; reform for, 6, 151–52; for Riis, 35–36, 99, 134; for Snyder, C. B. J., 149–57, 150, 154–56, 162; in Tammany Era, 36
Prohibition movement, 26
PS. *See* primary schools
Public Art for Public Schools (Cohen), 10, 89
public baths, 127–28, 128
public education: administration in, 9, 26–27, 38–40; athletic facilities for, 194; for children, 30–32, 30n, 31, 90, 100–1; culture of, 56; curriculum for, 86–87; ethics in, 33, 46–47; in Europe, 126–27; faculty in, 78; GS for, 11–12; High School of Performing Arts, 53–54, 54; history of, 38, 38–42, 41, 50–51, 50n; libraries for, 191; in New York City, 7, 47–48, 84, 183–84; pedagogy for, 86–98, 88–89, 91, 93–94, 98; policy for, 30–31, 127; politics of, 2–3, 37; for poverty, 100; in Progressivism, 89; PS for, 11–12; reform in, 71–72, 103–4; for Riis, 29–30; school codes for, 11–12; shortcomings in, 32n; for slums, 67–68; for Snyder, C. B. J., 4, 5, 6, 26–27, 99–104, 101, 149–57, 150, 154–56, 162; in United States, 104, 111, 156; Wehrum Report on, 137
"Public School Buildings in the City of New York" (Snyder, C. B. J.), 100, 101
public-school mandate: architecture and, 42–48, 44–45; for compulsory education, 152–53; history of, 28–33, 31; for Snyder, C. B. J., 33–42, 34, 38, 41

Ravitch, Diane, 39
refinements, 180–83
reform: for Board of Education, 100–2; in culture, 24–25, 36; for Dewey, 86; for GS, 28–29, 29n; in politics, 151; for poverty, 125–26; for Progressivism, 6, 151–52; in public education, 71–72, 103–4; for Riis, 3, 50; for Shaw, 122–23; for Snyder, C. B. J., 86–98, 88–89, 91, 93–94, 98; in Tammany era, 37, 46–47
religion, 200–1
Remington, Frederick, 24
Renaissance Revival architecture, 7, 7–8, 57–60
repairs, 120–22
retirement, 197–201, 198–99, 201
Revival Wadleigh High School, 142, 142–43
Richman, Julia, 89–90, 113, 123
The Right Time (Golden), 134
Riis, Jacob, ix, 170; architecture for, 53, 56, 63, 75, 138–39; H-Plan Schools for, 148; influence of, 6; Progressivism for, 35–36, 99, 134; public education for, 29–30; reform for, 3, 50; rooftop playgrounds for, 125; settlement houses for, 96; slums for, 35; social movements for, 68–69; vacation schools for, 96–97
The Rise of the New York Skyscraper (Landau), 136
Robinson, John Beverley, 66, 85–86
Robson, E. R., 65

Rohde, Gilbert, 161.
Romanesque Revival, 50, 52, 52–53, 55–56, 64, 151
rooftop playgrounds, 90–92, 94, 96–97, 124, 124–25
Roosevelt, Edith, 167–68
Roosevelt, Quentin, 167–68
Roosevelt, Theodore, 99, 166–68
Ross, Phyllis, 161, 164

safety: fireproofing, 72–73, 120–21, 180–81; health and, 70–73, 74–77, 75, 77–80, 80; mechanical innovations for, 74–77, 75, 77–80, 80, 85; for New York City Fire Department, 102–3; sanitation for, 183, 194; ventilation for, 81–82, 81–83, 121–22
St. Louis, 42–43
St. Mary's Park, 59–60, 67
St. Regis High School, 68
Salinger, J. D., 200
sanitation, 183, 194
Saratoga Springs, New York, 153
School Architecture (Donovan), 73, 74, 123
School Buildings of Today and Tomorrow (Harrison and Dobbin), 170
School for the Deaf, 192, 193
A Schoolmaster of the Great City (Patri), 39
Schuyler, Montgomery, 24
Sergeant, Edward A., 116
settlement houses, 95–96, 95n, 195
Seward Park, 96
Shaw, Adele Marie, 29, 35, 48; reform for, 122–23; Snyder schools for, 78–79, 87–88; truancy for, 127
Shephard Hall, 133
Shockley, Jay, 146n
Shonts, Charity Curtis, 15–16, 168
showers, 194
SHPO. *See* State Historic Preservation Office
Sidney Lanier High School, 164–65, 165
Simplified Collegiate Gothic architecture, 9, 9, 171–75, 171n, 174–75
Sinclair, Upton, 169–70
Skeffington, Shirley, 200–1, 201

skylights, 131–32, 132, 188
skyscrapers, 159
slums: in culture, 70–71; in New York City, 6, 29, 35–36; public education for, 67–68; tenement houses in, 51–52
Small Wonder (Zimmerman), 11
Snyder, Adam, 17
Snyder, Benjamin, 21, 21n
Snyder, Charity (née Shonts), 15–16, 168
Snyder, Charles B. J.: abundance for, 8–9; in administration, 197–99, 198; amenities for, 191–96, 192–93; career for, 23–24, 24–25, 26, 28–29, 166–72, 167; childhood of, 15–17; children for, 168; class sizes for, 12–13; construction for, 120–22, 180–83; creativity of, 7–8, 49–51, 51, 80–86, 81–82; death of, 201–3, 202–3; designs by, 51–60, 52–55, 58, 60–62, 62–69, 64–65, 67, 69–70; family home, 22–23, 23; functionality for, 122–35, 124, 128–29, 132–33, 135, 183–91, 184, 189; H-Plan schools for, 136–40, 140n, 141–42, 142–49, 144–45, 147–48; for Little, 50n; mechanical innovations for, 70–73, 74–77, 75, 77–80, 80; modernization for, 172–78, 173–75, 177, 179–80; New York City for, 18–23, 23, 104–6, 105–7, 108, 109–15, 110–16, 117–18, 119–20; politics for, 10–11, 45–46; Progressivism for, 149–57, 150, 154–56, 162; public education for, 4, 5, 6, 26–27, 99–104, 101, 149–57, 150, 154–56, 162; public-school mandate for, 33–42, 34, 38, 41; reform for, 86–98, 88–89, 91, 93–94, 98; reputation of, ix–xi, 1–2, 9–10, 42–48, 44–45, 119–20; retirement for, 197–201, 198–99, 201. *See also specific topics*
Snyder, Daniel, 17
Snyder, Earl Stimpson, 15
Snyder, Ella, 16
Snyder, Gail, 200
Snyder, George, 15–16
Snyder, Harriet Katherine (née de Vries), 23, 55, 199, 199
Snyder, Howard Halsey, 23, 164, 164n, 168, 199–200

Snyder, Jeremiah, 16, 21, 21*n*
Snyder, Kitty, 16–17, 168
Snyder, Orris, 16
Snyder, Philip, 17
Snyder, Robert Maclay, 35, 164, 164*n*, 168, 200–3, 202
Snyder schools, x–xi; for administration, 185; architecture for, 163–64, 163*n*; athletic facilities for, 123–24; auditoriums in, *129*, 129–34, *132–33*; for Board of Education, 73, 75, 153; budgets for, 155–56; Collegiate Gothic architecture in, 60, *61–62*, 62–63, 65, *69*, 113; for community, 193–94; for culture, 66–67, 94–96; for Dewey, 87; entranceways in, 106, *106–7*; history of, 1–4, *4–5*, 6–11, 7–9; for Hubbell, 97–98, *98*; Italian Palazzo architecture for, 172; Italian Renaissance architecture for, 111–12, *112*; learning in, 191; lighting in, 79–80, *80*, 129–32, *132*, 182; Manhattan Trade School for Girls, 176–78, *179*; moving partitions in, *93*, 93–94, 130; music rooms in, 191, *192*; naming of, 11–13; Naughton-tribute schools, 108, *109–11*, 110–11; for New York City, 170, 188; open-air classrooms in, 134–35, *135*; policy for, 85–86, 171; repairs for, 120–22; reputation of, 65–66, 77, 125–26; sanitation in, 183; School for the Deaf as, 192, *193*; for Shaw, 78–79, 87–88; showers in, 194; in Staten Island, *115*, 115–16; study halls in, 158–59; for teachers, 178; technology in, 157–58; ventilation in, *81–82*, 81–83; for Wharton, G. W., 153–54. *See also specific schools*
social class, 161
social movements: for children, 56–57; leadership for, 39–40; for poverty, 70–71; for Riis, 68–69; in United States, 34–35
spaces, innovations in, 87–88, *88*
Spanish-Mission-style architecture, 114
Stagg, David, 33
standardization, 170–71, 181, 181*n*

State Historic Preservation Office (SHPO), x, 4
Staten Island, *115*, 115–16, 153, *154*
Stern, Robert A. M., ix–x, 1, 43, 78, 152
"Streetscapes" (Gray), 10, 142
Strong, William, 36, 151
students: auditoriums for, 195–96; learning for, 158–59, 185–86; manual training for, 87–89, 96–97, 123, 160; water for, 183
study halls, 158–59
Stuyvesant High School, 123, *132*, 155–56
Sullivan, Louis, 104
swimming pools, 194
Switzerland, 81
Sylvie's Elementary School, 172, *173*

Tammany Era: for culture, 19, 32–33; Progressivism in, 36; reform in, 37, 46–47
teachers: administration and, 185–86; Brooklyn Teacher Training School, 124; New York Training School for Teachers, 64, 154–55; Snyder schools for, 178
technology, 157–58
tenement houses, 51–52
Thomas, George, 152
Thomas Jefferson High School, 176, 191
Toynbee Hall, 96
truancy, 127
Tudor arches, 116, 119, 119*n*, 147, 172, *173*, *174, 175*
Turner, Paul, 2
Twain, Mark, 188
Tweed, Boss, 32

Ultan, Lloyd, 66
Unger, Barbara, 66
United States: architecture in, 40, 166; ASHVE, 80–82, 80*n*; colleges in, 2; England compared to, 126–27, 151–52; Europe and, 139; Gary Plan in, 168–69; Gilded Age in, 16–17; Great Depression in, 127, 143; Great Migration in, 30; history of, 10; immigration in, 55–56; New York City for, 99–100; poverty in, 70–71, 127–28, *128*; Prohibition movement in, 26; public education in, 104,

111, 156; social movements in, 34–35; World War I for, 167–68
University Settlement House, 96
Upjohn, Richard, ix
Up the Down Staircase (Kaufman), 73, 74

vacation schools, 96–97
van der Rohe, Mies, ix
ventilation: heating and, 84–85, 182–83; for safety, *81–82*, *81–83*, 121–22
vocational education, 151; for Cooper Union, 123; for culture, 187; for H-Plan schools, 177–78; at Manhattan Trade School for Girls, 176–78, *179*, 187; at West Side Vocational High School, 88–89, *89*
de Vries, Harriet Katherine, 23, 55, 199, *199*

Wadleigh High School for Girls, 43, 153, 158–60, 162–63
Wald, Lillian, 35
Walsh, P. J., 102

Washington Irving High School, 176–78, *179*, 185–90, *189*
water, 183
Wehrum, Charles, 28, 83
Wehrum Report, 137
West Side Vocational High School, 88–89, *89*
Wharton, Edith, 19
Wharton, George, 46, 153–54, 159
Wheelwright, Edmund, 40, 47–48, 49–50
White, Stanford, 40, 57
Whitman, Walt, 3
Wilson, Woodrow, 187
windows, 173–75, *174–75*, 182, 188
Wirt, William, 168
World Fair, 6, 42–43
World War I, 167–68
World War II, 2–3
Wright, Jennifer Nadler, 11
Wright, Roy, 11

Zimmerman, Jonathan, 11

After twenty-four years as an English professor at Peace College and raising three daughters in Raleigh, North Carolina, **Jean Arrington** (1946–2022) relocated to New York City in 2005, where she taught at Borough of Manhattan Community College until 2017. During her NYC stint, she was fascinated by Snyder and his beautiful schools. To showcase this remarkable man and his amazing accomplishments, Jean gave walking tours highlighting various Snyder schools, gave lectures for architectural and historical organizations, and wrote articles for local newspapers.

Cynthia Skeffington LaValle, Snyder's great-granddaughter of Babylon, New York, has worn a few hats throughout her life—always in the healthcare field—registered nurse, computer programmer, project manager, and management consultant. In 2019, when Jean, with health concerns, could use some assistance, Cindy managed the project and team that brought this book to the finish line.

SELECT TITLES FROM EMPIRE STATE EDITIONS

Patrick Bunyan, *All Around the Town: Amazing Manhattan Facts and Curiosities*, Second Edition

Salvatore Basile, *Fifth Avenue Famous: The Extraordinary Story of Music at St. Patrick's Cathedral*. Foreword by Most Reverend Timothy M. Dolan, Archbishop of New York

William Seraile, *Angels of Mercy: White Women and the History of New York's Colored Orphan Asylum*

Andrew J. Sparberg, *From a Nickel to a Token: The Journey from Board of Transportation to MTA*

New York's Golden Age of Bridges. Paintings by Antonio Masi, Essays by Joan Marans Dim, Foreword by Harold Holzer

Daniel Campo, *The Accidental Playground: Brooklyn Waterfront Narratives of the Undesigned and Unplanned*

John Waldman, *Heartbeats in the Muck: The History, Sea Life, and Environment of New York Harbor, Revised Edition*

John Waldman (ed.), *Still the Same Hawk: Reflections on Nature and New York*

Gerard R. Wolfe, *The Synagogues of New York's Lower East Side: A Retrospective and Contemporary View, Second Edition*. Photographs by Jo Renée Fine and Norman Borden, Foreword by Joseph Berger

Joseph B. Raskin, *The Routes Not Taken: A Trip Through New York City's Unbuilt Subway System*

North Brother Island: The Last Unknown Place in New York City. Photographs by Christopher Payne, A History by Randall Mason, Essay by Robert Sullivan

Stephen Miller, *Walking New York: Reflections of American Writers from Walt Whitman to Teju Cole*

Tom Glynn, *Reading Publics: New York City's Public Libraries, 1754–1911*

Craig Saper, *The Amazing Adventures of Bob Brown: A Real-Life Zelig Who Wrote His Way Through the 20th Century*

Joanne Witty and Henrik Krogius, *Brooklyn Bridge Park: A Dying Waterfront Transformed*

David J. Goodwin, *Left Bank of the Hudson: Jersey City and the Artists of 111 1st Street*. Foreword by DW Gibson

Nandini Bagchee, *Counter Institution: Activist Estates of the Lower East Side*

Susan Celia Greenfield (ed.), *Sacred Shelter: Thirteen Journeys of Homelessness and Healing*

Elizabeth Macaulay-Lewis and Matthew M. McGowan (eds.), *Classical New York: Discovering Greece and Rome in Gotham*

Susan Opotow and Zachary Baron Shemtob (eds.), *New York after 9/11*

Colin Davey with Thomas A. Lesser, *The American Museum of Natural History and How It Got That Way*. Forewords by Neil deGrasse Tyson and Kermit Roosevelt III

Wendy Jean Katz, *Humbug! The Politics of Art Criticism in New York City's Penny Press*

Lolita Buckner Inniss, *The Princeton Fugitive Slave: The Trials of James Collins Johnson*

Angel Garcia, *The Kingdom Began in Puerto Rico: Neil Connolly's Priesthood in the South Bronx*

Jim Mackin, *Notable New Yorkers of Manhattan's Upper West Side: Bloomingdale–Morningside Heights*

Matthew Spady, *The Neighborhood Manhattan Forgot: Audubon Park and the Families Who Shaped It*

Robert O. Binnewies, *Palisades: 100,000 Acres in 100 Years*

Marilyn S. Greenwald and Yun Li, *Eunice Hunton Carter: A Lifelong Fight for Social Justice*

Jeffrey A. Kroessler, *Sunnyside Gardens: Planning and Preservation in a Historic Garden Suburb*

Elizabeth Macaulay-Lewis, *Antiquity in Gotham: The Ancient Architecture of New York City*

Ron Howell, *King Al: How Sharpton Took the Throne*

Phil Rosenzweig, *Reginald Rose and the Journey of "12 Angry Men"*

For a complete list, visit www.fordhampress.com/empire-state-editions.